WIMBLEDON
2018

WIMBLEDON IN PICTURES

THE CHAMPIONSHIPS
2 JULY - 15 JULY 2018

An AI mosaic of 8,400 photos, created with IBM Watson
wimbledon.com/poster

IN PURSUIT *of* GREATNESS

#WIMBLEDON

The Championships' Official Poster 2018 was produced by IBM, the AELTC's long-term Technology Partner, who used their Watson visual recognition interface
to create this striking image using 8,400 separate photographs from the Club's photographic archive

WIMBLEDON
2018

By Paul Newman

ROLEX

Published in 2018 by Vision Sports Publishing Ltd

Vision Sports Publishing Ltd
19-23 High Street
Kingston upon Thames
Surrey
KT1 1LL
www.visionsp.co.uk

ISBN: 978-1909534-85-8

Written by: Paul Newman
Additional writing by: Ian Chadband
Edited by: Jim Drewett and Alexandra Willis
Production editor: Ed Davis
Proofreaders: Lee Goodall and Eloise Tyson
Designed by: Neal Cobourne (our-kid-design.com)
Photography: Bob Martin, Thomas Lovelock, Adam Warner, Anthony Upton, Ben Queenborough, Ben Solomon, Dave Shopland, David Levenson, Dillon Bryden, Florian Eisele, Ian Walton, Jed Leicester, Joe Toth, Joel Marklund, Karwai Tang, Matt Harris, Simon Bruty, Steve Lewis, Tim Clayton
Picture editors: Neil Turner, Ellie Mears, Jordan Pettitt, Richard Ward, Sammie Thompson
Picture research: Sarah Frandsen

The All England Lawn Tennis Club (Championships) Limited
Church Road
Wimbledon
London
SW19 5AE
England

Tel: +44 (0)20 8944 1066
www.wimbledon.com

Printed in Slovakia by Neografia

This book is reproduced with the assistance of Rolex.

FOREWORD
By Chairman Philip Brook

I would like to welcome you all to the Official Annual of The Championships 2018, a celebration of the 132nd Championships, and of the 150th anniversary of the founding of the All England Club.

It was a Championships of beautiful weather, fascinating tennis and historic milestones, and I would like to highlight a few of these.

Firstly, 2018 marked His Royal Highness The Duke of Kent's 50th Championships as our President. His service to Wimbledon has been unwavering, and I would like to record my thanks to him. We were delighted to welcome our Patron, HRH The Duchess of Cambridge, HRH The Duke of Cambridge, our President HRH The Duke of Kent, and also the newly-married HRH The Duchess of Sussex, making her first visit to the Royal Box.

We were also very proud to have welcomed Billie Jean King and Rod Laver as our Special Guests to mark 50 years since they won the first Open Singles Championships at Wimbledon.

Congratulations to all our champions, to Novak Djokovic on the occasion of a memorable fourth Wimbledon singles title, his 13th Grand Slam title, and to Angelique Kerber on her first Wimbledon title, joining Steffi Graf, Michael Stich and Boris Becker as Open era German Wimbledon singles champions. And to those who achieved British success – Alfie Hewett and Gordon Reid, who completed a hat-trick of Gentlemen's Wheelchair Doubles titles, Jamie Murray, who reached a third mixed doubles final, and Jack Draper, who battled hard to reach the boys' singles final.

We witnessed four fantastic five-set matches, two in the quarter-finals, as Kevin Anderson dethroned Roger Federer and Rafael Nadal and Juan Martin del Potro went baseline to baseline, and two in the semi-finals, Anderson's epic against John Isner, and Nadal and Djokovic's absorbing 52nd encounter.

After her absence last year, Serena Williams returned to our Championships just 10 months after welcoming daughter Alexis Olympia to the world, and thrilled us with her run to an extraordinary 10th Wimbledon ladies' singles final.

We held the inaugural Quad Wheelchair Tennis doubles event at Wimbledon, in the form of an exhibition match won by Andy Lapthorne and David Wagner, that next year will become a full Championships event.

Our grass courts performed superbly amid the hot weather, the enhancements to our Grounds were all very well received, and we launched Wimbledon Broadcast Services as we became the Host Broadcaster, offering television coverage of all 18 courts for the first time.

Lastly, we spoke to space from Centre Court, with Mats Wilander interviewing Astronaut Commander Drew Feustel live aboard the International Space Station. Drew carries with him two very special Wimbledon coins, which will be used for the Finals Weekend next year.

Finally, to all of those who attended or watched The Championships in the glorious sunshine, thank you for your support, and I hope this annual will prove to be a memorable and enjoyable read.

Philip Brook

CHAMPION!

A 1ST WIMBLEDON VICTORY.
A 3RD GRAND SLAM® TITLE.

This watch is a witness to a thrilling victory on Centre Court. Worn by a player whose relentless determination and discipline earned her a third Grand Slam® title. Rolex congratulates Angelique Kerber on her remarkable first triumph at The Championships, Wimbledon. It doesn't just tell time. It tells history.

OYSTER PERPETUAL DATEJUST 36

ROLEX

INTRODUCTION
By Paul Newman

Even before a ball had been struck in anger it was clear that comebacks would be a central theme at The Championships 2018. As the 132nd edition of the world's most celebrated tennis tournament approached, we were wondering whether some of the sport's biggest names had the capacity to recapture their former glories.

Would Serena Williams, seven times a Ladies' Singles Champion at the All England Club, be the same force following her return to competition as a 36-year-old mother? Could Petra Kvitova, the champion of 2011 and 2014, crown her remarkable comeback from the horrors of a knife attack by winning the title for a third time? Would Maria Sharapova, making her first appearance at The Championships for three years, rekindle the flame she had lit with her triumph 14 years earlier? Would we see the Angelique Kerber of 2016, when she had been the game's outstanding female competitor, or would we be watching the player who had struggled to live up to her exploits in the following season?

Similar question marks hung over the comebacks of many of the leading men. Novak Djokovic, three times a champion on Centre Court, had gone nearly two years without reaching the final of a Grand Slam tournament and had only just started to rediscover his form following an elbow operation. Stan Wawrinka, who, like Djokovic, had missed the last six months of 2017, had been experiencing an equally difficult comeback, in his case after knee surgery. Milos Raonic and Kei Nishikori were also finding their way again following lengthy injury lay-offs, while Nick Kyrgios had been forced to miss Roland-Garros because of an elbow problem.

For British tennis fans, however, one question loomed over all others. Would Andy Murray be fit to play? The 31-year-old Scot had had a difficult time ever since limping out of The Championships 2017, when he had performed wonders just to reach the quarter-finals. Attempted comebacks at the US Open and Australian Open had both ended prematurely and in January he opted for surgery. Murray's recovery programme thereafter was not without setbacks. The former world No.1 pulled out of his scheduled comeback tournament in the Netherlands and finally made his reappearance just 13 days before the start of The Championships. Murray lost to Kyrgios first time out at The Queen's Club and played two more matches the following week at Eastbourne,

Above: Andy Murray arrived at Wimbledon to practise but decided with a "heavy heart" to withdraw on the eve of The Championships because he was not far enough along in his comeback after hip surgery

Right: Eight-times champion Roger Federer honed his perfectly grooved service action on No.3 Court

where he beat Wawrinka but was outplayed by his fellow Briton, Kyle Edmund. As he headed for the All England Club to practise, the champion of 2013 and 2016 was still undecided as to whether he would be fit enough to play.

Two days before The Championships Murray said he was still taking things day by day and had yet to make a decision on whether or not to play. "Wimbledon for me is obviously special for a lot of reasons," he added. "I always want to be here competing. It feels a little bit odd coming into the tournament this year. Normally at this stage I feel really nervous, lots of pressure, and I expect a lot of myself around this time of year. I've always loved that and enjoyed that in a way. It has been difficult, but I've enjoyed it, whereas this year it feels very, very different."

The following day, with the start of The Championships just 19 hours away, Murray announced, "with a heavy heart", that "playing best-of-five-set matches might be a bit too soon in the recovery process". He told British reporters that he felt "at ease" with his decision to withdraw – for the first time since 2007 – and said he was sure he would be back in future years.

Murray posted a picture of himself on Instagram giving a thumbs-down. "I need to look at the bigger picture with regards to my health right now," he said in a message to fans. Just to show that he had not lost his sense of humour, he added: "If anyone needs a coach over the next couple of weeks give me a buzz!" That drew plenty of responses. "Let's make it happen," Kyrgios said. "I know you like a challenge." Sloane Stephens was quite specific. "Warm-up is at 10.30, court 5," she said. "See you there?"

Murray was by no means the only player who had faced a race against time to be fit. Rafael Nadal, Juan Martin del Potro, Simona Halep and Sharapova had all pulled out of their warm-up tournaments as they recovered from their exertions at Roland-Garros, while Williams was recovering from the pectoral muscle injury that had forced her to withdraw before her fourth round match in Paris. The 23-times Grand Slam singles champion, who had played only three tournaments since beginning her

HAPPY BIRTHDAY TO US

The All England Lawn Tennis & Croquet Club, one of the world's great sporting institutions and host to the world's premier tennis event, looked in fine fettle as it celebrated its 150th birthday at The Championships 2018.

It was time to reflect again on a wonderful story: how the All England Club was formed in 1868 as a croquet club but learned to embrace lawn tennis and forged a Championships that was to transform the history of sport.

Today, of course, the Club remains central to global tennis but – just as importantly – it has retained its unique character as a private club with Members throughout the year enjoying its playing and social facilities as well as lifelong friendships.

To mark the occasion, a group of Members assembled for a special recreation of a famous 1870 photograph (*top right*) showing the Club's croquet players gathered outside the pavilion at the old Worple Road ground. In the modern version (*above*), the Members – who these days still play on the Club's croquet lawns off Bathgate Road – are looking very elegant in front of the modern Wimbledon Clubhouse.

Some things have changed, though. It will not have escaped your notice that the gentlemen in 1870 may have been a little more hirsute and that they don't appear to have any female company. Fortunately things have moved on since then, and who knows what future developments await 150 years further down the line?

To help celebrate the All England Club's origins as a croquet club, a group of famous volunteers put down their rackets and took part in a mini croquet challenge, with Andy Murray (top), Simona Halep, Serena Williams (middle row) and Roger Federer, Johanna Konta and Novak Djokovic (bottom row) all trying their hands. Inevitably, Federer, who'd been practising with his kids, turned out to be a natural. "It's great," he declared. "It's given me a lot of confidence for Wimbledon!"

Water, water – and a touch of Pimm's – everywhere at a very warm Wimbledon! And very welcome it was too, particularly for one police sniffer dog

comeback in March, had been unable to practise her serve until she arrived at the All England Club. However, any fears that she might not be ready were dispelled when Williams posted a video of herself on Centre Court with her baby daughter, Alexis Olympia, in the week before The Championships.

"Once upon a time there was a girl from Compton and she had a dream of playing at Wimbledon – and her dream came true," Williams told her daughter, who was dressed in Wimbledon white. "Yes, Olympia, your dreams can come true too. Do you know who that little girl was? That little girl was your momma."

She added: "There's a twist in this story. Your momma is going to play there again this year. And did you know what? You get to see her play – well, on TV, because you might be a little excited in the matches. But the moral of the story, Olympia, is that from Compton to Wimbledon you can dream big."

In another charming scene Williams lay on a bed with Olympia as her daughter played with a mini tennis racket and her mother's hair. "Tell me about your morning," Williams said to her. "Mine was good. I went to practise. I hit on Centre Court and then I hit on another court. I had a fun time. How was your day? Did you play? Did you eat? Did you have some milk?"

Of the leading players who were happy to report no serious fitness issues, a number were in ominous form. Roger Federer, who had again skipped the clay court season, Marin Cilic, who was runner-up to the Swiss in 2017, and Caroline Wozniacki, who had finally won her first Grand Slam title at the Australian Open in January, all won grass court titles in the build-up to The Championships.

So far it had been a grass court season marked by glorious weather. In the first 36 days of the British grass court summer a total of just two hours of play had been lost to rain and parts of the country had experienced the warmest and driest June on record.

Forecasters were predicting no end to the heatwave, which would hopefully provide the perfect backdrop as the All England Club celebrated a number of milestones. The Championships 2018 marked the 150th anniversary of the founding of the Club and 50 years since the beginning of Open tennis; Billie Jean King and Rod Laver, the singles champions in 1968, would be the Chairman's Special Guests at The Championships. It was the 50th Championships since His Royal Highness The Duke of Kent had become President of the Club. By the end of the Fortnight the Duke would have attended The Championships for a total of 285 days and made 349 trophy presentations. But who would be receiving their trophies from him this year? It was time to find out.

It was great to see Serena Williams back as she brought baby Alexis Olympia along to see her mother's Centre Court realm

@OLYMPIAOHANIAN/INSTAGRAM

It's hotting up

The sun was definitely out and the forecast promised plenty more good weather to come as the players prepared themselves for The Championships 2018.

Defending champions Roger Federer, who had a fresh spring in his step after winning his 98th tournament in Stuttgart the previous month, and Garbiñe Muguruza (*both right*) looked ready for the fray after having enjoyed over a week's competitive break.

It was definitely hot work, though, as former champions Rafael Nadal (*opposite, top*) – having enjoyed some much-needed rest following his 11th Roland-Garros triumph – and Maria Sharapova (*opposite, left*), grabbed a much-needed drink, and it's not often you see Juan Martin del Potro (*opposite, bottom left*) feeling the need to don a cap.

For British teenage wild card Katie Swan (*opposite, far right*) it was time to daydream a little about what was to come, but as for two-times Ladies' Singles Champion Petra Kvitova (*opposite, centre*), you could have sworn she had been keeping one eye on the FIFA World Cup as she took the chance to demonstrate some impressive keepy-uppy skills on the practice courts.

WIMBLEDON 2018
Gentlemen's Singles Top 16 Seeds

Roger FEDERER
Switzerland • Age: 36
Wimbledon titles: 8
Grand Slam titles: 20

1

Rafael NADAL
Spain • Age: 32
Wimbledon titles: 2
Grand Slam titles: 17

2

Marin CILIC
Croatia • Age: 29
Wimbledon titles: 0
Grand Slam titles: 1

3

Alexander ZVEREV
Germany • Age: 21
Wimbledon titles: 0
Grand Slam titles: 0

4

Juan Martin DEL POTRO
Argentina • Age: 29
Wimbledon titles: 0
Grand Slam titles: 1

5

Grigor DIMITROV
Bulgaria • Age: 27
Wimbledon titles: 0
Grand Slam titles: 0

6

Dominic THIEM
Austria • Age: 24
Wimbledon titles: 0
Grand Slam titles: 0

7

Kevin ANDERSON
South Africa • Age: 32
Wimbledon titles: 0
Grand Slam titles: 0

8

John ISNER USA	9	13	**Milos RAONIC** Canada
David GOFFIN Belgium	10	14	**Diego SCHWARTZMAN** Argentina
Sam QUERREY USA	11	15	**Nick KYRGIOS** Australia
Novak DJOKOVIC Serbia	12	16	**Borna CORIC** Croatia

Ladies' Singles Top 16 Seeds

Simona HALEP
Romania • Age: 26
Wimbledon titles: 0
Grand Slam titles: 1
1

Caroline WOZNIACKI
Denmark • Age: 27
Wimbledon titles: 0
Grand Slam titles: 1
2

Garbiñe MUGURUZA
Spain • Age: 24
Wimbledon titles: 1
Grand Slam titles: 2
3

Sloane STEPHENS
USA • Age: 25
Wimbledon titles: 0
Grand Slam titles: 1
4

Elina SVITOLINA
Ukraine • Age: 23
Wimbledon titles: 0
Grand Slam titles: 0
5

Caroline GARCIA
France • Age: 24
Wimbledon titles: 0
Grand Slam titles: 0
6

Karolina PLISKOVA
Czech Republic • Age: 26
Wimbledon titles: 0
Grand Slam titles: 0
7

Petra KVITOVA
Czech Republic • Age: 28
Wimbledon titles: 2
Grand Slam titles: 2
8

Venus WILLIAMS USA — **9**

Madison KEYS USA — **10**

Angelique KERBER Germany — **11**

Jelena OSTAPENKO Latvia — **12**

13 — **Julia GOERGES** Germany

14 — **Daria KASATKINA** Russia

15 — **Elise MERTENS** Belgium

16 — **CoCo VANDEWEGHE** USA

DAY
1

MONDAY
2 JULY

n a rapidly changing world there was something reassuring about the scene as the players walked out for the first match on Centre Court at The Championships 2018. The sense of timelessness that pervades the most famous stage in world tennis was underlined by the familiar sight of Roger Federer, the defending champion and the only player to have won the gentlemen's singles eight times, entering the stadium alongside Serbia's Dusan Lajovic, his first round opponent.

Above: Roger Federer might have had a new clothing sponsor, but the superlative skills definitely remained untouched

Previous pages: Federer and Dusan Lajovic are given a rapturous welcome by the expectant Centre Court crowd

There was, nevertheless, something unusual about the scene, although television viewers might have been more aware of it than those in the stadium. Federer's kit, which is often a talking point on the first day of The Championships, bore the logo not of Nike, his sponsors for the last 20 years, but that of Uniqlo. At the very moment that Federer walked out on to court the Japanese company issued a press release announcing that it had recruited him as a "global brand ambassador".

While a change of kit sponsor might seem a minor matter for the vast majority of players, this was big business. Uniqlo did not reveal details of the deal, but it was widely reported that it was worth $300m over 10 years – which would make it three times more lucrative than Federer's previous Nike agreement – and would not be affected by any decision he might make to retire.

At Federer's post-match press conference following an emphatic 6-1, 6-3, 6-4 victory over Lajovic, it was no surprise that the first question was about his kit. "I was excited to wear Uniqlo," Federer said. "It's been a long time coming." As Uniqlo do not make tennis shoes, Federer was still, for the moment, wearing Nike footwear. He also said he was in negotiations with Nike over the future of his 'RF' logo. "The RF logo is with Nike at the moment, but it will come to me at some point," he said. As for the tennis, that was much more simple. "I was really able to enjoy the match out there because I got off to a good start," Federer said. "It's wonderful to be back."

Federer was attempting to repeat his remarkable performance of 2017, when he won the titles at both the Australian Open and Wimbledon after taking a six-month break to recover from a knee injury at the end of 2016. A number of other top players followed suit in 2017 by not competing in the second half of the year in the hope of resolving physical issues. However, most struggled on their return, including Federer's Davis Cup colleague, Stan Wawrinka, who had knee surgery after The Championships 2017. After winning only three matches in his first four tournaments after his comeback at the start of 2018, the former world No.3 took another three-month break, but on returning at Rome in May he still looked a shadow of his former self. In his last grass court tournament before The Championships he won only four games against Andy Murray, who was playing only his second match after an 11-month lay-off.

The All England Club has never been the happiest hunting ground for Wawrinka, but against all the odds the world No.224 sprang a major upset on Centre Court by beating Grigor Dimitrov, the No.6 seed, 1-6, 7-6(3), 7-6(5), 6-4. Dimitrov, who had enjoyed the biggest win of his career at the end of 2017 by winning the ATP Finals in London, looked in control after winning the first set in just 23 minutes, only for Wawrinka to launch a determined comeback. "Mentally it was a big surprise to fight so well after losing the first set," Wawrinka said afterwards.

Following pages: Open up the special fold-out pages to reveal a unique and breathtaking panoramic view of Centre Court in all its glory on the first day of The Championships 2018

Below: 2014 semi-finalist Grigor Dimitrov became the first big name casualty in the gentlemen's singles when the Bulgarian succumbed to an inspired Stan Wawrinka on Centre Court

Four other men's seeds lost on the opening day, with Borna Coric's 6-7(6), 2-6, 2-6 defeat to Daniil Medvedev a particular surprise given that the 21-year-old Croatian had beaten Federer in the final at Halle eight days earlier. Richard Gasquet (No.23 seed) was beaten in straight sets by his fellow Frenchman, Gael Monfils, while Filip Krajinovic (No.28 seed) and Leonardo Mayer (No.32 seed) went down to Nicolas Jarry and Jan-Lennard Struff respectively.

There were even greater upsets in the ladies' singles, with Sloane Stephens and Elina Svitolina, seeded No.4 and No.5 respectively, both falling at the first hurdle. Stephens, who had won her first Grand Slam singles title at the US Open 10 months previously, had arrived at the All England Club fresh from her first appearance in the final at Roland-Garros, but the 25-year-old American appeared to pay for her lack of grass court matches and was beaten 1-6, 3-6 by Croatia's Donna Vekic, a proven performer on the surface. "It was frustrating," Stephens said afterwards. "I wasn't making the shots I wanted to make. I wasn't being as consistent as I wanted to. My feet were a little bit slow."

Vekic, the world No.55, won the grass court title in Nottingham last year and is also a former runner-up at Edgbaston. "I think grass really suits my game," she said. "I try to play aggressively." On this occasion Vekic won despite having been unable to sleep after watching Croatia's footballers win a dramatic penalty shoot-out victory over Denmark in the World Cup the previous evening. "That was crazy," she said.

Left: Stan Wawrinka made a welcome comeback from his injury-beset year to fight back from a set down in four absorbing sets on Centre Court

Below: Donna Vekic caused an opening day shock with her emphatic 6-1, 6-3 defeat of in-form US Open champion and Roland-Garros finalist Sloane Stephens

Selfie heaven

You have to hand it to Wimbledon's multi-tasking stars. They don't just entertain their fans by playing great tennis; these days, they also keep them happy afterwards by helping them take the best possible 'selfies'. As you can see, Novak Djokovic, Roger Federer, Serena Williams, Rafael Nadal and Eugenie Bouchard are all experts at assisting admiring photographers. Yet perhaps they could all learn from the police officer taking a snap of himself with some colleagues on Centre Court. Talk about the long arm of the law...

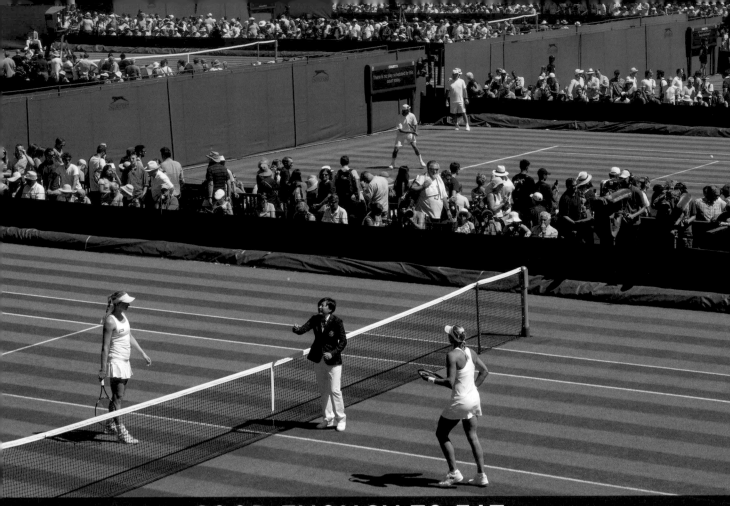

GOOD ENOUGH TO EAT

Wimbledon's grass courts are renowned as the best in the world and that's all down to Neil Stubley, Head of Courts and Horticulture at the AELTC, and his 16-strong team, who do such a wonderful job making the playing conditions as perfect as possible.

Certainly, as The Championships got under way the courts looked an absolute picture of pristine, emerald beauty, with top players like Karolina Pliskova quick to praise their quality at the start of two potentially sun-baked weeks.

Of course, tending the most prized pieces of turf in global sport does not come without pressure and the most rigorous scrutiny but Stubley was confident his courts of perennial ryegrass could handle the predicted hot spell.

"Once you get above 28, 29 degrees, the plant naturally starts to stress because it's a living surface. We're at that top level right now but as we can afford to get the irrigation on in the evenings because we've got such good weather – it's looking like this for the second week as well – at the moment we're nicely in control."

The grass almost looked good enough to eat in the opinion of Novak Djokovic. "I love tasting the grass of Wimbledon," smiled the three-times Gentlemen's Singles Champion, reflecting on his tradition of nibbling on a blade or two after each triumph. "The first time I did it, it was the sweetest dessert I've ever tasted in my life. Hopefully I'll get to taste it one more time before I finish my career."

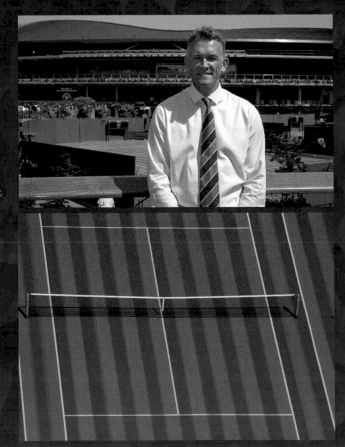

The importance of grass court ability and experience was also underlined in Tatjana Maria's 7-6(3), 4-6, 6-1 victory over Svitolina, who had not lost to an opponent ranked outside the world's top 50 for nine months. Maria, the world No.57, had won her first tour title at the previous month's Mallorca Open grass court event. The 30-year-old German's game style appeared to unsettle Svitolina, who made 44 unforced errors.

Nevertheless, Magdalena Rybarikova's previous grass court excellence was to no avail against Sorana Cirstea, who beat the No.19 seed 7-5, 6-3. Rybarikova, who was the first seed to lose in either singles event, had reached the semi-finals at The Championships last year and the previous month's final at Edgbaston. CoCo Vandeweghe, another who usually thrives on grass, also suffered a surprising defeat. Katerina Siniakova trailed the No.16 seed 5-3 in the final set but recovered to win 6-7(3), 6-3, 8-6 after more than three hours on No.3 Court. With Anastasija Sevastova (No.21 seed) and Zhang Shuai (No.31 seed) also losing, to Camila Giorgi and Andrea Petkovic respectively, the day ended with six ladies' seeds falling by the wayside. Agnieszka Radwanska, the No.32 seed, hung on by the skin of her teeth, saving six match points before beating Elena-Gabriela Ruse 6-3, 4-6, 7-5.

One of the biggest talking points of the previous week had been the seeding of Serena Williams at No.25 despite her lowly world ranking. Williams, who had been unseeded at Roland-Garros, started The Championships ranked No.181 in the world, having played only three tournaments since her comeback began in March following the birth of her daughter last autumn. The All England Club, however, reserves the freedom not to follow the world rankings automatically in making its seedings and took note of the seven-times champion's Wimbledon pedigree, not to mention the good form she had shown in Paris.

The anticipation is tangible as the crowds pour into the Grounds to claim the prime positions for the first day of Wimbledon, with some getting the bonus of a close-up view of the likes of world No.2 Caroline Wozniacki practising

Above: British teenage wild card Katie Swan was embraced by her family after her shock 6-2, 6-2 victory over Irina-Camelia Begu on Court 14

Above right: Another young Briton, Harriet Dart, also acquitted herself well, taking the second set before losing to big-serving No.7 seed Karolina Pliskova on Court 12

Playing her first match at The Championships for two years, Williams beat Arantxa Rus 7-5, 6-3. Having worn a black catsuit at Roland-Garros, the American chose a more conventional outfit on her return to SW19, although she was wearing compression tights for health reasons. Williams needed six match points to see off her Dutch opponent and explained afterwards that her serve, which has so often been a key weapon, was a work in progress following the pectoral muscle injury which had meant she had been unable to practise it until she arrived at the All England Club. "As time will go on, it will get better," she said. "My serve is a little playing catch-up, but it's doing better than I could have hoped."

Williams' sister, Venus, started slowly but was eventually a comfortable 6-7(3), 6-2, 6-1 winner over Johanna Larsson, while Caroline Wozniacki wasted no time against Varvara Lepchenko, winning 6-0, 6-3 in just 59 minutes.

Andy Murray's absence and Johanna Konta's modest form meant that hopes of British success were not as high as in past years, but 19-year-old Katie Swan gave home supporters good reason to cheer on the opening day when she bridged a gap of 168 places in the rankings to beat the world No.36, Irina-Camelia Begu, 6-2, 6-2 in just 52 minutes to record the first Grand Slam singles victory of her career. Swan, one of five highly promising young British women aged between 19 and 23 who were given wild cards, is mentored by Murray, whose management company recruited her to its stable at the start of the year. "He was my idol growing up," Swan said. "It's almost surreal being in his company."

Harriet Dart, another young Briton, won a set against Karolina Pliskova, the No.7 seed, before losing 6-7(2), 6-2, 1-6, while the two British men in action on the first day also went out. Aljaz Bedene, who represented Britain until last year but now flies the flag of Slovenia, the country of his birth, beat Cameron Norrie 4-6, 7-6(4), 7-6(4), 6-4, while Milos Raonic had too much firepower for Liam Broady, winning 7-5, 6-0, 6-2.

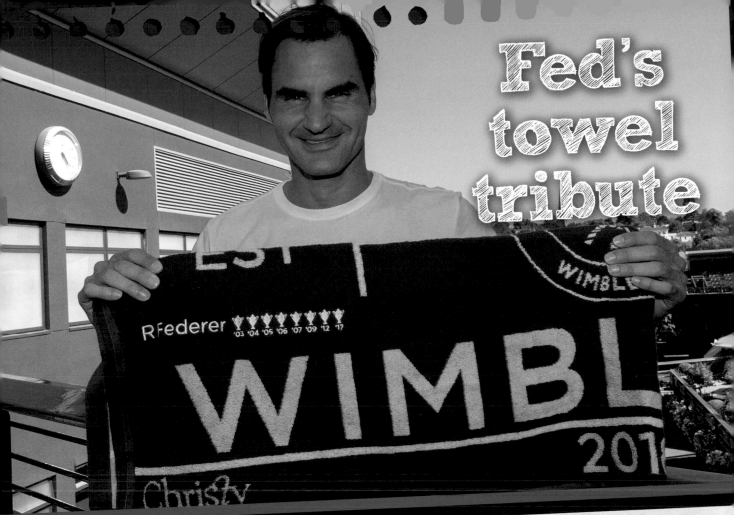

Fed's towel tribute

Eight times and counting: Roger Federer was delighted to be presented with his commemorative towel

● Now, we all love a Wimbledon towel, don't we? Not least the players. So, to mark Roger Federer's return as a record-breaking eight-times defending Gentlemen's Singles Champion, the All England Club teamed up with the great man to release 1,888 special limited edition 2018 Championships towels embroidered with his name, his eight trophies and each year of victory. Roger even proudly hung one over his chair during his first round match against Dusan Lajovic, while the rest were snapped up within 20 minutes at the No.1 Court Shop, with the proceeds going to the Wimbledon and Roger Federer Foundations.

To make sure a certain nine-times champion didn't feel left out, a set of special towels featuring all her triumphs was also presented to a delighted Martina Navratilova. "I used to have to steal my towels," she admitted with a guilty smile. "They're very dear to all of us players and make good presents – but I'm going to hold on to this one forever!"

● The Wimbledon towels are also wonderful for burying your head in when you're lost in thought. During a changeover in her match with Agnieszka Radwanska, Romanian Elena-Gabriela Ruse still had one draped completely over her head when she rose from her seat and blindly walked straight into a startled Ball Boy. Although it was completely her fault, the Ball Boy, like a true gentleman, apologised profusely. They're trained well at Wimbledon!

● One of the legion of Federer fans on Centre Court received a proper reward for her admirable persistence. As he took time signing autographs at the end of his match, a young girl manoeuvred around trying to catch his eye while holding a banner which pleaded, "ROGER CAN I HAVE YOUR HEADBAND PLEEEASE!!" Eventually, he spotted it, delved deep in his bag and pulled out the required souvenir for his supporter, who couldn't quite believe she was now the owner of the first Uniqlo 'Fed-band'.

● Among the day one victors was newly-wed Sam Querrey who, after beating Australia's Jordan Thompson, revealed how after his wedding to model Abby Dixon the previous month the pair had flown over to prepare for The Queen's Club tournament before going straight into Wimbledon mode. Watching big Sam playing tennis for four weeks? "I don't think Abby counts this as a honeymoon," said the 2017 semi-finalist with a wry smile.

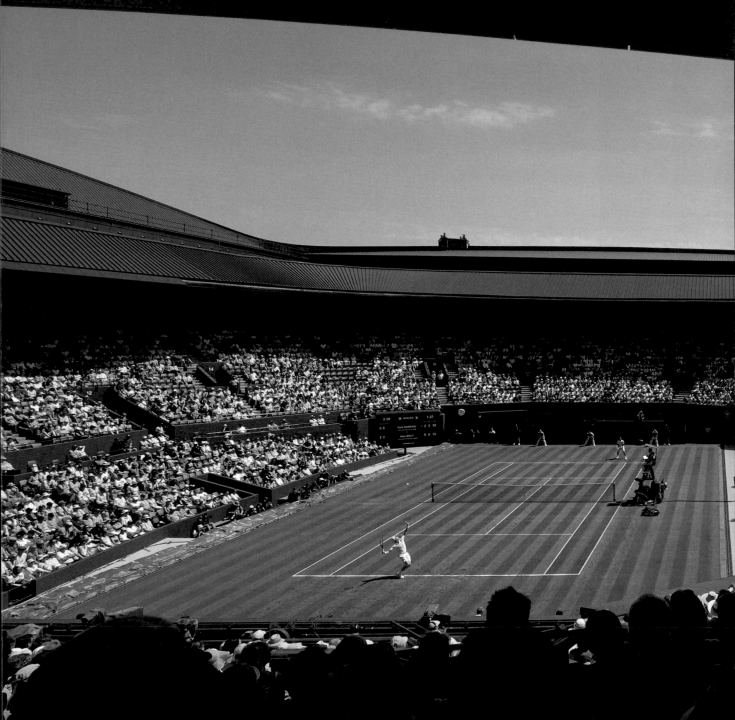

DAY
2
TUESDAY
3 JULY

If this was shaping up to be the year of the comeback, there could be little doubt which story had the potential to outdo all others. After Petra Kvitova, the Ladies' Singles Champion of 2011 and 2014, was the victim of a terrifying knife attack in her home in December 2016, doctors thought it unlikely that she would ever play again because of her horrific hand injuries. However, she returned to competition five months later and recorded some remarkable results over the next year.

In the first six months of 2018 she had won five tour-level tournaments and 38 matches, more than any other woman, and in winning at Edgbaston had demonstrated her grass court excellence. By the time The Championships began, the 28-year-old Czech was regarded by many as the favourite to win the title.

However, in one of the biggest upsets of the Fortnight, Kvitova was beaten 4-6, 6-4, 0-6 in the first round by the world No.50, Aliaksandra Sasnovich, who had lost first time out in both her warm-up tournaments. The 24-year-old Belarusian went for her shots, served well and kept focused throughout. "It was a good match but I can play better as well," she said afterwards.

Nevertheless this was a match decided largely by Kvitova's state of mind. The Czech looked drawn and ill at ease throughout and admitted afterwards that nerves had got the better of her. "I was probably my biggest opponent," Kvitova said. "It's all just down to nerves. It's nothing to do with any physical kind of movement, of the body or anything. It's just the tightness in my body. I didn't really have a clear mind. I was thinking a little bit too much. Of course, my hand is not moving as easily as it used to, so I was tight. I didn't move that well either."

She added: "I probably wanted it too much again. I joked just now that I'm probably going to skip the Grand Slams in future. When I was younger, I played better at the Grand Slams than at the other tournaments. Now I play better at the other tournaments rather than the Grand Slams."

Despite her disappointment, Kvitova kept everything in perspective, saying that she was pleased just to be playing again. "I've already won the biggest match of my life and career," she said.

Kvitova was not the only mighty oak to come tumbling down as Maria Sharapova, making her first appearance at The Championships for three years, was felled by a fellow Russian who had never previously won a match at the All England Club. The world No.132, Vitalia Diatchenko, won 6-7(3), 7-6(3), 6-4 after a remarkable match, played over more than three hours in lengthening shadows on No.2 Court.

Sharapova never looked entirely relaxed, but led by a set and 5-2. However, Diatchenko, matching Sharapova stroke for stroke from the baseline and chasing the ball to all corners, fought tenaciously. Sharapova twice led by a break in the deciding set but was unable to drive home her advantage and double-faulted on Diatchenko's first match point. "I definitely had several chances," Sharapova said afterwards. "Although not playing my best tennis, I opened up a few doors and was a couple of points away from winning."

Although Sharapova won the ladies' singles title in 2004, was runner-up in 2011 and has reached the semi-finals on three other occasions, she has also suffered some seismic defeats at the All England Club, including those to Alla Kudryavtseva (world No.154) and Michelle Larcher de Brito (world No.131) in 2008 and 2013 respectively. Sharapova missed The Championships 2016 through suspension following a drugs offence, was injured the following summer and did not play any warm-up tournaments this year after a gruelling clay court season. It meant that she had not played a competitive match on grass since her semi-final defeat to Serena Williams at The Championships 2015. "I love this place," she had tweeted during practice week. But perhaps time has taken its toll.

"The transition from clay to grass has been tougher for me as I've got older," Sharapova admitted. "That's just a matter of training, getting through the soreness in the first week or so."

Former champion Maria Sharapova was another high-profile early casualty as she suffered a shock defeat to fellow Russian Vitalia Diatchenko

Garbiñe Muguruza began the defence of her ladies' singles title with a 6-2, 7-5 victory over Britain's Naomi Broady, while Simona Halep, the world No.1 and top seed, beat Japan's Kurumi Nara 6-2, 6-4. In a meeting between two former finalists, Angelique Kerber beat Vera Zvonareva 7-5, 6-3. Zvonareva, who came through qualifying, was playing in her first Grand Slam tournament for more than three years following the birth of her first child. Caroline Garcia, the No.6 seed, was beaten 6-7(2), 3-6 by Belinda Bencic, while Anastasia Pavlyuchenkova, the No.30 seed, lost 4-6, 6-4, 3-6 to Hsieh Su-Wei.

Johanna Konta, a semi-finalist 12 months earlier, was made to work hard for her 7-5, 7-6(7) victory over Natalia Vikhlyantseva, the world No.103, but thought the experience would stand her in good stead. "The way I competed and the way I just kept going after every single point, I think I can take a lot from that," Konta said after needing six match points to complete her victory. "I think it's the tough matches, the ones where there's quite a bit of ebb and flow, when you save set points or you save break points, those are the matches where you come away feeling quite tough."

Another Briton, Katie Boulter, enjoyed her first singles victory at The Championships, beating Veronica Cepede Royg 6-4, 5-7, 6-4. "I'm ecstatic," the world No.122 said afterwards. "It's something I've dreamed of my whole life." Two other young British women lost but performed creditably. Katy Dunne relished her Centre Court chance before losing 3-6, 6-7(5) to Jelena Ostapenko while Gabriella Taylor fought back after a difficult first set against Eugenie Bouchard, who won 6-0, 4-6, 6-3. Heather Watson is a veteran in these parts in comparison with her young compatriots, but the 26-year-old was beaten 4-6, 5-7 by Kirsten Flipkens, a result that ensured Boulter would replace her as British No.2.

Jay Clarke, another British wild card, made a good impression on his Championships debut before losing 6-4, 3-6, 6-7(3), 6-3, 4-6 to Ernests Gulbis, while Kyle Edmund, the highest-ranked home singles player, beat Alex Bolt, a qualifier, 6-2, 6-3, 7-5. With England playing Colombia in the World Cup later in the day, Edmund, a keen football fan, was pleased to finish quickly.

Edmund, who reached his first Grand Slam semi-final at the Australian Open in January, was inevitably the focus of British media interest going into The Championships, but was taking everything in his stride.

MORE THAN JUST A NEW ROOF

It was a wonderful experience visiting the magnificent new No.1 Court this year. For although the arena's new retractable roof will only be completed for The Championships 2019, here was a unique opportunity for visitors to get a proper feel for the stadium's grandeur.

"The old No.1 Court is disappearing and we have a completely fixed roof which actually feels higher than the one on Centre Court," explained Robert Deatker, the Estate Director at the All England Club. "It gives it a roomy feel, and different acoustics. I think there'll be a very exciting, one-off feel to watching the tennis there this year."

Robert was not wrong. The No.1 Court crowds were to witness some of the most dramatic matches of The Championships, including two-times Ladies' Singles Champion Petra Kvitova's sensational second day defeat by Aliaksandra Sasnovich.

Yet the fascination of the massive No.1 Court project spread beyond the arena. Walking from Southfields to the All England Club, visitors were left in awe of a 'one Championships only' attraction – the nine gigantic 100-ton roof trusses being housed on two practice courts and two acrylic courts at Aorangi Park.

In October, one of Europe's biggest cranes will carry out the complex operation to move, lift and drop them into place and then we can see one of tennis' great roofed arenas in all its glory.

It isn't just No.1 Court – and its seven newly refurbished hospitality suites – itself, but its handsome new environs that make this project so very special. On the site of the old Court 19, spectators could now enjoy the opening of the Walled Garden, a new two-level public plaza that fitted in seamlessly with the traditional English country garden theme, as well as a new food market and food court. That made it easier for fans on the Hill to enjoy a leisurely lunch before following matches on a spectacular new 6 x 18 metre Big Screen, one of the largest outdoor screens in the country.

The world No.17 agreed that he had noticed more fans recognising him but insisted: "It's not like I'm a big deal or anything like that. A few more selfies, autographs, especially around this time of year, around the grass court season. It's a good thing."

Dominic Thiem, the runner-up at Roland-Garros, retired with a back injury against Marcos Baghdatis, but was the only player not to finish his first round match in either singles event. That was probably a consequence of new rules which meant that players could be fined up to the total of their first round prize money if they delivered below-par performances because of existing injuries. That had become an increasing problem at Grand Slam tournaments, with injured players taking the court because they did not want to lose their prize money. Under the new rules, players who withdrew with injury before their first round match – thereby enabling 'lucky losers' from the Qualifying Competition to take their place in the draw – still received half of what they would have won for losing in the first round. Nine lucky losers – seven men and two women – were given their chance this year.

Thiem was one of six men's seeds who lost on the second day. David Goffin was surprisingly beaten in straight sets by Matthew Ebden, while Jack Sock, Pablo Carreno Busta, Marco Cecchinato and Fernando Verdasco went out to Matteo Berrettini, Radu Albot, Alex de Minaur and Frances Tiafoe respectively. A total of 21 seeds (a Championships record) failed to make it past the first round – 11 in the gentlemen's singles and 10 in the ladies' singles.

Rafael Nadal and Novak Djokovic never looked in danger of joining the early fallers. Nadal beat Dudi Sela 6-3, 6-3, 6-2, while Djokovic beat Tennys Sandgren 6-3, 6-1, 6-2. Nadal, who had not played since winning his 11th Roland-Garros title, said there was "room to improve" but added: "After a while without playing on grass it's very important to start with a straight victory." Djokovic said that a gusting wind on No.1 Court had made the conditions challenging but thought he had played "quite a solid match".

In beating Federico Delbonis 6-3, 6-4, 6-2, Feliciano Lopez beat Roger Federer's record of 65 consecutive appearances in Grand Slam tournaments. The 36-year-old Spaniard has not missed one since playing at Roland-Garros in 2002. Lopez, who had lost all 13 of his matches against Federer, admitted: "When I was about to break the record, I thought: 'Wow, I'm going to beat Federer at something'."

Following pages: Canada's Denis Shapovalov, one of the sport's most exciting new talents, unleashes a spectacular backhand in his four-set win over Frenchman Jeremy Chardy on Court 16

Below: British teenager Jay Clarke had plenty of moments to savour in his match against Ernests Gulbis on Court 18, but the experienced Latvian eventually progressed in five sets

Caring Kyrgios

Fiery Australian Nick Kyrgios showed another side to his character after a Ball Girl was hit by one of his serves

CHAMPIONSHIPS Day 2 NOTEBOOK

• There's never a dull moment with Nick Kyrgios around and the maverick Australian's latest Wimbledon odyssey began in typically colourful fashion – but also rather painfully for one poor Ball Girl.

A 135mph ace flew past Denis Istomin's racket, reared up and smacked her in the shoulder, understandably prompting her to try to hold back a few tears. Kyrgios consoled her and was thoroughly impressed by her toughness. "She took it like a champ," he said. "I would have been crying, for sure."

• During Kyle Edmund's win over Australian Alex Bolt, No.1 Court had a fit of the giggles when some wag cried: "C'mon Andy!" It was an old joke being recycled for a new home hero, the same thing that Andy Murray used to hear when he was bursting on to the scene only to have someone shout: "C'mon Tim!" And while it's still hardly the wittiest outburst, there could be no more obvious sign that Edmund, after Murray and Henman, may really have made it at Wimbledon.

• You never quite know what to expect from Ernests Gulbis, one of the more enigmatic characters of men's tennis, as the teenage British wild card Jay Clarke discovered at the first changeover of their Court 18 match. The eccentric Latvian moseyed absent-mindedly over to the wrong side of the net, took a sip of water from Clarke's bottle and was about to delve into his bag too until the 19-year-old gave him a gentle tap on the rear and told the hardened pro 10 years his senior, in the nicest possible way, to clear off back to his own bag. Gulbis grinned apologetically and did as he was told. "He was pretty out of it at the start of the match," mused Clarke. "I don't know what he was thinking." Gulbis lost the first set but eventually woke up to win in five.

• There was great sadness in tennis when news emerged in August 2017 of how Roberta Vinci, Italy's popular multiple Grand Slam doubles winner (*below*), had all her tennis trophies stolen from her house in Taranto. The burglary included the loss of the Wimbledon ladies' doubles trophy that she won with fellow Italian Sara Errani in 2014 so the 35-year-old, who retired from the sport at the Italian Open in May, was thrilled to be invited over for a special occasion at the All England Club where she was presented with a replacement trophy.

DAY
3
WEDNESDAY
4 JULY

For years, logic had suggested that Caroline Wozniacki would be one of the regular title contenders. Wozniacki won the girls' title at the All England Club in 2006, has an outstanding record at Eastbourne, where she usually hones her preparations for The Championships, and loves playing on grass, which she believes suits her game. Yet, for a decade and more, the Dane had not managed to progress beyond the fourth round.

Perhaps 2018 would be different. Not only did the 27-year-old arrive fresh from winning the title at Eastbourne, where Angelique Kerber and Johanna Konta were among her victims, but she had also lifted the pressure on herself by winning her first Grand Slam singles title – at the 43rd attempt – at the Australian Open at the start of the year.

A quickfire victory over Varvara Lepchenko in the first round at this year's Championships had confirmed Wozniacki's good form, but day three delivered the world No.2's annual serving of Wimbledon woe. Wozniacki was beaten 4-6, 6-1, 5-7 by Ekaterina Makarova, a player she had defeated in seven of their eight previous meetings. Makarova went for her shots from the start, with the match statistics telling their own story. The 30-year-old Russian's strategy of all-out attack brought her 37 unforced errors to Wozniacki's 22, but, crucially, she also hit 46 winners to her opponent's 23. Makarova nevertheless needed six match points to complete her victory. "I told myself I was not going to lose this match," she said afterwards. "I had so many match points, but I forgot it and started over."

There was an invasion of flying ants during the match – "I want to focus on playing tennis and not eating bugs," Wozniacki told the umpire at one stage – but later insisted that the insects had not affected the result and was philosophical in defeat. "It's frustrating because I feel like I could have gone and done something really great here," she said. "I did everything I could. I fought as hard as I could. I can't even be mad at myself because I played up to the level that I can. I think she played above her level and really raised it and got a little lucky and played well when she needed to."

She added: "I played someone who went all-in with every single shot. In the second set, I think that showed to me that that was in my head, how I wanted it to go. Then she started again hitting a lot of lines, a lot of crazy shots that were going in."

The result, which ensured that Simona Halep would remain on top of the world rankings after The Championships, extended Makarova's remarkable record at Grand Slam tournaments. Although the world No.35 has never reached a Grand Slam singles final, her list of victims at the sport's four biggest tournaments includes Serena and Venus Williams, Kerber, Petra Kvitova, Garbiñe Muguruza, Victoria Azarenka, Halep, Marion Bartoli and Ana Ivanovic.

Agnieszka Radwanska, who was beaten 5-7, 4-6 by Lucie Safarova, was the only other ladies' seed to go out on the third day, but Wozniacki's departure left only three of the top eight seeds still in the competition. However, their number included Karolina Pliskova, another player with a poor Championships record despite her good results elsewhere on grass. The 26-year-old Czech, seeded No.7, finally reached the third round at the seventh attempt by beating Azarenka 6-3, 6-3 in a meeting of two former world No.1s. Pliskova, who had gone out in the second round 12 months earlier when seeded No.3, said she had tried to put less pressure on herself this year. "I'm very happy with my victory as it is the first time I am in the third round here," she said. "The last few years I was waiting for a good result and it still didn't come. Maybe this year is the time. I am feeling great."

Australian Open champion Wozniacki, who had never been past Wimbledon's fourth round in 11 previous attempts, suffered another frustrating early exit

TENNIS MOTHERS ON THE MARCH

The return of Serena Williams to SW19, bringing baby daughter Alexis Olympia with her, helped shine a fresh spotlight on the six working tennis mums featuring in the ladies' singles.

Williams, Victoria Azarenka, Kateryna Bondarenko, Tatjana Maria, Vera Zvonareva and Evgeniya Rodina are all faced with special challenges, having to make considerable sacrifices as they attempt to juggle their careers with the demands of motherhood, and though they all conceded it wasn't easy, they reckoned they'd have it no other way.

Williams was emotional about missing Olympia's first steps during the first week because she was practising, while Azarenka talked of her guilt over the amount of time she's away from her one-year-old son, Leo.

"It's difficult for me because I schedule everything around him and try to maximise my time with him," explained two-times Grand Slam champion Azarenka, who lovingly writes Leo's name on her match shoes. "So whenever he's sleeping, that's when I'm working, and other times I'm a full-time mom. It's more challenging, but I wouldn't change it."

On this special mums' Wednesday, Azarenka (*above*), Maria and Williams all enjoyed the limelight on Centre Court, although Azarenka and Maria – a first round winner over Elina Svitolina – lost out to Karolina Pliskova and Kristina Mladenovic respectively.

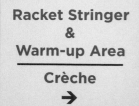

Racket Stringer & Warm-up Area

Crèche

→

Tatjana Maria (top) and her daughter Charlotte are clearly big fans of Wimbledon's fun-filled creche. "Here, it's the best. You bring your children, they eat together, do activities. It's beautiful to see her after you've played a match," she smiled.

strawberr...

THE MUMS WHO WON

How hard is it for a mother to win Wimbledon? Well, only four women have ever achieved the feat – and only one in the modern era.

Blanche Hillyard, who competed in the first ever ladies' singles in 1884, won one of her six titles as a mother-of-one and three more after having her second child. Her great rival, Charlotte Sterry (née Cooper), won four titles before starting a family and returned to win again as a mother-of-two in 1908.

The great seven-times Ladies' Singles Champion Dorothea Lambert Chambers won four titles in five editions as a mother between 1910 and 1914, missing 1912 only because she gave birth to her second son. We then waited another 66 years as the dramatic improvement in athleticism at the top of the game and the advent of professionalism made being a champion tennis-playing mum a vastly more difficult proposition.

Yet the graceful, modest Australian Evonne Goolagong Cawley, who first lifted the title as a teenager in 1971, delighted everyone by winning again in 1980 (*left*) as a mother to three-year-old Kelly.

So now it's over to you, Serena…

Serena Williams moved up a gear from the first round to beat Bulgaria's Viktoriya Tomova 6-1, 6-4 but said she had not been surprised at the number of top players who had been beaten. "It's hard," she said. "Everyone's playing hard. No one's giving you anything for free. Today I didn't get anything for free. In my first round, I didn't get anything for free." The seven-times Ladies' Singles Champion admitted that she had felt under stress in her opening match, but believed she was now moving in the right direction. "There's so many things that I want to improve on, but that's kind of how I always feel," she said.

Venus Williams also moved into the third round but once again had to come from a set down before beating Romania's Alexandra Dulgheru 4-6, 6-0, 6-1. The 128-strong draw for the ladies' singles featured a total of eight Romanians, including one with a remarkable story. Mihaela Buzarnescu, aged 30, who has a PhD in sports science, had never played in a Grand Slam tournament until the 2017 US Open, but after a career plagued by injuries had shot up the world rankings. At the start of 2017 she was playing in minor tournaments in Uzbekistan, Egypt and Turkey, but after winning seven tournaments on the International Tennis Federation (ITF) circuit she had risen to No.72 in the world rankings by the end of the year, which meant she could start playing regularly on the main Women's Tennis Association (WTA) tour.

By the time Buzarnescu arrived at the All England Club she had played a remarkable 100 matches in the previous 12 months and climbed to No.28 in the world. She had to come from behind to beat Aryna Sabalenka, the Eastbourne runner-up, in three sets in the first round, but brushed aside the challenge of Britain's Katie Swan in the second, winning 6-0, 6-3 in just 74 minutes.

After two days of turmoil in the gentlemen's singles some order was restored, with Lucas Pouille the only seed to go out. The Frenchman, seeded No.17, was beaten 4-6, 2-6, 7-6(8), 6-3, 2-6 by Austria's Dennis Novak, a qualifier ranked No.171 in the world.

Roger Federer rarely looked in any trouble against Lukas Lacko, who at Eastbourne had just played in only his second tour-level singles final and had arrived at The Championships having already played 11 matches on grass in the build-up. However, that experience proved to no avail as the 30-year-old Slovakian was swept aside by Federer, who completed a 6-4, 6-4, 6-1 victory in an hour and a half to take his number of successive winning sets at The Championships to 26. The 36-year-old Swiss gave a serving masterclass, dropping only nine points on his serve in the whole match. From 4-3 and 40-30 in the opening set until 4-1 and 30-0 in the third, the eight-times Gentlemen's Singles Champion won 35 service points in a row.

"Sometimes your serve matches up better against certain players," Federer said afterwards. "When you want to serve well I think what's important is your point-for-point mentality. You maybe say that the first point is as important as a break point, so the concentration is the same. You try to remember all the things you've done throughout the entire match, what has worked, what hasn't worked.

Left (clockwise from top left): *Czech Lucie Safarova, Romania's Mihaela Buzarnescu, and Serena Williams all roared their way into the third round of the ladies' singles*

Below: Austrian qualifier Dennis Novak continued his surprise run by knocking out French No.17 seed Lucas Pouille on Court 18

Well that was unexpected!

Such had been the glorious weather that everyone felt almost a little indignant about the Wednesday evening stoppage for rain that came out of the blue and spoiled the fun, briefly turning parasols into umbrellas and forcing players like Stan Wawrinka off the courts. As it turned out, though, it was the only rain break of the entire Fortnight, making this the most sun-blessed tournament since the 2010 edition, which saw no interruptions at all.

Milos Raonic (**below**), watched by an awe-struck No.2 Court crowd (**right**), struck a 147mph serve – the second fastest ever at Wimbledon – in his win against Australian John Millman

"I don't need that much time, especially after a short previous rally, to go through all of that and reassess everything very quickly. I think I can do that very well. Then it's more than just serving. It's also first-strike tennis, serve and first shot, serve and taking the right decisions as you go along."

It was a day when there was plenty of big serving on show from some big men. Milos Raonic (6ft 5in) hit 34 aces in beating John Millman 7-6(4), 7-6(4), 7-6(4) and Sam Querrey (6ft 6in) hit 17 in a 7-6(4), 6-3, 6-3 victory over Sergiy Stakhovsky. However, 61 aces (making it a record 12,862 across his career) were still not enough for Ivo Karlovic (6ft 11in), who was beaten 7-6(5), 6-3, 6-7(4), 6-7(4), 11-13 in just under four hours by Jan-Lennard Struff. Madison Keys, who has one of the best serves in the women's game, was asked whether she enjoyed watching the biggest servers in the men's game. "I'm going to be totally honest with you," the American said after her 6-4, 6-3 victory over Thailand's Luksika Kumkhum. "I find it kind of boring. Sorry."

Three more of the game's biggest servers were also in action, but John Isner (6ft 10in), Kevin Anderson (6ft 8in) and Marin Cilic (6ft 6in) were unable to complete their matches because of rain. Yes, rain. The only showers to disrupt The Championships 2018 started to fall just before 7pm. Play had already finished on Centre Court, but five other men's matches were eventually called off for the day, though Cilic and Guido Pella resumed very briefly on No.1 Court. Cilic was leading by two sets to love, but went a break down in the third on the final point of the day. It was to prove a significant moment, as we would discover less than 24 hours later.

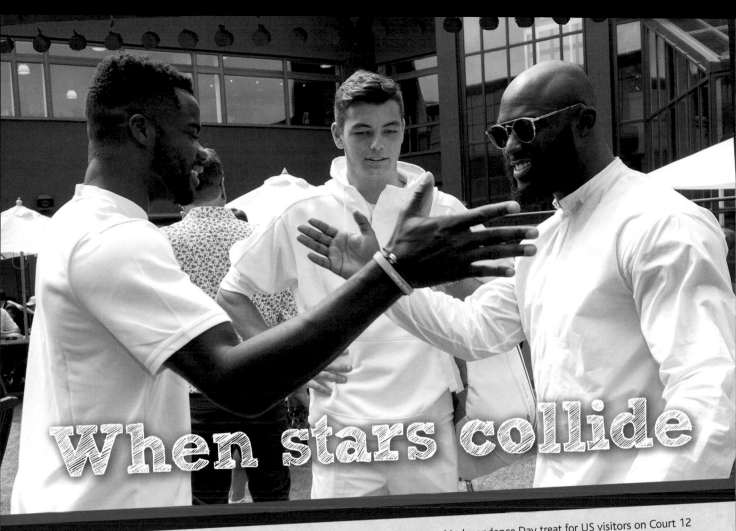

When stars collide

American footballer Leonard Fournette (right) greets rising US star Frances Tiafoe (left) and Taylor Fritz (middle) during his tour of the All England Club

• One distinguished US visitor attending The Championships on day three was American football star Leonard Fournette, the power-packed Jacksonville Jaguars running back. One of the NFL's hottest properties, the 23-year-old admitted he had never played tennis in his life. "But if I practised at it, I might be top five," he added breezily. In the meantime, an athlete tipped for greatness reckoned he was just going to watch Serena and Roger on Centre Court because "I'm ready to see greatness in my eyes, man".

• On a day of monster serving, Milos Raonic crashed down the biggest of all, a 147mph serve to the body that, as one TV commentator chuckled, nearly "tattooed" his browbeaten opponent, Australian John Millman. It proved to be the fastest delivery of the entire Championships, just 1mph slower than Taylor Dent's 2010 record, leaving everyone to gulp at the thought of just how quick Canada's 2016 finalist might have been had he not been suffering from a virus.

The straight-sets defeat after three tie-breaks proved not to be Millman's only problem. The Queenslander had been told by officials that his underwear was too bright beneath his thin shorts and thus breached the all-white clothing rule so his dad, Ron, was sent on an emergency mission to a local shop to buy something more suitable.

• We had a real Independence Day treat for US visitors on Court 12 with three big-serving Americans ensuring this would be no yawn on 4 July. Madison Keys and Sam Querrey did their bit with comfortable victories but the drama came with a frustrated John Isner seeing a two-set lead disappear against Belgian Ruben Bemelmans while losing patience with Hawk-Eye, insisting that it wasn't working properly, and receiving a code violation for his behaviour. Eventually, the first rain of the week in the fifth set meant he could cool down overnight with the match still in the balance.

• Wimbledon hasn't had many guests quite as unwelcome as the swarms of flying ants that descended on the Grounds for a second straight year, a natural phenomenon that tends to occur in hot weather, which unfortunately bugged spectators and players alike for a brief period in the late afternoon.

While a few players had to swat the legions of creatures away as the ants embarked on their 'nuptial flight', none seemed quite as fazed as No.2 seed Caroline Wozniacki, who asked the umpire during her second round defeat to Ekaterina Makarova if they could find some insect repellent.

The Dane felt that the invasion died down pretty swiftly and she refused to blame her performance on being distracted by the insects. "I don't think it had any impact," she shrugged. "But it was definitely a first for me here."

DAY
4

THURSDAY
5 JULY

G oing into The Championships 2018 no man other than Roger Federer and Rafael Nadal had a better recent record at Grand Slam level than Marin Cilic. The 29-year-old Croatian had reached his first Wimbledon final the previous summer, only to have his chances of beating Federer scuppered by a painful foot blister.

Six months later Cilic pushed Federer much harder in the Australian Open final before the Swiss won after five hard-fought sets. Given that Cilic had also won his second grass court title at The Queen's Club the previous month, the former US Open champion was regarded as one of the favourites for the gentlemen's singles title.

The ease of Cilic's opening victory over Yoshihito Nishioka suggested that the No.3 seed would not have too much trouble next time out against Guido Pella, a 28-year-old Argentinian who had just won a singles match at The Championships for the first time. Indeed, Cilic appeared to be coasting when he took the first two sets on No.1 Court on Wednesday for the loss of only four games. Even when he dropped serve at 3-3 in the third set there did not appear to be any cause for concern in the world No.5's camp.

That break of serve was the last action of a rain-interrupted evening and proved a foretaste of what was to come when the match resumed in bright sunshine at 1pm the following day. In a remarkable turnaround, Pella sprang one of the biggest surprises of The Championships to win 3-6, 1-6, 6-4, 7-6(3), 7-5.

Even when Pella served out for the third set, winning his first two service games of the day to love, few would have expected the world No.82 to maintain his momentum, but he then recovered from 3-1 down in the fourth set and took the tie-break with something to spare. By now Cilic's two biggest weapons, his serve and forehand, were misfiring badly, while Pella's confidence was rising. There were no breaks of serve in the decider until the 12th game, in which three successive forehand errors by Cilic handed Pella the biggest victory of his career.

Cilic insisted that he had not felt burdened by expectations as one of the pre-tournament favourites. "I was still focusing on my game," he said. "I was just not feeling as comfortable as yesterday with my hitting.

I was not as accurate. I was missing some easy balls and giving him a chance to come back. It was not just the pressure. It was me not executing well on the court."

Pella said that his coach had told him to play more aggressively on the resumption. "Yesterday the match started so badly for me," he said. "Today was very different because I started to feel very good. I closed out the third set with some big serves and after that I started to feel better and better."

It was a day book-ended by significant upsets as Garbiñe Muguruza, the defending champion, went out of the ladies' singles in the last match on No.2 Court. Beaten 7-5, 2-6, 1-6 by Belgium's Alison van Uytvanck, Muguruza made the earliest exit by a defending Ladies' Singles Champion at Wimbledon since Steffi Graf lost in the first round in 1994. The result underlined Muguruza's reputation for inconsistency. The Spaniard was runner-up to Serena Williams on Centre Court in 2015, won Roland-Garros in 2016 and beat Venus Williams here in the 2017 final, but has also suffered a number of surprising early defeats in tournaments.

Van Uytvanck, the world No.47, had lost in the first round in her three previous appearances at The Championships. With nothing to lose, the 24-year-old Belgian went on all-out attack after the first set. "I was in the zone and just hitting every ball and it was going my way," she said afterwards. Muguruza agreed. "She played big," the No.3 seed said. "She took a lot of risk, and it worked for her. I also think that my level today was not where I wanted it to be."

As well as Cilic, three other men's seeds departed as Diego Schwartzman, Denis Shapovalov and Damir Dzumhur lost to Jiri Vesely, Benoit Paire and Ernests Gulbis respectively, while John Isner saved two match points before completing a 6-1, 6-4, 6-7(6), 6-7(3), 7-5 victory over Belgium's Ruben Bemelmans. Isner hit 64 aces in the match, which had been called off the previous evening with Bemelmans leading 4-3 in the decider. Kevin Anderson also found his serving rhythm, hitting 34 aces in his 6-3, 6-7(5), 6-3, 6-4 victory over Andreas Seppi.

Stan Wawrinka's match against Thomas Fabbiano was another that had spilled over into a second day. Although Fabbiano had taken the first two sets on Wednesday, the Italian had just saved two set points when serving at 5-6 in the third when Jake Garner, the umpire, called a halt to proceedings despite Wawrinka's pleas. Fabbiano, a qualifier, held serve when the match resumed and then saved two more set points in the

All power to Belgian Alison van Uytvanck, who celebrated perhaps the biggest shock of the week by knocking out defending Ladies' Singles Champion Garbiñe Muguruza on No.2 Court

NEW IN AT NUMBER ONE

Kyle Edmund ended the day as the last British player left in the singles draws following Johanna Konta's exit, but as he enjoyed his maiden victory on Centre Court over American Bradley Klahn he seemed to be growing quietly and impressively into his role as the big home hope.

The 23-year-old Yorkshireman, a self-effacing, laid-back figure with a big, bold game, appeared eminently level-headed and unfazed by all the hype and expectation that goes with being the British No.1 at Wimbledon, especially with the home fans desperate for someone to fill Andy Murray's golden shoes this year. "I've felt a little bit more attention," shrugged the modest Edmund. "But it's not like I'm a big deal or anything."

But it's obvious to observers that he could become a very big deal very soon. Having surged into the world's top 20 and earned his first victory over Murray in Eastbourne, the Australian Open semi-finalist is beginning to look and feel as if he belongs in the elite. "You go from being a little kid dreaming of it, then when it becomes reality, sometimes it can be a bit surreal," he admitted. "At the end of the day it's my job. You have to believe in yourself. There's a reason why you're there."

He could certainly be encouraged by a resounding endorsement from the man he's attempting to emulate. "I'm really happy that Kyle's doing really well," said Murray. "It's great for British tennis, with the stage of my career I'm at, to have another player at the top of the game. Hopefully, he'll be competing for the biggest tournaments – he's improving all the time as a top player."

tie-break before winning 7-6(7), 6-3, 7-6(6). Although Wawrinka had failed to build on his opening round victory over Grigor Dimitrov, the world No.224 was happy with his fitness and his level of tennis following knee surgery. "Now it's about getting back the confidence, winning some tough matches," he said.

Feliciano Lopez's record 66th consecutive appearance in a Grand Slam tournament ended in a 4-6, 1-6, 2-6 defeat by Juan Martin del Potro. Nick Kyrgios eased to a 6-3, 6-4, 7-5 victory over Robin Haase, but his fellow Australian, Bernard Tomic, the world No.184, was beaten 6-2, 3-6, 6-7(7), 5-7 by Kei Nishikori. Tomic had come through the Qualifying Competition after falling 125 places in the world rankings since The Championships 2017.

Rafael Nadal and Novak Djokovic both won in straight sets again. Nadal, nevertheless, was made to work for his 6-4, 6-3, 6-4 victory over Mikhail Kukushkin during an oppressively hot day on Centre Court. The Roland-Garros champion was handed two time violations by the umpire after taking too long at the start – the All England Club had announced earlier in the year that it would strictly enforce the one-five-one minute rule for warm-ups – and tardiness before the start of the third set.

Djokovic needed only 91 minutes to beat Horacio Zeballos 6-1, 6-2, 6-3 on his debut on No.2 Court. The Serb enjoyed the experience. "What was different was the walk to the court, with everybody cheering you on, wishing you luck, and then after the match congratulating you," he said. "That was quite special, quite different."

World No.1 Simona Halep was in ruthless mood on day four, reeling off the last 10 successive games to complete a 7-5, 6-0 win over China's Zheng Saisai

Kyle Edmund made only his second appearance on Centre Court, having lost to Gael Monfils 12 months earlier. The 23-year-old Briton beat qualifier Bradley Klahn 6-4, 7-6(0), 6-2. Edmund did not have to defend any break points and made just 13 unforced errors. "You grow up watching Centre Court and dreaming of winning there, so you'll always remember the first match you win there," Edmund said afterwards.

Edmund was the last British singles player standing for the fourth successive Grand Slam tournament after Katie Boulter and Johanna Konta both lost. Boulter could be satisfied with her performance in losing 3-6, 4-6 to No.18 seed Naomi Osaka, but Konta would surely have hoped for better than a 3-6, 4-6 defeat to a fired-up Dominika Cibulkova on Centre Court.

Cibulkova, nevertheless, was in theory the toughest opponent any seed could have met in the second round. The Slovakian would have been seeded No.32 – and therefore could not have faced another seed until the third round – but for the All England Club's decision to seed Serena Williams despite the American's lowly world ranking. Cibulkova controlled the majority of the rallies against Konta and had to defend only one break point. "When she's playing well, she really goes for her shots," Konta, the No.22 seed, said afterwards. "She was hitting winners from five metres behind the baseline."

On the same court last year Konta had beaten Simona Halep to become the first Briton to reach the ladies' singles semi-finals for 39 years. As a consequence she had reached a career-high position at No.4 in the world, but after this defeat and other disappointments over the previous 12 months the 27-year-old would now drop to No.50. Nevertheless, she remained positive. "I am not terribly worried about losing a number next to my name," Konta explained. "This year I actually feel like I'm heading in the direction I want to be heading in. I think I'm improving. I think sooner or later those results will come."

Angelique Kerber took time to get going against Claire Liu, the 2017 Girls' Singles Champion, but won 3-6, 6-2, 6-4. Halep, the No.1 seed, also made a slow start, but won the last 10 games to beat Zheng Saisai 7-5, 6-0. After two rounds, Halep was the only top 10 seed left in the top half of the draw but insisted that the fate of other leading players would not affect her. "It doesn't mean that I will win the tournament because they lost," she said. "Every match is really difficult here."

The next big thing

Stefanos Tsitsipas gets airborne in typically flamboyant style to hit a crucial winner against America's Jared Donaldson

CHAMPIONSHIPS Day 4 NOTEBOOK

• The spirit of Boris Becker was rekindled on Court 18 where Stefanos Tsitsipas, the brilliant Greek teenager who does love to hurl himself around the grass like the old German wunderkind, sealed a game in the fifth set of his win over Jared Donaldson by diving headlong to meet the American's searing pass with an incredibly acrobatic backhand volley. "Wow, welcome to the future of men's tennis!" declared the commentator – and we knew exactly what he meant.

• Ten years since she won the Wimbledon girls' singles title as a 14-year-old, Laura Robson, commentating for the Tennis Channel during The Championships, underwent a successful hip surgery in an attempt to rebuild a promising career interrupted cruelly by injury woes. Sharing a post-op photo on social media, she wrote: "Posting a pic so people might finally stop asking when I'm playing at Wimbledon this year." Like a real trooper, she was soon to be seen back at work on her crutches.

• To mark the 70th anniversary of the National Health Service, the All England Club was delighted to invite the inspirational Professor Dame Elizabeth Nneka Anionwu, honoured for her services to nursing in the 2017 Queen's New Year's Honours List, to represent NHS England as a guest in the Royal Box.

The All England Club also chose this occasion to announce the appointment of Dr Fenella Wrigley, of the London Ambulance Service, as the first Chief Medical Officer of the AELTC and The Championships from 2019.

• A year on since the terrible injury that befell Bethanie Mattek-Sands, who ruptured a patella tendon and dislocated a kneecap on Court 17, the flamboyant American made the most heartwarming return to Wimbledon – and a winning one too – with her great friend and doubles partner Lucie Safarova.

The 33-year-old had the previous week already made an emotional trip back to Court 17 to bring some closure to the awful episode that sidelined her for eight months but there were no more tears to be shed as she and Safarova, five-times Grand Slam doubles champions, got back to business on Court 5 to beat 16th seeds Alla Kudryavtseva and Lyudmyla Kichenok in the first round.

"It kind of felt like old times," declared the pink-haired Bethanie, who has a scar running across her reconstructed right knee. "Lucie and I were the same on the court. It didn't even feel like 12 months went by and it was really special that I got my win with my bestie beside me. We had a lot of fun and I'm really happy to be back."

DAY
5
FRIDAY
6 JULY

A

As the surprising outcomes in the ladies' singles continued, with defeats for Venus Williams and Madison Keys taking the number of top 10 seeds left standing to just two, it was tempting to suggest that the draw was opening up for Serena Williams.

However, the 36-year-old American was having none of it. "A lot of the top players are losing, but they're losing to girls that are playing outstanding," Williams said after securing her place in the last 16 with a 7-5, 7-6(2) victory over Kristina Mladenovic. "I think, if anything, it shows me every moment that I can't underestimate any of these ladies. They are just going out there swinging and playing for broke."

From the moment Williams played an exhibition event in Abu Dhabi in December 2017, less than four months after the birth of her daughter, Alexis Olympia, and a month after her marriage to the internet entrepreneur, Alexis Ohanian, it was clear that the former world No.1 would do everything within her powers to climb back to the summit.

Not even a difficult birth and subsequent health complications could weaken Williams' desire to return. Olympia was delivered by emergency caesarean section, after which Williams was confined to bed for six weeks. She suffered a pulmonary embolism and underwent surgery to prevent blood clots from reaching her lungs. The former world No.1 said at The Championships that the experiences had made her "appreciate that I'm out here, that I'm alive, that I'm able to be here and do well".

Williams made her return to the tour in March at Indian Wells and Miami, 14 months after her last competitive appearance at the 2017 Australian Open, which she won when eight weeks pregnant. However, it was clear from her results (two wins and two defeats) that she still had plenty of work to do. She did not play again until Roland-Garros, where she beat two top 20 players, Ashleigh Barty and Julia Goerges, before a pectoral muscle injury led to her withdrawal just before she was due to face Maria Sharapova in the fourth round.

"I felt good going into Roland-Garros," Williams said after her latest victory here over Mladenovic. "I had a long time of training – serious training every day, all the time. I felt really, really, really, really good going into that. I also didn't have any pressure on me. It almost felt weird."

She added: "I don't necessarily have to win another Wimbledon in my career. I don't have anything to lose. I have absolutely nothing to prove. Everything is a bonus."

Whereas Williams' first two opponents at The Championships had both been ranked outside the world's top 100, Mladenovic, who had been in the top 10 the previous summer, provided a serious test. The Frenchwoman led 5-3 in the opening set, but Williams' fightback demonstrated how her game – and in particular her serve – was back in good order. She closed out her victory with two successive aces. "I'm feeling pretty good," she said. "I haven't had any problems yet. I think taking those three weeks of just doing absolutely no serving, just a ton of rehab for my shoulder, really helped."

In making such an impressive comeback, Williams was underlining her status as a role model for women in general and for mothers returning to work. "Women are really strong," she said. "We are real fighters. We fight for absolutely everything we get, every opportunity we get, whether it's tennis, any other sport, a company, a CEO position, a board position."

Williams had been happy to share photographs and videos of her daughter with the public via social media. When it was pointed out to her that some other players preferred to keep their children out of public view, she replied: "It's 2018. I'm so modern. I didn't even think about it. For me, it was so natural. She's so fun. I just want to share those moments with everyone."

Left: While her little sister Serena beat one 'Kiki', last year's finalist Venus Williams was defeated by another, Dutchwoman Kiki Bertens, on No.1 Court

Following pages: This young fan had the right idea on yet another hot day at The Championships, splashing around in the water feature at the top of the Hill

OPEN TENNIS: 50 YEARS YOUNG

To celebrate the 50th anniversary of Open tennis at Wimbledon, how wonderful it was to see Billie Jean King and Rod Laver, the two champions from that inaugural Open Championships of 1968, back together in the Royal Box as Special Guests of All England Club Chairman Philip Brook.

The two trailblazers, Billie Jean at 74 and Rod at 79, enjoyed reminiscing about that landmark Championships where the pair of them led off the dancing at the Champions' Dinner (*right*).

The memory brought a smile to Laver, who remembered he had been a bit worried about whether he'd only show off his two right feet on the dance floor. "A bit of a nerve-wracking situation," he recalled with a laugh.

The pair, who went on to win 23 Grand Slam singles titles between them, became great friends over the years and their admiration for each other as legends of the game has only grown apace.

"I couldn't have been more pleased to have won my first 'prize money' Wimbledon with Rod Laver there. That's just poetic, it's perfect," reflected Billie Jean, who also recorded an episode of *Desert Island Discs* at Wimbledon during her visit. "I just love that guy and to watch him play – aaaah, I wish he could still play – he was just so beautiful to watch."

Billie Jean, reckoned Rod, was "probably a saviour when it came to ladies' Open tennis" – the key figure in the drive to ensure that the women's game received the publicity and rewards it deserved.

Richard Lewis, the All England Club Chief Executive, said of the great duo: "It's wonderful to have them here with us as we celebrate how Wimbledon was a driving force behind bringing tennis into the Open era and helping make the sport what it is today."

The seven-times Ladies' Singles Champion had a big impact on the match that decided her next opponent. Keys, the No.10 seed, admitted after her 5-7, 7-5, 4-6 defeat to Evgeniya Rodina that she had made the crucial mistake of thinking ahead to meeting her fellow American in the next round when she led 5-2 in the first set. Keys lost the next nine games and went on to make a total of 48 unforced errors. "I don't think I did a good job of keeping in the moment and playing the person who was in front of me," Keys said afterwards. "I started playing not to lose, which doesn't usually work out well for me."

Rodina, a 29-year-old Russian who had earned her place in the draw via the Qualifying Competition, was the only mother other than Williams left in the competition. The world No.120 had returned to the tour in the summer of 2013, nine months after the birth of her daughter, Anna.

The only player in the draw older than Williams was her 38-year-old sister, Venus, who was beaten 2-6, 7-6(5), 6-8 by the Dutchwoman Kiki Bertens. The five-times Ladies' Singles Champion recovered after a slow start, but Bertens kept her nerve to secure a place in the fourth round for the first time. Williams, the runner-up to Garbiñe Muguruza 12 months earlier, said afterwards that she had "just run out of time", but was in monosyllabic mood when asked about the future. Did she expect to return next year? "Yeah," Williams replied, without any further comment. Williams was the eighth of the top 10 seeds to lose and was almost followed by a ninth before Karolina Pliskova recovered from a set and 1-4 down to beat Mihaela Buzarnescu 3-6, 7-6(3), 6-1.

In the gentlemen's singles, two of the younger guard caught the eye. Stefanos Tsitsipas, aged 19, became the first Greek man in the Open era to reach the fourth round of a Grand Slam tournament when he beat Thomas Fabbiano 6-2, 6-1, 6-4, while Alexander Zverev continued his recent habit of winning five-set matches by beating Taylor Fritz 6-4, 5-7, 6-7(0), 6-1, 6-2.

Tsitsipas, the world No.35, whose all-action style has made him an immediate hit with the public, had climbed 157 places in the world rankings since The Championships 2017. At 6ft 4in tall and with flowing brown hair he does not look dissimilar to Zverev, who was already at No.3 in the world despite having usually failed to find his best form at Grand Slam tournaments. However, the 21-year-old German had just reached the quarter-finals at Roland-Garros, where he won three successive five-set matches.

After losing two of the first three sets in fading light on Thursday evening to Fritz, Zverev took immediate control when their second round match resumed and dropped only three more

French favourite Gael Monfils celebrated a fine 5-7, 6-4, 6-4, 6-2 win over last year's semi-finalist Sam Querrey on Centre Court

World No.3 Alexander Zverev fought back from two sets to one down in his resumed second round match against American Taylor Fritz

games. "Stopping at 2-1 down was not a nice feeling, but I played better than yesterday," Zverev said afterwards. "I think I showed today that I am playing my best tennis."

Both Tsitsipas and Zverev still have a long way to go before they might even go close to emulating the feats of Roger Federer, who beat Germany's Jan-Lennard Struff 6-3, 7-5, 6-2 in the 200th tour-level grass court match of his career. Federer, who in the first round had passed Jimmy Connors' Open era record of 102 matches played at The Championships, extended his number of consecutive sets won at the All England Club to 29 despite a big-hitting display by Struff, who was attempting to reach the fourth round of a Grand Slam tournament for the first time.

The crowd on Centre Court were even treated to a Federer 'SABR' shot ('sneak attack by Roger'), with the 36-year-old Swiss charging forward to return a serve on the half-volley. Federer, who went on to win the point with a volley, first used the tactic in 2015, but it had been seen only rarely in recent times. "I can never practise it because how do you?" Federer said. "I just feel like it's not really what you do in a practice with other guys. They would be like: 'Really?' I can only really practise it with my coach."

Three more 30-somethings continued to make impressive progress. Kevin Anderson hit 22 aces in beating Philipp Kohlschreiber 6-3, 7-5, 7-5, while Gael Monfils and John Isner both reached the fourth round for the first time in their 10th appearances at The Championships. Monfils beat Sam Querrey, a semi-finalist last year, 5-7, 6-4, 6-4, 6-2, and Isner did not have to defend a single break point in his 6-3, 6-3, 6-4 victory over Radu Albot. Another American, Mackenzie McDonald, reached the fourth round on his Championships debut by beating Guido Pella 6-4, 6-4, 7-6(6).

The gentlemen's doubles was still in its early stages, but the top two seeds both went out. Oliver Marach and Mate Pavic, the No.1 seeds, let slip a two-set lead in the first round against Federico Delbonis and Miguel Angel Reyes-Varela, who won 4-6, 6-7(3), 6-4, 7-5, 6-2. Lukasz Kubot and Marcelo Melo, the No.2 seeds and defending champions, were beaten 7-6(5), 4-6, 6-7(4), 6-7(8) in the second round by Jonathan Erlich and Marcin Matkowski.

Route 66

Feliciano Lopez was all smiles as he was presented with a gift to mark his 66th consecutive Grand Slam appearance

• The evergreen Spanish serve-and-volleyer Feliciano Lopez was knocked out in the second round on Thursday by Argentina's Juan Martin del Potro, yet the Grand Slam Board did not want the 36-year-old's outstanding achievement of having competed in a record 66th consecutive Grand Slam to pass by without recognition. A gathering was convened to mark the occasion the following day, at which Lopez was presented with a set of photographs from his run of 66 – one from each Slam – and three bottles of wine from the year 2002, the start of his streak.

The man who's been to every Grand Slam for the last 16 years was rightly proud of his achievement, not least because of the individual – a certain Roger Federer – he had surpassed to get there.

"It's only a number," said Lopez, "but I'm really proud of my consistency. It's not about the number of Grand Slams played; it's about how many years I have been playing at the top level. This is the most important thing."

• Daniil Medvedev, one of the best young players on the circuit, bowed out at the hands of Adrian Mannarino in a hard-fought five-setter but the Russian departed with his reputation enhanced – except in one area. The 22-year-old made a dozen Hawk-Eye challenges and not one was upheld, the worst record of anyone at Wimbledon in 2018. On the ladies' side, Simona Halep may be the world No.1 but she was bottom of the class on challenges – getting none right in six.

• After an exhausting five hours and two minutes, El Salvador's Marcelo Arevalo and Chilean Hans Podlipnik-Castillo beat British pair Jay Clarke and Cameron Norrie 6-4, 6-7(5), 5-7, 6-4, 22-20. It seemed nailed on to be the longest match of The Championships. Little did we know...

• This was the most eco-friendly Wimbledon to date with the All England Club introducing a host of different measures to minimise the impact of The Championships on the environment.

More than 400,000 plastic straws, usually accompanying a refreshing Pimm's, had been used at The Championships 2017 so – as part of the Club's wider sustainability plans – they were replaced with recyclable paper straws for 2018.

The AELTC also provided 87 free water refill points and 21 water fountains for the public, thus doubling the amount since 2014, and introduced 10 new electric vehicles for the first time as part of its Jaguar Land Rover courtesy car fleet.

Rafael Nadal was one of the first to hail the new measures. Asked for his thoughts on the plastic reduction, he said: "100 per cent support on this. I am an ocean lover. All the things that we do to protect our beautiful planet are more than welcome."

DAY
6

SATURDAY
7 JULY

It has become a hugely popular tradition on Middle Saturday for The Championships to celebrate achievements in other sports. Once again the Royal Box was packed with a dazzling array of sportswomen and men, who were each given a rousing reception when introduced to the crowd.

The tradition felt particularly appropriate this year as Middle Saturday coincided with the England football team's World Cup quarter-final against Sweden, which kicked off at 3pm, two hours after play started on Centre Court. Some of the Royal Box guests recorded good-luck video messages which were broadcast on the big screen on the Hill, with Chris Robshaw capturing the spirit of the nation. "Bring it home boys," the former England rugby union captain roared.

Rafael Nadal was the day's first winner on Centre Court and was conducting his post-match interview following his 6-1, 6-2, 6-4 victory over Alex de Minaur when he heard cheers celebrating England's opening goal in Russia. "England is coming home or what?" Nadal asked with a smile. The world No.1 was not suggesting that the team were heading out of the World Cup but referring instead to the 'Football's Coming Home' song adopted by England fans. At his later press conference Nadal thanked Sir Bobby Charlton, one of England's World Cup heroes of 1966, for respecting tennis by staying in the Royal Box until the end of his match rather than leaving to find out what was happening in Russia. News of the final result – a 2-0 victory that sent England into the World Cup semi-finals for the first time in 28 years – was posted on the Big Screen with a message of congratulations from everyone at Wimbledon.

82

Britain's Kyle Edmund, who had posed for the cameras the previous day with his Swedish coach, Fredrik Rosengren, with both men proudly wearing their national football teams' shirts, caught glimpses in the locker room of what was happening in Samara as he prepared for his third round encounter with Novak Djokovic, which started less than 20 minutes after the final whistle. There was an upbeat mood in Centre Court, fuelled both by England's deserved victory and by anticipation of what the last home player in either singles event might achieve against a former champion still striving to recapture former glories after two difficult years.

During Djokovic's struggles, Edmund had flourished. The 23-year-old Briton stood at No.17 in the world rankings, an improvement of 33 places since his last appearance at The Championships. In the interim he had played in his first Grand Slam semi-final at the Australian Open and reached his first tour-level final, on clay in Marrakech. Grass had not been his most productive surface in the past, but he was through to the last 32 at The Championships for the first time.

The atmosphere around the court made it feel almost like a Davis Cup tie and at the start Edmund seemed keen to use that to his advantage. Normally reserved and undemonstrative, he celebrated winning points with a clenched fist, made the first break in the seventh game and took the opening set to a huge roar from the crowd.

Djokovic, however, was less than happy with some spectators, particularly after receiving a time violation from the umpire for taking too long between points. "They were slightly unfair to me," Djokovic said afterwards. "I thought the crowd's reaction after [the time violation] was quite unnecessary. A couple of guys were really pretending they were coughing and whistling while I was bouncing the ball, more or less to the end of the match."

The Serb, nevertheless, thrives on adversity and he raised his game significantly in the second set. Edmund held firm until a double fault at 3-4 cost him his serve, after which Djokovic served out to level the match. An early break put the No.12 seed in charge in the third set and he went on to complete a 4-6, 6-3, 6-2, 6-4 victory in just under three hours. For the first time in 11 years Britain would not have a singles player competing in the second week.

A wide-eyed Novak Djokovic and British favourite Kyle Edmund were locked in a match of high intensity on Centre Court before the Serb finally prevailed in four sets

COME ON ENGLAND (AND KYLE!)

England's bid to win football's World Cup, which provided such an enjoyable backdrop to The Championships 2018, saw players, staff and fans all get caught up in the fun, with things coming to a head as Gareth Southgate's team met Sweden in the quarter-finals on Saturday afternoon.

Kyle Edmund (*above*) – who like fellow English player Katie Boulter (*right*) and numerous spectators had been wearing his national shirt with pride – enjoyed plenty of pre-match banter with his Swedish coach Fredrik Rosengren (*below*) before the pair joined forces in a brave but eventually unsuccessful effort to defeat Novak Djokovic on Centre Court.

Fans around the Grounds watched England's 2-0 win on mobile phones before a congratulatory message was flashed up on the Big Screen to cheers on the Hill, which brought a smile to the face of Sir Bobby Charlton (*opposite*), who – gentleman that he is – stayed seated until the conclusion of Rafael Nadal's win over Alex de Minaur.

CONGRATULATIONS
TO THE ENGLAND TEAM
FROM EVERYONE AT
WIMBLEDON

Hot on the Hill

During this glorious spell of weather no day was hotter than the first Saturday, with temperatures soaring to beyond 31 degrees Celsius around the Grounds. It was the perfect day to relax on the Hill (while discovering your newly purchased Wimbledon towel could act as a handy sunshade), to enjoy some refreshment, maybe grab yourself a Pimm's and cheer on the players strutting their stuff on the Show Courts.

Djokovic said afterwards that the match had been settled by "a couple of points here and there". Edmund, despite his disappointment, had enjoyed the occasion. "Playing on Centre Court is always like a dream," he said. "From playing last year in my first match here, this is the best it's been in terms of atmosphere. At points in the match it was really loud. It was a great atmosphere to be in."

No.1 Court was the place to be for the day's biggest upsets, with none greater than Simona Halep's 6-3, 4-6, 5-7 defeat by Chinese Taipei's Hsieh Su-Wei. The world No.1 led 5-2 in the final set and had a match point at 5-4, but became the ninth of the top 10 ladies' seeds to lose, leaving Karolina Pliskova as the sole survivor into the second week. Halep was the first top seed in the ladies' singles to lose to an unseeded opponent since Ana Ivanovic was beaten by Jie Zheng in 2008.

Hsieh, aged 32, has made a habit of upsetting the biggest names on the biggest stages, having also beaten Johanna Konta at Roland-Garros in 2017 and Garbiñe Muguruza at this year's Australian Open. Those

Hsieh Su-Wei could hardly believe it when she defeated the world's top player, the in-form Simona Halep, on No.1 Court in one of the shocks of The Championships 2018

victories over Konta, Muguruza and Halep were her only wins over top 10 opponents.

The world No.48's unpredictable mix of single-handed and double-handed strokes, lobs, drop shots and clever variations of pace and spin can unsettle even her practice partners. "I normally drive the girl crazy before because when I practise, in two shots I do a drop shot," she said. "If I don't drop shot, I hit as hard as I can. The girl is like: maybe I should have someone travel with me so I don't drive the other girl crazy. Now I am a little bit better. I try to practise normally with the girls and not to go too crazy on the drop shot."

Halep, who won her first Grand Slam singles title at Roland-Garros during an exhausting first six months of the year, said she had been "too tired" and had "pain everywhere" but also admitted to "an unprofessional attitude". The Romanian said Hsieh had deserved to win but added: "I just was too negative to myself, talking too much. I think because I was tired, I couldn't stay focused for every ball."

The following match on No.1 Court also produced a major surprise as the world No.138, Ernests Gulbis, beat the world No.3, Alexander Zverev, 7-6(2), 4-6, 5-7, 6-3, 6-0. It was Zverev's second successive five-set match and his third day in a row on court after his second round victory over Taylor Fritz had taken two days to complete. The 21-year-old German admitted afterwards that he had felt tired after not eating for 24 hours because of a stomach bug. "It felt like somebody just unplugged me in the middle of the fourth set," he said.

Gulbis, a former semi-finalist at Roland-Garros, has had an up-and-down career. The 29-year-old Latvian, a free spirit who is rarely afraid to speak his mind, has been troubled by injuries in recent times and fell out of the world's top 500 last year. Before arriving at The Championships he had recorded only one tour-level main draw victory in 2018, having beaten Gilles Muller at Roland-Garros after coming through qualifying to reach the main draw, as he did here.

Kei Nishikori closed out a long day on No.1 Court by beating Nick Kyrgios 6-1, 7-6(3), 6-4. The unpredictable Kyrgios looked out of sorts in the first set, which took just 16 minutes, and was given a code violation for smashing the ball away in anger towards the end of the second set. "I was pretty uptight," he said afterwards. "A lot of nerves. I just struggled with a lot of things today. I just never settled. Obviously getting broken in the first game didn't help me. I just panicked. Everything just went south, I guess."

Elsewhere Juan Martin del Potro, who had yet to drop a set, beat Benoit Paire 6-4, 7-6(4), 6-3, while Milos Raonic completed a 7-6(5), 4-6, 7-5, 6-2 victory over Dennis Novak. Frances Tiafoe, who at 20 was attempting to become the youngest American man to reach the fourth round for 28 years, let slip a two-set lead against Russia's Karen Khachanov, who won 4-6, 4-6, 7-6(3), 6-2, 6-1.

Jelena Ostapenko, Belinda Bencic and Daria Kasatkina, all aged 21, went through to the fourth round with straight-sets victories. Ostapenko beat Vitalia Diatchenko 6-0, 6-4, Bencic beat Carla Suarez Navarro 6-1, 7-6(3) and Kasatkina reached the second week for the first time with a 7-5, 6-3 victory over Ashleigh Barty. Angelique Kerber, showing the form that had taken her to the final in 2016, made only five unforced errors in beating Naomi Osaka 6-2, 6-4. The No.11 seed could hardly have imagined that she would be the highest-ranked player left in the top half of the draw, but it had been a remarkable first six days. Now it was time to draw breath, enjoy the traditional watering of the courts on Middle Sunday and prepare for the second week. If it proved as thrilling as the first, we were in for a treat.

Jessica Ennis-Hill waves to the crowd as Centre Court salutes the sporting stars invited to the Royal Box on Super Saturday

Super Saturday strikes gold

CHAMPIONSHIPS NOTEBOOK
Day 6

• Middle Saturday has become by tradition 'Super Saturday' at Wimbledon, the day that illustrious sports figures are invited to sit in the Royal Box by All England Club Chairman Philip Brook. The icons who took a bow on Centre Court this year, it had to be said, made a particularly fine team.

Six British Olympic champions in Lizzy Yarnold and Amy Williams (skeleton), Nicola Adams (boxing), Jessica Ennis-Hill (athletics), Jack Laugher (diving) and Adam Peaty (swimming) attended, as well as two Paralympic champions, skiing gold medallist Menna Fitzpatrick and her guide Jennifer Kehoe.

Also saluted were world champion boxers Carl Froch and David Haye, and golfers Matt Kuchar, Sergio Garcia and Tommy Fleetwood. Wheelchair tennis stars Gordon Reid and Alfie Hewett were joined by double European diving gold medallist Lois Toulson, multi-medal-winning gymnast Nile Wilson and cyclist and renowned adventurer Mark Beaumont.

Former England captains Andrew Strauss (cricket) and Chris Robshaw (rugby) were there alongside Welsh rugby's flying doctor JPR Williams (once a junior tennis champion himself).

British tennis luminaries Judy Murray, Anne Keothavong, Paul Hutchins and Leon Smith joined China's double Grand Slam champion Li Na and the incomparable duo of Rod Laver and Billie Jean King, Wimbledon's first Open era champions, who shared the limelight with footballing knight and England World Cup hero Sir Bobby Charlton.

• Ten years on from their iconic 2008 final, Rafael Nadal and Roger Federer took another step closer to a rematch with Centre Court victories before Rafa offered the tantalising prospect that, never mind playing each other, we might one day even see them teaming up to play competitive doubles. "You never know," said Nadal, admitting their crowded calendars might be a bit of a problem. "But why not? He is able to do it, I am able to do it."

• Ernests Gulbis was delighted that his sensational defeat of No.4 seed Alexander Zverev meant that, for the first time, two Latvians had made the second week, with Jelena Ostapenko also progressing by beating Vitalia Diatchenko. "Cool," said Gulbis. "Back home it's big because we don't have a lot of athletes. We're a small nation. Whatever happens, it's big."

• Hsieh Su-Wei was a delight on court with her unorthodox shots bamboozling world No.1 Simona Halep. She calls it 'Su-Wei style' and as she doesn't even quite know what she's going to do next, how can her opponents? Off court too, she made everyone smile as she explained her improved 2018 form. "I was trying to enjoy, not just tennis, but life, the food like the strawberries and cream, the burgers and lobster, all the shops!" she enthused. Evidently, she was enjoying Wimbledon as much as we were enjoying her.

NEXT MATCH - NO.1 COURT

Angelique KERBER (11)
V
Belinda BENCIC

DAY 7

MONDAY
9 JULY

s there a day's tennis anywhere to match day seven at The Championships? It is the only date in the tournament calendar, other than a finals weekend, when every man and woman left in singles competition at a tournament is scheduled to play. Provided the weather has not intervened and no long-running matches have disrupted scheduling plans, all 16 remaining men and 16 remaining women play their fourth round matches on Manic – or Magic – Monday at The Championships.

Above: Roger Federer continued on his imperious way, his serve still unbroken as he brushed aside France's Adrian Mannarino on Centre Court

Previous pages: Spectators getting themselves ready for Wimbledon's 'Manic Monday', when all 32 remaining singles players battle for quarter-final places

'Manic' would have been a good description of the first week given the scattering of the seeds. By the time the second week had started the sense of drama at the All England Club appeared to have spread to the British Government. David Davis, who had been leading the country's negotiations to leave the European Union, had resigned overnight as Brexit Secretary and by the afternoon Boris Johnson, the Foreign Secretary, had followed suit. Where would the upheavals end? There was no knowing what the political outcome might be, but at this rate we were heading for a finals weekend at Wimbledon that fascinatingly might feature Evgeniya Rodina against Alison van Uytvanck and Mackenzie McDonald against Jiri Vesely.

However, just when it seemed that the world was turning upside down, logic and predictability returned to the court, for one day at least. Manic Monday still featured an abundance of drama, but at the end of the fourth round only two of the 16 singles matches had been won by the lower-ranked player. Kiki Bertens (world No.20) beat Karolina Pliskova (world No.8) and Camila Giorgi (world No.52) knocked out Ekaterina Makarova (world No.35).

For the first time in the Open era, eight of the 16 players left in the gentlemen's singles were aged 30 or over. That equalled the record for any Grand Slam tournament, eight having also reached the fourth round at Roland-Garros in 1969 and 2017. By the end of the day, five of the 30-somethings had made the quarter-finals, which matched the Open era record for any Grand Slam event, set here 12 months earlier.

Roger Federer, at 36 the oldest singles player left standing, appeared barely to break sweat in his 6-0, 7-5, 6-4 victory over Adrian Mannarino despite another sweltering day on Centre Court. Mannarino won only one point on his serve in the 16-minute opening set and appeared to be heading for a speedy exit when he went 0-40 down at the start of the second, but the 30-year-old Frenchman recovered to make a decent fight of it. He also became the first man at The Championships 2018 to have break points against Federer, though all four went unconverted.

With three big servers – Kevin Anderson, Milos Raonic and John Isner – completing his half of the draw, Federer had a theory about the conditions. "Because it's been so hot and the ground has been so hard, there's been more bounce in it and it's been easier to move," he said. "When it's damp, wetter, with more humidity in the air, I think it's more tricky for, let's say, the baseliner, maybe even for a big server, because it's harder for him to move as well. It's definitely helped a certain style of player, maybe the big servers, maybe the good baseliners."

Raonic, the 2016 runner-up, eased to a 6-3, 6-4, 6-7(5), 6-2 victory over McDonald, Isner beat Stefanos Tsitsipas 6-4, 7-6(8), 7-6(4) while Anderson ended a run of five successive defeats against Gael Monfils, winning 7-6(4), 7-6(2), 5-7, 7-6(4). Isner and Anderson both reached their first singles quarter-finals at Wimbledon at the 10th attempt.

Although Rafael Nadal had reached the final every year he had played at SW19 between 2006 and 2011, the world No.1 had failed to progress beyond the fourth round since. "It's true that I have not been in the quarter-finals, but I've played good tennis here," he insisted. "I lost a couple of matches that I could have won. Sometimes just a few points change the final result."

Kei Nishikori punched the air in delight after finally ending the fine run of Latvian qualifier Ernests Gulbis on No.2 Court

Pineapple bling

Manic Monday saw one of Wimbledon's fancier dressed fans turn himself into a walking, talking version of the Gentlemen's Singles Trophy. All the names of the champions adorned a golden outfit that was complemented by his golden nails, shoes and shades. He even designed a pineapple hat, although he could shed no light on one of Wimbledon's enduring mysteries: why exactly does the exotic fruit sit atop the famous Challenge Cup? Nobody knows but the best guess is that pineapples were such 19th century delicacies that they were seen as an indication of high status – fitting as no trophy comes more highly prized than this one.

This time Nadal had arrived "thinking that I can do a good result" and proved his point with a fourth consecutive straight-sets victory, beating Vesely 6-3, 6-3, 6-4 to reach the quarter-finals for the fourth Grand Slam tournament in a row, which he had last achieved in 2012.

The 11-times Roland-Garros champion rejected a suggestion that the conditions favoured him, with the ball bouncing higher than usual because of the harder surface. Nadal pointed out that most players left in the draw were either former Wimbledon champions or big servers. "I don't see a lot of players from clay in the quarter-finals," he added.

Novak Djokovic beat Karen Khachanov 6-4, 6-2, 6-2 to secure a place in the quarter-finals for the eighth time, a record bettered in the Open era only by Federer, Jimmy Connors and Boris Becker. In reaching his 41st singles quarter-final at all Grand Slam tournaments Djokovic also equalled Connors' total, which is second only to Federer's tally of 53.

Djokovic and Khachanov did not start on No.1 Court until after 7pm because Anderson had needed nearly three and a half hours to beat Monfils. That had left Djokovic concerned he might suffer the same fate as last year, when his fourth round match did not get on court until the following day. "Post-match I heard that the organisers were planning to cancel my match if Monfils and Anderson went to a fifth," he said afterwards. "Luckily for me it didn't happen." The match eventually finished at 8.50pm, by which time Djokovic was struggling to see the ball clearly because of the fading light.

Kei Nishikori reached the quarter-finals for the first time by beating Ernests Gulbis 4-6, 7-6(5), 7-6(10), 6-1. Gulbis slipped and hurt his left knee during the second tie-break and struggled thereafter. Juan Martin del Potro won the first two sets against Gilles Simon but lost the third before play was ended for the day because of the light.

Evgeniya Rodina enjoyed the tournament of her life but ultimately was second best to Serena Williams in the battle between the two mums left in the draw

THE HOST WITH THE MOST

Wimbledon put itself in the picture like never before in 2018 as it took over the host broadcasting of The Championships and introduced exciting new broadcast technology to give fans the biggest and best possible view of all the action.

The new Wimbledon Broadcast Services (WBS), which took over from the BBC as Host Broadcaster, provided multi-camera coverage of all 18 Championships courts for the first time where previously only 15 had been covered.

It also introduced 'Net Cam' on both Centre Court and No.1 Court, while its coverage of Centre Court in 4K HDR ensured an ultra-high definition picture that almost felt like being there.

The All England Club's broadcast links with the BBC remained characteristically strong, with viewers able to watch all Centre Court matches in Ultra HD on BBC iPlayer, thanks to the WBS innovations.

"Wimbledon has a rich tradition of broadcast innovation," said the AELTC's Head of Broadcast and Production Paul Davies, "and so we are delighted that never before have our global audiences had the opportunity to get so up close and personal to the action on SW19's hallowed lawns."

Taking its coverage in-house ran alongside Wimbledon's multi-million pound project to renovate part of its broadcast centre, introducing new edit suites and state-of-the-art transmission centres that will help continue to deliver the finest possible experience for fans watching The Championships throughout the world.

The rout of the leading ladies' seeds was completed when Bertens beat Pliskova 6-3, 7-6(1) to make the last eight for the first time. She would now meet Julia Goerges, who also made her first quarter-final here by beating Donna Vekic 6-3, 6-2. Pliskova's defeat meant that for the first time since the seedings had been introduced in 1927, none of the top eight had reached the quarter-finals. Pliskova, nevertheless, refused to see it as a missed opportunity. "I don't think the draw is open," she said. "You still have to beat the players."

Serena Williams pointed out that it was not correct to say that none of the world's top 10 had reached the quarter-finals because the line-up included Angelique Kerber. The German had been seeded No.11 because that reflected her world ranking at the time of the draw, but had actually climbed one place in the rankings by the start of The Championships through her results at Eastbourne the previous week. Williams said her own seeding at No.25 might also have distorted the overall picture. "I've never been ranked where I am," she said after her 6-2, 6-2 victory over Rodina, the world No.120. "Usually I'm one of those few seeds left that's still fighting and still in the tournament."

The meeting of Williams and Rodina brought together the last two mothers in the singles competition, but there were not too many other similarities between them. Williams, who as the world No.181 became the lowest-ranked player ever to reach the quarter-finals, took charge from the moment she won the first three games. Williams, who would now face Giorgi after the Italian's 6-3, 6-4 victory over Makarova, felt she still had much room for improvement. "This is only my fourth tournament back," she said after reaching her 13th Wimbledon quarter-final. "I feel like I'm getting to where I want to be. For me, there's so much farther I want to go to get back where I was, and hopefully go beyond that."

Serena had revealed two days earlier that she had been out practising when her 10-month-old daughter, Alexis Olympia, walked for the first time. The former world No.1 was asked what sport her daughter might eventually play. "Ice skating could be fun," she said. "I would hope she doesn't play tennis. It's a lot of work, plus I don't want her to have pressure from what I did, you guys talking about: 'Are you going to be able to do as good as your mom?' I don't want her to have that."

Belinda Bencic had made a fine return after injury problems but went down in two hard-fought sets to Angelique Kerber on No.1 Court

Kerber, who beat Belinda Bencic 6-3, 7-6(5), said she was taking no notice of the fact that she was the highest seed left in the competition. "I am not feeling the pressure because I am not looking at who is left or not from the seeds," Kerber said afterwards. "I'm just looking forward to my next match. Every single day that I'm here I'm trying to do my best. This is all I'm focusing on."

Jelena Ostapenko reached the quarter-finals for the second successive year with a 7-6(4), 6-0 victory over Aliaksandra Sasnovich. The 2017 Roland-Garros champion trailed 2-5 in the opening set but fought back after being handed a code violation for coaching from her entourage. "I didn't really hear anybody saying anything," Ostapenko said afterwards. "That code violation made me even more motivated and angry, so I just started to play better."

Daria Kasatkina came from behind to beat Van Uytvanck 6-7(6), 6-3, 6-2 and reach the last eight for the first time, while Dominika Cibulkova secured her quarter-final place by beating Hsieh Su-Wei 6-4, 6-1.

Jamie Murray, who had won the mixed doubles title with Martina Hingis 12 months earlier, had a day to remember. Murray and Bruno Soares reached the gentlemen's doubles quarter-finals by beating the British brothers Ken and Neal Skupski 6-3, 6-4, 6-4. Murray then enjoyed a dramatic victory alongside Victoria Azarenka in the mixed doubles. The Centre Court roof was closed for the first time at The Championships 2018 to enable their second round match against Robert Farah and Anna-Lena Groenefeld to be completed under lights, a reflection of the new rules surrounding use of the roof to complete matches. Murray and Azarenka trailed 1-5 in the decider but completed a 7-6(6), 6-7(6), 7-5 victory at 9.43pm to round off a wonderful day.

Jamie Murray and Victoria Azarenka – now known as 'Muzzarenka' – knocked out No.7 seeds Robert Farah and Anna-Lena Groenefeld in the second round of the mixed doubles

Isner into the unknown

John Isner celebrates his victory, while over in the Royal Box Thomas Bjorn, Europe's Ryder Cup captain, sits behind Britain's four-time Olympic sailing champion Sir Ben Ainslie (below right)

● John Isner couldn't help laughing as he turned up for interviews having reached the quarter-finals – remarkably for the first time – thanks to his win over Stefanos Tsitsipas. "Ah, this is what this press room is like... it's been eight years," sighed the giant American, suggesting he'd never done anything at his Wimbledon "house of horrors" since THAT match against Nicolas Mahut in 2010.

Asked if he hoped that tennis-loving US President Donald Trump – who was due to arrive in Britain later in the week on an official visit – might watch him if he reached the semi-finals, Isner, whose dad Bob ran for Congress as a Democrat in 2016, said: "I'd love to have Trump come watch me. That would be awesome. Maybe I'll tweet at him if I win on Wednesday. I know a lot of people won't like that but I don't care."

● Roger Federer, fresh from reaching an amazing 53rd Grand Slam singles quarter-final, had the perfect answer when asked about whether Sunday's FIFA World Cup final in Moscow, due to kick off two hours after the start of the gentlemen's singles final, might act as a distraction and somehow detract from the atmosphere on Centre Court.

"Maybe you should ask the question over in Russia, how they're going to feel about Wimbledon being played at the same time. I'm more concerned the World Cup final will have issues because the Wimbledon final is going on," responded Federer with a smile. "They'll hear every point. 'Wow, love-15, 15-30...' The players are going to look up in the crowd and not understand what's going on at Wimbledon!"

● Camila Giorgi booked a Centre Court date with Serena Williams by winning her match against Ekaterina Makarova, but when asked for her thoughts about the way her next opponent – one of the sport's greatest icons – played the game, the reserved Italian offered an unexpected response. "I don't follow tennis, women's tennis," shrugged Giorgi to the surprise of the assembled journalists, although she followed up with: "But I think is going to be a good match [against Serena]. I will be focused on my game."

● It was 'tee time' in the Royal Box as some of the world's best golfers, including South African icon Ernie Els, English stars Lee Westwood, Ian Poulter, Paul Casey, Matthew Fitzpatrick and Tyrrell Hatton, as well as

European Ryder Cup captain Thomas Bjorn, enjoyed a spectacular afternoon.

Another golfing great, Sergio Garcia, who had been in the Royal Box on Saturday, felt it was a tremendous honour to be invited back for a second year running even if he sensed his navy jacket might not be quite as spectacular as a certain green number he had worn the year before. "Don't worry," tweeted the 2017 Masters champion. "I'm planning on winning it back!"

DAY
8

TUESDAY
10 JULY

For all the upsets of the first four rounds in the ladies' singles, the line-up on quarter-finals day was not exactly short on big names. It included three players who had won Grand Slam titles in Serena Williams, Angelique Kerber and Jelena Ostapenko, as well as Dominika Cibulkova, who had been runner-up at the Australian Open in 2014. Six of the eight quarter-finalists were seeds, while Cibulkova would have been seeded but for the presence of Williams.

Even the lowest-ranked player of the eight, Camila Giorgi, had a good record on grass, the world No.52 having won more singles matches at The Championships than at any of the other Grand Slam tournaments. Giorgi, Kiki Bertens, Julia Goerges and Daria Kasatkina were appearing in their first Wimbledon quarter-finals, while Giorgi and Goerges had never played in a singles quarter-final at any Grand Slam event.

The day began with spectators looking skywards towards the spectacular flypast marking the celebrations of the RAF's 100th anniversary, but attention quickly refocused on the tennis. The opening match on Centre Court between Kerber and Kasatkina promised much and quickly lived up to all expectations.

Kerber, the world No.10, was the highest-ranked player left in the draw. The 30-year-old German had been a Wimbledon semi-finalist as long ago as 2012, but it was not until 2016 that she made her

biggest breakthrough after working hard on her fitness in pre-season and adding some aggression to her redoubtable defensive game.

The results of the changes were immediate. Kerber won her first Grand Slam title at the 2016 Australian Open, reached the following Wimbledon final, in which she lost to Williams, and became world No.1 after winning the US Open. In her annus mirabilis she also won an Olympic silver medal and was runner-up at the year-end WTA Finals.

However, the success came at a price. Kerber sometimes looked uncomfortable under the spotlight and in 2017 her results tailed off badly. She reached only one final, failed to go beyond the fourth round at any of the Grand Slam events and fell from No.1 in the world to No.21. Once again it took a change of direction between seasons to turn her fortunes around. Kerber parted company with her long-time coach, Torben Beltz, and hired Wim Fissette instead after the Belgian stopped working with Johanna Konta.

The upturn in Kerber's results was instant. She won her first title for 16 months in Sydney, made the semi-finals of the Australian Open before losing one of the matches of the year to Simona Halep (who took the final set 9-7) and arrived at The Championships 2018 having reached the quarter-finals or better in nine of the 11 tournaments she had played in the first half of the season.

The last of those tournaments had been at Eastbourne, where Kasatkina had proved a formidable opponent in the quarter-finals before losing a third set tie-break. Two weeks later they met again, this time on Centre Court, in a highly entertaining encounter.

Kerber won 6-3, 7-5 but Kasatkina showed why she is one of the game's most exciting young players. The 21-year-old Russian is a delightful shot maker who is just as likely to play a devilish drop shot as

Above: At lunchtime, spectators at Wimbledon were privileged to witness what was hailed as a 'once in a lifetime flypast' of 100 aircraft – one of the biggest ever undertaken – to mark the 100th birthday celebrations of the Royal Air Force

Camila Giorgi went for her shots as usual and became the first player to take a set off Serena Williams at The Championships 2018, but the Italian eventually succumbed 6-3, 3-6, 4-6

to throw all her weight into a thumping backhand. She has a wonderful touch, though she also has the capacity occasionally to miss by a mile when she goes for a big winner.

The contrast with the ruthlessly consistent Kerber made for a fascinating confrontation. There were 10 breaks of serve, while Kasatkina hit more than twice as many winners as Kerber (33 to 16) and twice as many unforced errors (31 to 14). The Russian also saved six match points. The last game featured five deuces as Kasatkina kept herself alive with some bold returns and spectacular winners.

"We both played on a really high level, starting from the first point," Kerber said afterwards. "For me it was important to play aggressively, to take the challenge of how she was playing and to try to move well and get a lot of balls back."

Kasatkina was happy with her performance but admitted that she had sometimes gone for too much and had simply hit some "crazy shots". However, the world No.14 said she had not felt any pressure or fear in the final game. "My head was just empty," she said. "I was just going on the next point and playing, playing, playing."

At about the same time as Kerber was winning on Centre Court, her next opponent, Ostapenko, was completing a 7-5, 6-4 victory over Cibulkova on No.1 Court to become the first Latvian woman ever to reach a Wimbledon singles semi-final. The world No.12, a powerful ball-striker who loves to go for her shots, cracked 33 winners to just six by Cibulkova, who had won both their previous meetings but was rarely in contention this time.

Some six weeks earlier Ostapenko had cut a sorry figure when she lost in the first round in defence of her title at Roland-Garros. "I had so much pressure, but it's all gone now and I'm just going out there and enjoying it," Ostapenko said.

The second quarter-final on Centre Court saw Williams take on Giorgi, who was the highest-ranked player the seven-times Ladies' Singles Champion had faced so far. The Italian's slight frame belies her power. Giorgi had hit 144 winners in her first four matches (of the remaining players only Goerges, with 163, had struck more) and had also recorded the Fortnight's joint second fastest serve by a woman; Venus Williams had hit the fastest at 123mph followed by Giorgi, Serena Williams and Naomi Osaka, all on 119mph.

In a match full of bold hitting, the serves proved decisive. Williams struggled to handle Giorgi's in the opening set, which the Italian took after breaking in the sixth game. In the second and third sets, however, it was Williams who turned up the power. In the final set she was serving an average of 5mph faster than she had in the first and hit her fastest serve of the tournament at 122mph.

Giorgi did not have any break points in the second and third sets, while Williams broke once in each to complete a hard-fought 3-6, 6-3, 6-4 victory. "Every time I play Giorgi she always plays that level so I knew going in it would not be an easy match," Williams said afterwards. "I just kept fighting."

"Everything right now is a little bit of a surprise, to be here, to be in the semi-finals. I always say I plan on it, I would like to be there, I have these goals, but when it actually happens, it still is, like: 'Wow, this is really happening.'"

Following pages: All hail Wimbledon's ever-splendid Ball Boys and Girls, pictured here slightly off-guard as they prepare for their official portrait, another annual Wimbledon tradition

Below: Jelena Ostapenko rediscovered her 2017 Roland-Garros-winning form as she swept aside Dominika Cibulkova 7-5, 6-4 on No.1 Court

WIMBLEDON IS OUT OF THIS WORLD

Wimbledon's mission to boldly go where no Grand Slam had gone before saw a unique link-up between the All England Club and NASA to broadcast a live interview with tennis-loving astronaut Drew Feustel aboard Mission 56 on the International Space Station.

Commander Feustel had been in the Royal Box with his wife Indira and fellow British astronaut Tim Peake at The Championships 2017 and it was there while watching the tennis with Philip Brook, Chairman of the AELTC, that the idea of him taking a memento from Wimbledon into space during his six-month-long scientific expedition was hatched.

So the Club commissioned two gold coins, featuring the Mission 56 logo on one side and Wimbledon's logo on the other, which will be used for the Finals Weekend coin tosses at The Championships 2019.

The coins could be seen floating around inside the space station as seven-times Grand Slam singles champion Mats Wilander (*right*) and Celina Hinchcliffe interviewed Feustel for The Wimbledon Channel, during which the Commander revealed, mind-bogglingly, how he'd watched – among several other matches – Roger Federer playing on Centre Court from outer space. Well, we always knew Roger was on another planet...

Flying over the eastern coast of the US, Feustel – proudly wearing a Wimbledon T-shirt – told Wilander

how "magical" he'd found his SW19 experience. Asked by Mats if he'd have preferred to be an astronaut or a Wimbledon champion, he smiled: "All of us are born with certain skills and mine wasn't tennis! I'll stick to science and floating in space."

However, he hoped he might combine his two loves. "Having coordinated with the USTA, we have some very small rackets and we're going to see if we can play a game here in space," he said. "But without the assistance of gravity, it could be pretty tough!"

If Williams felt surprised at making her 11th Wimbledon singles semi-final it was hard to imagine what Goerges must have felt after reaching her first at the age of 29 thanks to a 3-6, 7-5, 6-1 victory over Bertens. The German had lost in the first round in each of the previous five years and had never gone beyond the third round. The match was tight until Goerges' greater firepower made the difference in the latter stages as Bertens lost eight of the last nine games.

"I don't have many words today to describe the moment I'm going through right now," Goerges said afterwards. "It's pretty unreal for me at the moment to get to that stage at a Grand Slam. It's obviously always been a dream for every player to be in the semis at Wimbledon."

The quarter-final line-up in the gentlemen's singles was completed by Juan Martin del Potro, whose fourth round encounter with Gilles Simon had been called off the previous evening because of fading light at the end of the third set. Del Potro, who hit 27 aces, went on to win 7-6(1), 7-6(5), 5-7, 7-6(5), but Simon

pushed hard. The Frenchman saved four match points when Del Potro served at 5-4 in the fourth set and led 5-4 in the tie-break before the Argentinian secured his quarter-final meeting with Rafael Nadal.

The biggest surprise so far in the mixed doubles was provided by Jay Clarke and Harriet Dart, aged 19 and 21 respectively. The British wild cards, who had never played together before, had already knocked out the No.13 seeds, Max Mirnyi and Kveta Peschke, and followed that with a 6-3, 6-4 victory over the No.1 seeds, Mate Pavic and Gabriela Dabrowski. Dart had arranged to go on holiday the following day but said she would now have to change her plans. Henri Kontinen and Heather Watson, champions in 2016 and runners-up in 2017, were beaten 2-6, 6-7(4) by Ivan Dodig and Latisha Chan.

Britain's Jamie Murray and his Brazilian partner, Bruno Soares, let slip a lead in their gentlemen's doubles quarter-final against Raven Klaasen and Michael Venus, who won 6-7(5), 7-6(5), 5-7, 7-6(4), 6-4. However, the home country would have two representatives in the semi-finals. Joe Salisbury and Denmark's Frederik Nielsen overcame seeded opposition for the third round in a row when they beat Ben McLachlan and Jan-Lennard Struff 7-6(6), 4-6, 7-6(2), 7-6(4), while Dominic Inglot and Croatia's Franko Skugor beat Robin Haase and Robert Lindstedt 6-3, 6-7(2), 7-6(1), 6-4.

The Invitation events, which are always very popular with the public, got under way, bringing together some familiar faces from the recent and not-so-recent past. The field for the Ladies' Invitation Doubles included Li Na, China's greatest ever player, who retired after playing her last competitive match at The Championships 2014, and Martina Navratilova, who had made her debut here in 1973.

Juan Martin del Potro let out a roar of ecstasy tinged with relief after finally wrapping up victory via a fourth set tie-break in his resumed contest with Gilles Simon

The court jester is back!

So, which player do you think attracts the most internet hits to watch him play? Roger or Rafa? No, it's a 62-year-old son of an Iranian hill tribesman who never ranked beyond 192 as a player but who's long been world No.1 at making fans laugh and marvel at his unmatched showmanship and dazzling trick shots. Yes, Mansour Bahrami remains the ultimate court jester.

Teaming up with Goran Ivanisevic in the Gentlemen's Senior Invitation Doubles against Jacco Eltingh and Paul Haarhuis, more than 176,000 fans watched Wimbledon's Facebook live stream to see magic Mansour in action – and they weren't left disappointed. At one point he was on his knees in a rally before chasing down a lob and blindly smashing an over-the-shoulder winner with his back to the net.

"I never had a tennis lesson in my life. I played as a kid with a dustpan and a ball and that's how I learned the basics," shrugged the moustachioed Merlin of tennis, trying to explain his wizardry. "It's when I see people laughing, I love it most. I'm the happiest man out there."

Bryan back on top

Jack Sock and Mike Bryan (right) were all smiles on No.3 Court as they claimed a victory that sent Bryan back to the top of the world rankings

• What a day for Mike Bryan. Even without injured twin Bob, by winning his gentlemen's doubles quarter-final alongside Jack Sock against India's Divij Sharan and New Zealander Artem Sitak, the 40-year-old ensured that he would return to the top of the doubles rankings as the oldest-ever world No.1. "Congrats big bro," came the Instagram message from Bob, the younger by two minutes. "Even though I'm not there to physically celebrate with you, I'm always there in spirit."

• Andy Murray looked perfectly at home while making his BBC Sport debut as a member of their analysis and commentary team – as well as one half of an unlikely comedy double act.

In the studio, fellow pundit Tim Henman asked his mate: "Who is more boring? Me or you? If we put it to the public, what would the result be?" To which Murray responded: "It would be tight. Can we set it up?"

Yes, they could, reckoned Sue Barker, unable to contain her mirth. So a website poll was created to resolve the burning question, with Tim left delighted to be voted as Wimbledon's most boring with a landslide 65 per cent share of the vote.

Murray also turned his hand to being a tipster, suggesting that Novak Djokovic was in the form to beat either Rafael Nadal or Roger Federer. Is he henceforth to be known as 'Mystic Muzza'?

• After her triumph over Camila Giorgi on Centre Court, Serena Williams paid a touching tribute to Jana Novotna, the former Ladies' Singles Champion she had got to know so well before the much-loved Czech's death from cancer at the age of 49 in November 2017.

At the first Championships since Jana's passing and on the 20th anniversary of her famous 1998 victory, Williams reflected: "It's incredibly sad and heartbreaking for not just the tennis world, but for just the world. She was so sweet.

"I was devastated but I know that her legacy and legend will live on. She did a lot for tennis and I feel honoured that I had a chance to get to know her."

• Busy Serena not only offered supreme entertainment for her A-list followers on Centre Court – including singer Justin Timberlake, his actress wife Jessica Biel and rap star Drake (*right*) – afterwards she then also made sure her fans were taken care of too.

One supporter was all fingers and thumbs trying to work his camera phone so Serena took it from him, organised a much better selfie and then gave him a high five too. Now that's Supermom multi-tasking...

DAY
9
WEDNESDAY
11 JULY

A ndy Murray was in the commentary box rather than out on the court, but in other respects it was just like old times on men's quarter-finals day. Roger Federer, Rafael Nadal and Novak Djokovic, the three other members of the 'Big Four' who had dominated men's tennis for more than a decade, were competing alongside each other in the last eight of a Grand Slam tournament for the first time in more than three years.

Between them they had dropped just one set in the first four rounds. Djokovic had been taken to four sets by Kyle Edmund in the third round, while Federer and Nadal had both lost only 36 games in their first four matches. That was the fewest games Nadal had dropped in his six runs to the quarter-finals at The Championships, while Federer had lost fewer games on only three of the previous 15 occasions when he had made the last eight.

Head-to-head records with their opponents suggested that the three men with 13 of the last 15 gentlemen's singles titles to their names would progress without too much difficulty. Federer had not dropped a set in any of his four matches against Kevin Anderson, Nadal had won six of his last eight meetings with Juan Martin del Potro and Djokovic had beaten Kei Nishikori 12 times in a row.

With Djokovic on his way to a 6-3, 3-6, 6-2, 6-2 victory over Nishikori in the first match of the day on Centre Court and Federer standing at match point in the third set against Anderson in the opening match on No.1 Court (the defending champion's first match away from Centre Court since 2015), everything was looking straightforward. How wrong we were. By the end of the day Federer had lost 6-2, 7-6(5), 5-7, 4-6, 11-13, while Nadal had survived only after battling to beat Del Potro 7-5, 6-7(7), 4-6, 6-4, 6-4 for more than four and three-quarter hours. HRH The Duchess of Cornwall and HRH The Countess of Wessex, who joined HRH The Duke of Kent in the Royal Box, could hardly have chosen a better day to visit The Championships.

Anderson had never gone beyond the fourth round in his nine previous appearances here, while Federer, the first man in the Open era to play at The Championships 20 years in a row, was aiming to extend a number of his own Wimbledon records, including the number of gentlemen's singles titles (eight), the number of men's semi-final appearances (12) and the number of matches played at the All England Club in the Open era (106).

In winning the first two sets 36-year-old Federer also equalled the record for the number of consecutive sets won at Wimbledon (34), which he had set in 2006. However, even at the start of the second set there had been a hint of what might follow as Anderson ended the defending champion's run of 85 consecutive games won on serve at The Championships.

Federer, nevertheless, retrieved that break, won the ensuing tie-break and went on to match point when Anderson served at 4-5 in the third set. The South African saved it by forcing Federer into a backhand error, broke in the following game and then served out for the set.

Anderson, who was serving beautifully, took the fourth set, after which it became a case of whose serve would falter first in the decider. Federer, whose game seemed at times to lack its customary zip, finally cracked at 11-11. A double fault gave Anderson his first break point of the set and the world No.8 converted it when Federer missed a forehand. After four hours and 14 minutes Anderson sealed his victory in the following game by forcing Federer into a backhand error on his first match point.

"I tried my best to keep fighting," Anderson said afterwards. "By the end I thought I did a great job, not thinking about things too much. I thought I was really in the flow of the match. Beating Roger Federer here at Wimbledon in such a close match will definitely be one that I'll remember. I just kept on telling myself that I had to keep believing."

Kevin Anderson seemed almost incredulous as he celebrated the biggest victory of his career

Federer, whose only other defeat here from two sets up had been against Jo-Wilfried Tsonga in 2011, insisted that he had felt good physically and mentally even at the end. "I know what kind of energy I need to bring to the fifth," he said. "I was able to bring that. To be honest, I didn't feel mental fatigue. Now I feel horribly fatigued and just awful."

The Swiss said he aimed to return in 2019. "I just love being around here," he said. "We have a good time as a family. I have great memories from here. My heroes all won here. Every time I come back here, I try to be like them."

Anderson's semi-final opponent would be John Isner, whose record at The Championships had been even more modest than the South African's. In his nine previous visits he had never gone beyond the third round.

The 33-year-old American's quarter-final against Milos Raonic was a showdown between two huge servers. Raonic hit 32 aces to Isner's 26, but the Canadian had only one break point, which he failed to convert when his opponent served for the third set at 5-4. Isner, who took three of his six break points, won 6-7(5), 7-6(7), 6-4, 6-3, the turning point coming in the tie-break at the end of the second set when he saved a set point with a smash.

Afterwards Isner described his feelings as "pure elation" and added: "This is amazing. It's by far the best Grand Slam I've ever played in my career – and I've been playing for 11 years. I'm super happy. To do it here at Wimbledon makes it even a little bit more special."

Djokovic had been the first man through to the semi-finals, an emphatic win over Nishikori underlining his rapidly improving form. The only hiccup came in the second set when Carlos Ramos gave him an official warning for bouncing his racket on the grass. After arguing with the umpire, a distracted Djokovic dropped his serve in the next game and went on to lose the set.

Left: Novak Djokovic was back to his elastic best as he defeated Kei Nishikori in four absorbing sets on Centre Court

Below: Nishikori played some fine tennis but somehow always brings the best out of Djokovic, who extended his lead in career meetings to 14-2

John Isner was ecstatic (**right**) at reaching his first Grand Slam semi-final after winning his monster-serving clash with Milos Raonic (**above**) on No.1 Court

"I thought it was unnecessary to get the warning," Djokovic said afterwards. "I didn't harm the grass. I know how I threw the racket. He [Nishikori] even threw his racket in the fourth set. The chair umpire said he didn't see it, so I got the warning and he didn't. I think it's not fair."

Djokovic saved three break points at 2-2 in the third set and then won 10 of the last 12 games. The Serb said afterwards that he felt "pretty close" to recapturing his best form. "I feel like I'm peaking at the right moment," he said. "I've worked very hard and very smart to get myself in the best possible shape for the biggest events and it doesn't get any bigger than Wimbledon."

England's footballers were playing Croatia in the World Cup semi-finals in the evening, but there was never any danger of Centre Court remaining anything other than packed as Nadal and Del Potro staged arguably the match of the tournament. A contest full of breathtaking rallies featured dive volleys, spectacular tumbles, ferocious ball-striking and wonderful athleticism from both men. The excitement reached fever-pitch in the fifth set when a superb 23-shot rally ended with Nadal chasing down a drop shot only for Del Potro to dive headlong to hit a winning volley.

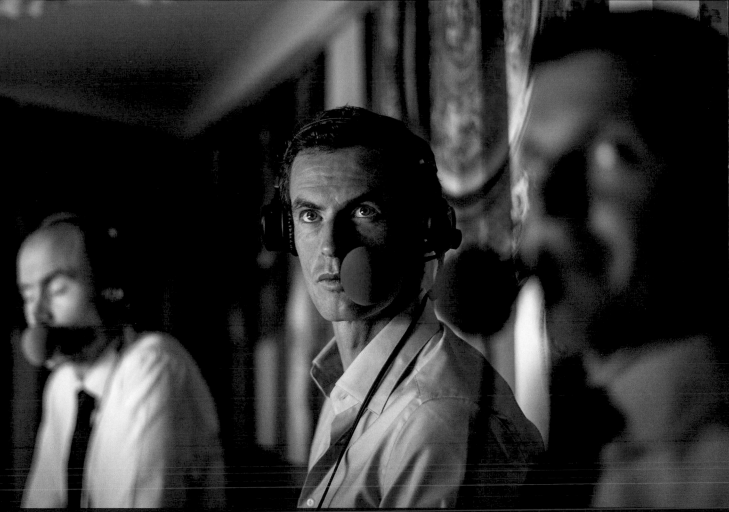

A CENTRE COURT NATURAL

When a teenage Andy Murray made his first Centre Court appearance way back in 2005, losing to David Nalbandian, the youngster made a superb impression during a five-setter. Thirteen years on, now entertaining and informing us all from the Centre Court commentary box as a knight of the realm, it was a delight to report that he made another rather distinguished debut.

Acting as co-commentator with Tim Henman and Andrew Cotter on the brilliant Rafael Nadal versus Juan Martin del Potro quarter-final, Murray proved a natural in front of the mike, demonstrating a fine command of statistics – Cotter even called him 'Statto' – while giving priceless insights about the two players that only someone who had faced (and beaten) them both could offer.

The sport's cognoscenti were suitably impressed at the depth of his knowledge and homework. "A well-researched Andy Murray reeling off the stats again during commentary," tweeted Stuart Fraser, the tennis correspondent of *The Times*. "Says that Rafael Nadal is the all-time No.1 in terms of points won on his second serve. He's right."

He even won over hard-to-please TV critics like Jan Moir, who purred in the *Daily Mail* that "Murray was insightful, thoughtful, good humoured and intelligent", although she couldn't help adding: "Admittedly, it was

delivered in the flat McMonotone of someone taking details of your complaint in a call centre in Edinburgh." The self-deprecating Murray would have laughed at that.

What was most evident, though, was just the sheer pleasure that Murray took in being a fan for one evening, watching a great match unfold and passing on his enthusiasm and passion to the viewer as he declared: "This set is one of the best sets of tennis I have ever seen live. Incredible."

Everyone at Wimbledon, of course, would have rather seen him on court than in a commentary booth but here was evidence that another career may well embrace him after he hangs up his racket.

Above: The denouement of Rafael Nadal's epic win over Juan Martin del Potro, which saw 'Delpo' win a 23-shot rally with a diving volley, then later tumble at match point down and the victorious Spaniard step over the net to console him (**right**), was so poignant that even John McEnroe said he was reduced to tears

Opposite: Nadal looked back to his Championship-winning best as he finally prevailed in a superb five-setter that his fellow world No.1 Simona Halep described as the best match she had ever seen

Del Potro's comeback from four wrist operations has helped to earn him huge popularity around the world. For years he could not hit double-handed backhands and instead had to play single-handed slices, but now he was playing without pain and with all his old power. He hit 33 aces to Nadal's three and 77 winners to his opponent's 67, but the Spaniard kept fighting back even after going two sets to one down. A subtle change of tactics proved crucial as Nadal played more drop shots and attacked the net more frequently.

The world No.1 broke in the fifth games of both the fourth and fifth sets and eventually closed out victory with a classic piece of serve-and-volley which left Del Potro lying flat out after stumbling in his attempt to reach Nadal's backhand winner. After raising his arms in celebration, Nadal stepped over the net and went to console the 29-year-old Argentinian, who was still lying on the ground. "I wanted to stay there for all night long," Del Potro said afterwards. "But Rafa came to me and we shared a big hug. It was kind of him."

Nadal agreed it had been "a very emotional match" full of high-quality tennis. "Especially in the last set there were some amazing points," he said. "Sorry to Juan Martin. He's an amazing opponent and an amazing player. In some ways he deserves victory too."

Twenty-four hours after learning that she would become the new world No.1 in doubles, Timea Babos and her partner, Kristina Mladenovic, suffered a surprising defeat. The No.1 seeds were beaten 6-7(4), 3-6 in the quarter-finals by Alicja Rosolska and Abigail Spears. Bethanie Mattek-Sands and Lucie Safarova, playing together for the first time since Mattek-Sands suffered a sickening knee injury at The Championships 2017, also went out, losing 7-5, 4-6, 2-6 to Gabriela Dabrowski and Xu Yifan.

Competitors in the Ladies' Wheelchair events prepared for The Championships against the imposing backdrop of the University of Roehampton's Southlands College

A Croatia v England semi (again!)

Goran Ivanisevic and Tim Henman, on the 17th anniversary of their own epic semi-final clash, shake hands ahead of England's World Cup semi-final encounter with Croatia

• A certain football match 1,600 miles away in Moscow was occupying plenty of minds as England prepared for their FIFA World Cup semi-final against Croatia. And though all the hope and hype seemed to be about 'football coming home', the voice of Wimbledon's favourite Croatian, 2001 Gentlemen's Singles Champion Goran Ivanisevic — who famously won his own Anglo-Croatian semi-final with Tim Henman on his way to the title — offered a sobering warning.

"For sure, you are coming home. But I hope not with the trophy," smiled Ivanisevic, who was later disappointed to see his Canadian charge Milos Raonic get knocked out in the quarter-finals by John Isner. To drown his sorrows, Ivanisevic went off to the pub to watch the semi-final amongst England fans. "And hopefully," he said, "I'm going to be the last one standing and laughing." He was too. Croatia won 2-1.

• England versus Croatia produced an absorbing match but Andy Murray wouldn't have known. The game was being monitored in the BBC commentary box while the Scot was co-commentating on the Nadal versus Del Potro quarter-final but that five-setter proved so magnificent, including a final set Murray said was one of the best he'd ever seen live, that he barely cast a glance at the football.

• Iva Majoli, Croatia's 1997 Roland-Garros winner who had been playing in the 2018 Ladies' Invitation Doubles, couldn't miss one of her nation's greatest sporting moments so flew out to Moscow to see the game.

Above and beyond the call of duty, though, she then promised to jet back to Wimbledon to join her Tunisian partner Selima Sfar for an 11.30am start against Britain's Fed Cup captain Anne Keothavong and double US Open champion Tracy Austin. The result? Another win for Croatia after extra time (10-7 in the champions tie-break to be exact).

• An Anglo-Croatian alliance had already seen Londoner Dominic Inglot and Sibenik's Franko Skugor win their gentlemen's doubles quarter-final on Tuesday but their alliance went out the window as they sat together to watch the big match. "I've got a feeling Franko's going to be really relaxed and chilled and I'll be all up in his face, so we'll see how he handles that," predicted Inglot. How Dom handled England's defeat, though, hasn't yet been confirmed...

• After England had lost their match with Belgium at the group stages of the World Cup, John McEnroe was asked what advice he would give Gareth Southgate's team. "Don't lose again!" barked Supermac. "You may never have this chance again. So take advantage of it." At least the great man's exhortations worked wonders for a while, and there can be no doubt that a new generation of young fans have been introduced to the joy of sport this summer by England's performances as well as yet another incredible Wimbledon.

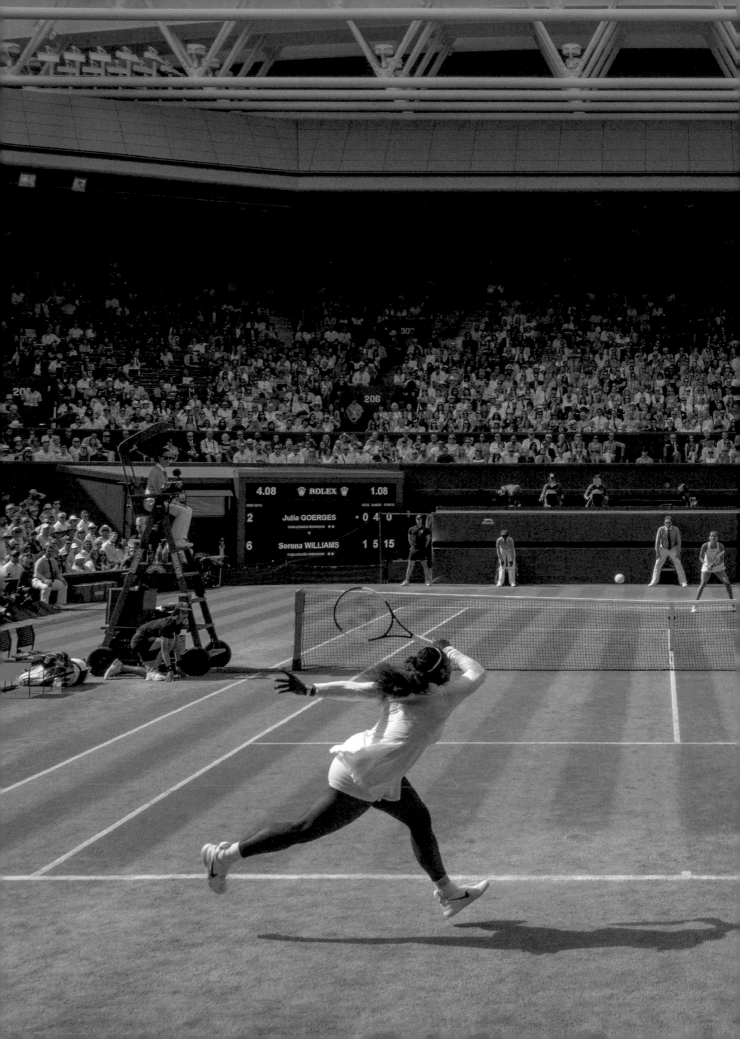

DAY
10

THURSDAY
12 JULY

Ever since Serena Williams won her first Grand Slam singles title at the age of 17 we had come to expect the unexpected from her. At the Australian Open in 2007 a clearly unfit Williams, ranked No.81 in the world after playing only five tournaments in the preceding 16 months because of severe knee trouble, became the lowest-ranked woman to win a Grand Slam title for 29 years. Three years later she was absent for 11 months after requiring two foot operations and having a large haematoma removed from her stomach, but reached the final of the US Open within three months of her return.

In 2012 the American suffered what remains her only first round defeat in 68 appearances in Grand Slam tournaments when she was beaten by the world No.111, Virginie Razzano, at Roland-Garros, but bounced back to win Wimbledon and embark on the best run of her career. By the time she had been crowned Australian Open champion at the start of 2017, when she was already eight weeks pregnant, Williams had won 10 of the previous 19 Grand Slam tournaments.

Now Williams needed just two more wins to secure what would surely be her greatest triumph. In only her fourth comeback tournament after a 14-month break following the birth of her daughter, Williams was through to her 11th Wimbledon ladies' singles semi-final. In her first five matches the world No.181 (the lowest-ranked ladies' singles semi-finalist in the history of The Championships) had yet to meet a player ranked in the top 50, but now faced an opponent in the form of her life.

Julia Goerges had never previously gone beyond the fourth round of any Grand Slam tournament and had fallen at the first hurdle in her last five appearances here, but her career had been revived following

changes to her coaching team, who convinced her that her big-hitting game could be successful on grass. The 29-year-old German went into her semi-final having hit more winners (199), more aces (44) and more unreturned serves (113) in the Fortnight than anyone else in the 128-strong draw.

With Angelique Kerber facing Jelena Ostapenko in the other semi-final, it would be the first time that two German women had featured in the last four of a Grand Slam tournament since Graf beat Anke Huber at Roland-Garros in 1993. Might we witness only the second all-German ladies' singles final here following Cilly Aussem's victory over Hilde Krahwinkel in 1931?

Goerges, however, had not taken a set off Williams in their three previous meetings, the most recent of which had been in Paris just five weeks earlier, and once again the American quickly took charge. Williams won 6-2, 6-4 in just 70 minutes.

Williams served well, found a good rhythm on her ground strokes and moved with improved fluency. From 2-2 she won four games in a row to take the first set and in the second faltered only when she was broken when serving for the match at 5-3. That lapse was quickly forgotten as she broke to love in the next game to become the first mother since Evonne Goolagong Cawley in 1980 to reach the final. Just 10 months after the birth of her daughter, 36-year-old Williams would be playing in her 30th Grand Slam singles final.

"It's been a crazy 10 months," Williams said afterwards. "I was still pregnant at this time last year. That's something I have to keep reminding myself. Going out there, being a mum, is super-cool. Knowing that no matter what happens, I have amazing support and unconditional love, it's such a great feeling."

Goerges was also in a positive mood. "Overall I felt I played great," she said. "I'd never got to this stage of a Grand Slam before. I'm working towards achieving it another time."

Kensington Palace announced that Meghan Markle, HRH The Duchess of Sussex, would be accompanying HRH The Duchess of Cambridge, Patron of the All England Club, to Saturday's final, two months after Williams had attended her friend's wedding to Prince Harry at Windsor Castle. "We've always had a wonderful friendship," Williams said. "Every year for a couple of years she comes out to Wimbledon, has

A fired-up Williams, back to something like her high-stepping best, looked on her way to her 30th Grand Slam singles final right from the start of the match

THE INCREDIBLE JOURNEY

If Serena Williams and all her supporters in the players' box, including husband Alexis Ohanian (*right*), seemed so emotional about her semi-final triumph over Julia Goerges, it was no surprise because the victory in itself marked the culmination of what the seven-times Ladies' Singles Champion called a "crazy" voyage back towards the summit of tennis.

Serena herself couldn't help but reflect on 10 extraordinary months which had transported her from being close to death with a pulmonary embolism following the difficult birth of her baby Alexis Olympia to being the inspirational mum who had amazed everyone by making it into a 10th Wimbledon ladies' singles final just four months after returning to tennis at the age of 36.

It was extra-special, she felt, because of everything she had been through. "It's no secret I had a super tough delivery. I lost count after, like, four surgeries. Because of all the blood issues I have, I was really touch-and-go for a minute," she revealed afterwards.

"I didn't actually know until after my agent, Jill [Smoller], who is actually more of a friend, was saying how much stress it was. I'm glad no one told me at the time I was going through that. Yeah, it was tough. There was a time I could barely walk to my mailbox.

"For me, it's such a pleasure and a joy to be in the final because less than a year ago I was going through so much."

Was it the toughest of her several comebacks? "I don't know if it's been the toughest because I have Olympia. For me, I only see joy out of it," she said. "In a way, it's by far the toughest, but in a way it's by far the best."

supported me. Now she's supporting me in a different role. But our friendship is still exactly the same. We always have supported each other, just been there for each other through a lot."

Williams was asked at her press conference if she ever felt like Wimbledon royalty. "If there was Wimbledon royalty, I would like to believe I would be Wimbledon royalty because I've done pretty well here in the past," she said. "Honestly, I'm just me. I don't feel any different. I know that sounds weird, but I don't. That's an attitude I always want to keep, something I want to teach my daughter to always just have this humility."

The other semi-final brought together two players with contrasting styles. Although Kerber had added some aggression to her game since her disappointing season in 2017, her strengths remained her athleticism, consistency and ability to make her opponents keep hitting the extra ball.

Ostapenko preferred all-out attack. The 21-year-old Latvian, a formidable ball-striker who always goes for her shots, had enjoyed a remarkable victory the previous year at Roland-Garros, where she had become the first unseeded player to win the Suzanne Lenglen Cup for 84 years. Although she had wilted under the pressure of defending her title in Paris 12 months later, the world No.12 had again flourished on grass. She reached the quarter-finals at Eastbourne and had now followed up her run to the quarter-finals at The Championships 2017 by going one round better.

Williams treated the Centre Court crowd to her familiar victory pirouette after her impressive win

Above: Jelena Ostapenko played with freedom but simply made too many errors in her straight-sets semi-final defeat by Angelique Kerber

Right: Kerber looked back to her best as she defeated Ostapenko to set up a repeat of the 2016 final against Serena Williams

On the day, however, it was Kerber's reliability that triumphed over Ostapenko's gung-ho approach as the world No. 10 won 6-3, 6-3 in 68 minutes. Ostapenko hit 30 winners to Kerber's 10, but the unforced error count was the more telling statistic. Kerber made just seven to Ostapenko's 36 as the Latvian's chances sank in a flood of mistakes. Afterwards Ostapenko insisted that she was working on her consistency. "It's not like I want to hit every ball so hard," she said. "Sometimes in the match that happens because I really want to hit a winner, I want to win the point. But in practice, of course I'm working on longer rallies."

Ostapenko thought the court surface had benefited Kerber. "I think the Centre Court is much slower than the other courts I played on before," she said. "She had really many advantages because of that. My shots were not that effective on such a slow court."

Kerber said it had been crucial to remain patient. "She is a player who tries to be aggressive from the first point," the 30-year-old German said. "For me it was important to move well, be patient and take my chances when I had the chance to step in and be aggressive."

Through to her first Grand Slam final since beating Karolina Pliskova at the US Open in 2016, Kerber said she expected her meeting with Williams – in a repeat of the final at The Championships 2016 – to be "a completely new match". She added: "We both learned a lot. She's coming back. For me, I'm coming back from 2017. I know that I have to play my best, best tennis to beat her, especially on the grass, on the Centre Court, where she has won so many titles."

While no home players had made it to the second week of the singles events, Britain would be guaranteed a presence in the mixed doubles final. Jay Clarke and Harriet Dart, making their debuts on Centre Court, beat the No.10 seeds, Juan Sebastian Cabal and Abigail Spears, 7-6(10), 7-5 to earn a semi-final meeting with their fellow Briton Jamie Murray and the Belarusian Victoria Azarenka, who beat the No.4 seeds, Jean-Julien Rojer and Demi Schuurs, 4-6, 7-5, 7-5.

However, Britain's Dominic Inglot and Croatia's Franko Skugor lost in the semi-finals of the gentlemen's doubles to Mike Bryan and Jack Sock, who were playing in their first Grand Slam tournament together. Bryan and Sock won 6-3, 6-1, 6-7(11), 6-7(4), 6-4 after failing to take six match points in the third set. Bryan, who at 40 had ensured that he would become the oldest player to top the men's doubles world rankings, had already won three Wimbledon titles alongside his brother Bob, who was absent with a hip injury. British hopes were also dashed in the other semi-final as Joe Salisbury and Denmark's Frederik Nielsen were beaten 6-7(6), 6-3, 3-6, 4-6 by Raven Klaasen and Michael Venus.

Three Britons played in the quarter-finals of the junior singles events for the first time for eight years, but losses for Emma Raducanu and Anton Matusevich left Jack Draper to fly the flag. By defeating Lorenzo Musetti 6-7(3), 6-3, 6-1, Draper became the first Briton since Kyle Edmund in 2013 to reach the last four of the junior singles events.

There were mixed fortunes for Britons as the Wheelchair events got under way. Alfie Hewett reached the singles semi-finals by beating Stephane Houdet 7-6(3), 6-4, but Gordon Reid went down 3-6, 3-6 to Joachim Gerard. In the ladies' singles Lucy Shuker lost 2-6, 1-6 to Aniek van Koot.

Evening settles at Wimbledon after another long and glorious day

New kid on the block

Wimbledon could be seeing a lot more of Cori Gauff as the USA's teenage sensation clearly has the firepower to trouble the very best

• Look out for the name Cori Gauff. The 14-year-old new sensation of junior tennis may have bowed out at the quarter-final stage of the girls' singles, having been beaten by Chinese No.10 seed Wang Xiyu, three years her senior, but the big-hitting kid from Florida known as 'Coco' still left a considerable impression on Court 18.

The newly crowned Roland-Garros junior champion, who cites Serena Williams as one of her heroes, served a 120mph thunderbolt, faster even than any player in the senior draw apart from Serena herself (125mph) and sister Venus Williams (123mph).

But her performance at Wimbledon at least guaranteed that after the tournament, Coco would become the youngest-ever ITF world No.1 junior at 14 years and four months.

• At The Championships 2017, John Isner's dietary habits were a subject of much fascination as it was revealed he had ordered 36 salmon nigiri rolls after one match. Yet as he prepared for Friday's semi-final with Kevin Anderson, the American revealed that he had got into a more chocolatey food fad this year.

"I've had a little bit of a sugar craving. After each win these 10 days, I've had a Kit Kat. I'm not going to change that now," smiled the 33-year-old a mite guiltily as he explained how usually he didn't "eat much unhealthy stuff".

• Julia Goerges (*right*), justifiably proud of herself after a tough, breakthrough four weeks of grass court tennis that was finally ended by Serena Williams, also fancied a gastronomic treat after reaching her first Grand Slam semi-final.

Asked what she was most looking forward to after her exhausting schedule, the German had two wishes. "Sleeping in my own bed. That's the biggest reward I think for me," she said, "and maybe I will get a doner kebab when I come back home, that's a good thing to do."

• The wait for that elusive Wimbledon title for wheelchair tennis legend Shingo Kunieda goes on. Japan's 34-year-old world No.1 has 22 Grand Slam singles titles to his name – nine Australian Open, seven Roland-Garros and six US Open titles – and was desperate to break his duck at Wimbledon as he pursued the calendar Grand Slam following victories in Melbourne and Paris. Yet Argentine Gustavo Fernandez beat him in a three-set thriller on Court 14, leaving Kunieda to sigh: "Every time the Grand Slam loss is really tough, but this year after Australia and France I wanted everything to win."

For several years it had been noticeable that players were enjoying longer careers, with some reaching their peaks even in their thirties. In the past the top players' results would tend to tail off in their mid-twenties – Bjorn Borg, John McEnroe and Mats Wilander won 25 Grand Slam singles titles between them but none after their 26th birthdays – but now Roger Federer and Rafael Nadal, the best players of their generation, were staying at the summit for much longer.

The gentlemen's singles at The Championships 2018 represented another significant landmark down that road. For the first time in the Open era at any Grand Slam tournament all four gentlemen's singles semi-finalists were over the age of 30. Kevin Anderson had recorded his best Grand Slam result at 31 the previous summer by reaching the US Open final, John Isner would be playing in his first Grand Slam semi-final at 33, and 32-year-old Nadal had won three of his 17 Grand Slam titles since turning 30. The only semi-finalist with a point to prove as a 30-something was 31-year-old Novak Djokovic, who had won the last of his 12 Grand Slam titles at 29.

The first semi-final brought together two men who had known each other since they played college tennis in the United States. Isner had been a top 30 player for more than seven years without ever threatening a significant breakthrough, though he had enjoyed the best week of his career earlier in 2018 by winning the Miami Open.

Anderson's career had followed a similar path until a difficult year in 2016. Troubled by a labrum tear in his hip, the former world No.10 had dropped to No.80 in the world by the start of 2017. However, a steady recovery saw the South African make his way back up the rankings and enjoy a superlative run at the US Open, where he lost to Nadal in the final.

With Isner standing 6ft 10in tall and Anderson 6ft 8in, both men made full use of their height to deliver huge serves. In winning all 95 of his service games, Isner had become the first man to reach the semi-finals without dropping his serve since such records began in 1992. He was also first on the list of most tour-level tie-breaks won in 2018 with 23. Anderson was in second place on 20.

You could have forgiven Centre Court ticket-holders for asking whether it would be possible to bring in camp beds as well as water, sandwiches and sun block. It was soon clear that expectations of a long match were well founded. After two hours and 27 minutes there had still not been a break of serve, but Anderson and Isner were just warming up. By the end of the day they had broken a series of records before Anderson finally triumphed 7-6(6), 6-7(5), 6-7(9), 6-4, 26-24 after six hours and 36 minutes.

After four hours and 44 minutes it became The Championships' longest semi-final, supplanting Djokovic's 2013 victory over Juan Martin del Potro. After five hours and 12 minutes it became the longest Centre Court singles match, beating Pancho Gonzales' 1969 victory over Charlie Pasarell. Nineteen minutes later it became the second longest singles match on any Wimbledon court, replacing Marin Cilic's 2012 win over Sam Querrey. After six hours and 33 minutes it became the second longest singles match at any Grand Slam tournament ahead of Fabrice Santoro's 2004 Roland-Garros victory over Arnaud Clement. The only match it did not threaten to eclipse was Isner's extraordinary 6-4, 3-6, 6-7(7), 7-6(3), 70-68 victory over Nicolas Mahut at The Championships 2010, which had lasted 11 hours and five minutes and took three days to complete.

Isner roared his defiance, hitting 53 aces in total, but it was still not enough to take him to his first Grand Slam final

Above: The long good Friday duel became a must for viewers on the Hill before the scoreboard told the final tale of Anderson's monumental win (**right**)

Opposite: An exhausted Anderson took his bow but admitted afterwards: "My feet are sore, they're swollen. The legs are pretty jelly-like"

AN EPIC IN EVERY SENSE

It was a match destined to go down in Wimbledon's annals as one of The Championships' most monumental contests. The longest duel ever witnessed on Centre Court, the numbers from Kevin Anderson's semi-final win over John Isner were quite something.

396

The number of minutes it took for Anderson to prevail, the most ever in a Wimbledon semi-final and the second most in any Grand Slam match in history after the famous 11 hours and five minutes (665 minutes in total) battle between Isner and Nicolas Mahut in 2010

99

The most games ever played in a Grand Slam singles semi-final before Anderson finally prevailed 7-6(6), 6-7(5), 6-7(9), 6-4, 26-24

50

The most games ever played in a single set on Centre Court and the second most in any set of a singles match played at Wimbledon after Isner's 70-68 fifth set against Mahut

175

The number of minutes it took Anderson to win the final set

247

The number of winners the two men struck, Anderson blasting 118 and Isner 129

264

The number of unreturned serves the pair delivered, 129 from Anderson and 135 from Isner

110

The number of successive service games won by Isner at The Championships until he was broken in the third set (Pete Sampras owns the record of 118, set between 2000 and 2001)

20

The most points ever played in a gentlemen's singles semi-final tie-break (in the third set)

102

The number of aces the pair served, the most seen in one Centre Court match (Anderson 49, Isner 53)

162

The combined height in inches of the two combatants, with Anderson at 6ft 8in beating Isner (6ft 10in) to the title of Wimbledon's tallest-ever finalist

After the longest match came a truly great one with Rafael Nadal (**above**) duelling late into the evening with Novak Djokovic under the Centre Court roof (**right**)

While the match was long, the rallies were not. Of the 569 points played, only 99 featured exchanges of more than four shots. There were only 16 break points: Anderson won four of his 11, while Isner won two of his five. Isner, whose fastest serve was timed at 142mph, hit 53 aces, which took his total for the Fortnight to 214, beating Goran Ivanisevic's 2001 record. Anderson reached 137mph and struck 49 aces.

Isner had taken his run of service games won to 110 by the time Anderson broke midway through the third set. Isner broke back immediately, however, and went on to win the tie-break to lead by two sets to one.

Anderson, nevertheless, had shown his resilience in beating Federer from two sets down 48 hours earlier. The world No.8 took the fourth set and once again had to keep serving to stay in the match in the decider. Isner, looking the more likely to falter, saved break points at 7-7, 10-10 and 17-17 and recovered from 0-30 down six times. At 24-24, however, Isner finally succumbed. He went 0-30 down after a remarkable point in which Anderson hit one shot left-handed after falling to the floor, went 0-40 down after the South African hit a forehand winner and at 15-40 netted a backhand. On Anderson's first match point in the following game Isner missed a forehand.

Anderson embraced Isner at the end but barely smiled before leaving the court. "John is such a great guy and I really feel for him," Anderson said in his interview immediately afterwards, seemingly close to tears. "If I'd been on the opposite side I don't know how you can take that, playing for so long and coming out short. I apologise if I'm not more excited right now, but there are so many mixed emotions."

At his press conference Anderson said he did not know what had got him through the match "other than just a will to try to succeed". Isner said he felt "pretty terrible" and added: "My left heel is killing me. I have an awful blister on my right foot. I've felt better."

With Anderson wondering how he would recover for Sunday's final, both men advocated changes to the no tie-breaks rule in deciding sets, which is used here and at the Australian Open and Roland-Garros. Anderson liked the US Open's use of fifth set tie-breaks at 6-6, while Isner suggested introducing them at 12-12. Richard Lewis, the All England Club's Chief Executive, said that such changes would be considered after The Championships when there had been time for reflection.

With the first semi-final finishing at 7.46pm, it was decided to play the second, between Djokovic and Nadal, under Centre Court's closed roof and artificial lights. Even so, there would be a strong possibility that the match would not finish that night. Under the All England Club's agreement with the local authority, matches must finish by 11pm in consideration of local residents, transport connections and the need for spectators to get home safely.

In the Open era no two players have met as frequently as Djokovic and Nadal. Djokovic led their head-to-head record by 26 wins to 25, but Nadal had won nine of their 14 meetings in Grand Slam tournaments. They had met at The Championships twice, Nadal winning their 2007 semi-final and Djokovic the 2011 final.

Both men are exceptional athletes and there were some spectacular rallies. Djokovic

Dutchwoman Aniek van Koot won a dramatic third set tie-break 13-11 against Japan's No.2 seed Yui Kamiji to seal a place in the Ladies' Wheelchair Singles final

won the first set 6-4 and retrieved an early break in the second, but at 2-3 Nadal broke again, following up an exquisite drop shot with a big forehand winner. The Spaniard served out to take the second set 6-3.

With both men in full flow, the third set produced some breathtaking tennis. It went to a tie-break, in which Djokovic led 5-3, only for Nadal to respond with two stunning drop shot winners and an unreturned serve to go 6-5 up. Djokovic saved three set points before Nadal saved one at 8-9. At 9-10, however, with the clock showing that the 11pm curfew had just passed, the world No.1 missed a backhand to give Djokovic the set. After nearly three hours both men had won 107 points each, but they would resume the following day with Djokovic leading 6-4, 3-6, 7-6(9).

Anderson was not the day's only marathon winner. Jack Draper, who was aiming to become the first Briton to win the boys' singles title for 56 years, was on court for four hours and 24 minutes before completing a 7-6(5), 6-7(6), 19-17 semi-final victory over Colombia's Nicolas Mejia to secure a meeting in the final with Tseng Chun Hsin, the No.1 seed. Draper, aged 16, needed 10 match points to complete his victory. "I can't feel my legs," he said with a smile when asked how he was feeling at his post-match press conference. "I was having loads of bananas, loads of electrolytes. That's what kept me going."

Jamie Murray would also be a British presence on the final day after reaching the mixed doubles final with Victoria Azarenka. They beat the home pair of Jay Clarke and Harriet Dart 6-2, 6-2 to set up a final against Alexander Peya and Nicole Melichar, who beat Michael Venus and Katarina Srebotnik 6-4, 6-4.

Barbora Krejcikova and Katerina Siniakova, the champions of Roland-Garros, beat Alicja Rosolska and Abigail Spears 7-5, 6-4 to set up a ladies' doubles final against Melichar and Kveta Peschke, who beat Gabriela Dabrowski and Xu Yifan 6-3, 4-6, 7-5. Stefan Olsson, who beat Britain's Alfie Hewett, and Gustavo Fernandez reached the Gentlemen's Wheelchair Singles final, while Diede de Groot and Aniek van Koot would contest the Ladies' Wheelchair Singles final.

A Ball Boy found himself at the heart of the action on Court 18 when Henri Leconte invited him to take over serving duties from him during the Gentlemen's Senior Invitation Doubles match between Leconte and Cedric Pioline and Richard Krajicek and Mark Petchey

Lefty legend

Kevin Anderson delighted the Centre Court crowd by scrambling to his feet and producing a very creditable left-handed groundstroke to stay in, and eventually win, a remarkable point

● It was a shot that will go down in Wimbledon folklore, the day a right-handed player fashioned a remarkable stroke with his left hand to help him win a crucial point en route to finally prevailing in the longest match ever played on the most famous court in tennis.

Kevin Anderson was locked at 24-24 in his seemingly endless battle with John Isner on Centre Court when he produced a magical piece of southpaw scrambling. Having been knocked over and seeing his racket forced from his grasp due to the power of Isner's serve, Anderson still had the presence of mind and speed of thought to grab his racket with his left hand while the American was hitting his return, get up and somehow manoeuvre the ball back across the net. To monstrous cheers, he went on to win a match-changing point.

Afterwards he enjoyed telling us how he did it. As a tennis-loving youngster growing up in South Africa, it transpired he had needed surgery on his right arm, leaving his dad and coach Michael to suggest he "learn to play left-handed" while regaining strength in his playing hand.

So he did and became reasonably adept. "But I didn't know that was going to come into play at this point in my career," laughed Anderson.

● John McEnroe echoed the feelings of many observers when he hailed Isner and Anderson and said: "It's a damn shame there is a loser here.

I hope this magnificent effort between these two will allow the powers that be to make a change for their sake, other players' sake and the sake of players coming up."

● What do you do for six and a half hours when you're waiting for your turn to go on court? Novak Djokovic and Rafael Nadal killed time in their own different ways. Novak showed himself locked into what was presumably a very lengthy game of marbles in the locker room, while Rafa revealed that in between doing 10 separate warm-ups to keep himself ready he whiled away a considerable bit of the time practising his golf putting.

● Britain's own 16-year-old marathon man Jack Draper, who outlasted Nicolas Mejia over four hours and 24 minutes, winning 19-17 in the third and final set of their boys' singles semi-final, not only demonstrated a champion's steel but also a gentleman's class on No.3 Court.

As he watched his Colombian opponent weeping, Draper thought: "Well, I can't celebrate too much because what if I was on the other side, I know I'd be destroyed if I'd lost. So I tried to comfort him."

DAY
12

SATURDAY
14 JULY

1 6 mph

Considering all the talk at the start of The Championships about this being the year of the comeback, the line-up for the final of the ladies' singles could hardly have been more appropriate. Angelique Kerber was on her way back after a disappointing 2017, while Serena Williams was just four months into her return after giving birth. Although it was only the third final here in the Open era not to feature a top 10 seed, and Williams – the world No.181 – was the lowest-ranked player ever to reach the final, it was a meeting of two players of the highest quality.

Above: Serena Williams gave it her all in her comeback final but there was to be no fairytale ending

Previous pages: Angelique Kerber tumbled to the Centre Court turf in joy as she realised she had just beaten the great Serena Williams in the Wimbledon ladies' singles final

Williams needed just one more Grand Slam singles title to equal Margaret Court's all-time record of 24. Kerber, meanwhile, had won two of her three Grand Slam singles finals, two of which had been against Williams. Kerber beat Williams in three sets in her first final at the Australian Open in 2016 but lost in straight sets at The Championships six months later. The meeting of the 30-year-old German and the 36-year-old American would be the first ladies' singles final at The Championships between two 30-somethings since Virginia Wade beat Betty Stove in 1977 and the first to feature a mother since Evonne Goolagong Cawley won in 1980.

A final of such quality drew the crowd it deserved. HRH The Duchess of Cambridge, Patron of the All England Club, was accompanied by HRH The Duchess of Sussex, who is a personal friend of Williams, on their first outing together without their husbands. Two familiar faces, however, were sadly absent from the Royal Box. Maria Bueno, three times a Ladies' Singles Champion at Wimbledon, had died the previous month, while Jana Novotna, the 1998 champion, had passed away the previous November at the age of just 49. Tiger Woods, Lewis Hamilton and Anna Wintour joined Alexis Ohanian, Williams' husband, in her players' box as the American sought her eighth Wimbledon singles title.

Williams had won six of her previous eight meetings with Kerber and was seen by most observers as the favourite. With hindsight, many had probably allowed their judgement to be swayed by the extraordinary story surrounding Williams' return. Kerber represented a step up in class compared with Williams' previous opponents. From the moment she broke in the opening game, the world No.10 looked the better all-round player and she needed only 65 minutes to complete a 6-3, 6-3 victory.

Kerber's athleticism enabled her to keep making Williams hit the extra ball. With the German pulling her from side to side, there were too many occasions when Williams struggled to get into position to play her shots. The relentlessly consistent Kerber made only five unforced errors while Williams made 24. Williams did not have her best serving day, but Kerber's left-handed serve was effective throughout. Williams had only one break point in the match.

Kerber went 2-0 up, lost the next three games, but then won four in a row to take the opening set. Williams held on in the second set until Kerber broke for 4-2. A forehand winner took Kerber to match point at 5-3, upon which Williams netted a backhand return. The players shared a long embrace at the end, a reflection of the respect and affection they have for each other.

"When I was a kid I was always dreaming of this moment," Kerber said afterwards. "To win Wimbledon, it's something really special in my career." She was the first German champion since her childhood idol, Steffi Graf, won the last of her seven Wimbledon titles in 1996. "The thing I took from her was her movement and the fact that she hit a lot of balls back, but also with intent," the new champion said afterwards.

Following pages: The Centre Court duel in front of an enthralled capacity crowd lasted 65 minutes as Kerber produced a consummate performance to triumph 6-3, 6-3

Below: Kerber played magnificently to win the rematch of the 2016 final

Angelique Kerber was understandably overcome with emotion at the end of the match (**above**), while Serena Williams was gracious in defeat, offering warm congratulations as the players embraced at the net (**right**)

Double Duchess

HRH The Duchess of Cambridge, Patron of the AELTC, and HRH The Duchess of Sussex appeared to truly savour their day out at a sun-drenched Wimbledon as they watched the conclusion to a breathless gentlemen's singles semi-final between Novak Djokovic and Rafael Nadal before seeing Angelique Kerber defeat tennis royalty in the shape of Serena Williams – a close friend of the Duchess of Sussex – in the hard-fought ladies' singles final.

The two royal sisters-in-law received enthusiastic cheers and happily waved to the delighted crowds from the balcony. The Duchesses also had the opportunity to meet a selection of young people from The Championships, including Tia Carter, who performed the coin toss, followed by a few Ball Boys and Girls, junior players and competitors from the Wheelchair events.

Above: Serena Williams received a huge ovation from the entire Centre Court crowd but she recognised that the biggest applause belonged to the new champion (**right**)

Opposite: Angelique Kerber became the first German since Steffi Graf 22 years earlier to lift the Venus Rosewater Dish

Kerber, who returned to No.4 in the world rankings, added: "I think without 2017 I could not have won this tournament. I think I learned a lot from last year, with all the expectation, all the things I went through. I learned so many things about myself. I also needed to find the motivation after 2016, which was amazing."

Wim Fissette, Kerber's coach, thought her best was yet to come. "Even physically she can do a lot better," he said. "Her serve can still improve and her offensive game, the more she feels success with it, the more she will use that. And the more experience she has, she will take that into the big matches to stay mentally calm."

Williams, who returned to No.28 in the world rankings, was close to tears in her post-match interview. Asked about her gracious acceptance of defeat, she said with a smile: "I'm just better at acting now, I guess."

She added: "It was a great opportunity for me. I didn't know a couple of months ago where I was, where I would be, how I would do, how I would be able to come back. It was such a long way to see

light at the end of the road. I think these two weeks have really shown me that I can come out and be a contender to win Grand Slams. This is literally just the beginning." Williams was asked what she would tell her daughter about the day. "I think it was a happy story," she said. "I'll probably change the ending."

Ohanian, Williams' husband, revealed his pride on Instagram. "Days after our baby girl was born, I kissed my wife goodbye before surgery and neither of us knew if she would be coming back," he wrote. "We just wanted her to survive. Ten months later she's in the Wimbledon final."

The final had not started until after 4pm because of a late finish to the second men's singles semi-final, which had resumed at 1pm. Novak Djokovic had just taken a two-sets-to-one lead over Rafael Nadal when play had finished for the day at 11pm the previous evening. It ended up being the second longest men's semi-final in Championships history, beaten only by the previous day's marathon between John Isner and Kevin Anderson.

Djokovic won 6-4, 3-6, 7-6(9), 3-6, 10-8 after five and a quarter hours of spell-binding play by both men. The match statistics told their own story, with both men hitting 73 winners, both making 42 unforced errors and Djokovic winning 195 points to Nadal's 191.

The two finalists depart the big stage, flanked by the Ball Boys and Girls offering them a guard of honour

GERMANY SALUTES ANGIE

Angelique Kerber's ladies' singles triumph, the first by a German player since Steffi Graf in 1996 (*right*), was greeted with considerable enthusiasm back home, brightening up what had otherwise been a disappointing sporting summer for her compatriots.

Germany's football team had been knocked out at the group stage at the World Cup in Russia, but as the nation's biggest-selling newspaper *Bild* proudly declared after Kerber's win: "The others have the World Cup, we have Wimbledon!"

Chancellor Angela Merkel led the messages of congratulations to the immensely popular 30-year-old that flooded in after Kerber's defeat of Serena Williams had earned her a third Grand Slam title, describing her triumph as "thrilling".

The win was met with equal delight within the German sporting community, with former Formula One world champion Nico Rosberg hailing her triumph as "mega" while the nation's leading tennis man Sascha Zverev posted on Instagram: "While I'm in the gym doing everything I can to one day be where I want to be my Hopman Cup partner @angie.kerber just became Wimbledon champion. Well done Angie I couldn't be happier for you."

Boris Becker, the three-time champion, tweeted that he, Graf and Michael Stich, Germany's trio of Wimbledon singles champions in the Open era,

would now have to share and probably "enlarge our living room!!!"

Kerber herself was thrilled to receive a message of congratulations from Graf. "She said she was happy for me, that I really had to enjoy every moment now and that I deserved it," reported Kerber. "It's always a great feeling to get a message from her."

Many praised the way Kerber had bounced back from a difficult year after her double Grand Slam triumph in 2016. *Stuttgarter-Zeitung* reported: "The harsh setbacks, the frustration, the unexpectedly weak results – all this is forgotten. Kerber has immortalised herself once again in German tennis history."

Above: It's hats off to Novak Djokovic and Rafael Nadal as the pair conclude one of the great Wimbledon semi-finals

Right: The amazing athleticism of Novak Djokovic (**top**) and Rafael Nadal (**below**) made for a remarkable five hour and 15 minute semi-final before the Serb finally prevailed

Although the sun was shining, the Centre Court roof remained closed, as it had been the previous evening. Both players would have had to agree to the roof being opened and Djokovic wanted it to stay closed. The common consensus was that the conditions favoured Djokovic, who is the better indoor player. Nadal was later asked if it had made sense to keep the roof shut. "No, but I will not talk more about this," the Spaniard replied. "I don't want you to write about this today."

It was soon clear that the rest of the match would be as tight as the first three sets had been. The opening game of the fourth set took 15 minutes before Nadal held serve after saving two break points. After an early exchange of breaks Nadal broke again in the eighth game before serving out to level the match.

In the deciding set Nadal saved a break point at 3-4 before Djokovic saved two at 4-4. Serving at 4-5, Nadal went 0-30 down but dug himself out of trouble with four successive unreturned serves. At 7-7 Djokovic saved three break points and had a match point in the next game, which Nadal saved with an audacious drop shot. At 8-9, however, Nadal went 0-40 down and then missed a forehand to give Djokovic his victory.

Nadal thought he had played "a great match" and said he could not have given much more. "I am proud of myself," he said. Djokovic said the match had been "extraordinary from every point of view" and called Nadal "probably the greatest fighter ever to play this game".

Djokovic admitted that over the previous 18 months he had experienced "moments of doubt, of frustration, disappointment, where you're questioning whether you want to keep it going in this way or that way". He added: "Speaking from this position right now, it makes it even better for me because I managed to overcome challenges and obstacles and get myself to the final of a Slam."

Mike Bryan equalled John Newcombe's record of 17 Grand Slam men's doubles titles when he partnered Jack Sock to a 6-3, 6-7(7), 6-3, 5-7, 7-5 victory over Raven Klaasen and Michael Venus. At 40 Bryan became

the oldest man in the Open era to win the title. It was the first Grand Slam men's doubles title he had won without his twin brother Bob, who had a hip injury. "I want to dedicate this title to him," Mike said afterwards. "This is really special. This is the biggest tournament in the world."

Barbora Krejcikova and Katerina Siniakova became the first former Girls' Doubles Champions here to win the ladies' doubles title. The Czechs, who had triumphed at Roland-Garros the previous month, beat American Nicole Melichar and Czech Kveta Peschke 4-6, 6-4, 6-0.

Poland's Iga Swiatek won the girls' title, beating Switzerland's Leonie Kung 6-4, 6-2. She confirmed afterwards that this would be her last junior Grand Slam tournament.

Diede de Groot retained her Ladies' Wheelchair Singles title, beating her fellow Dutchwoman Aniek van Koot 6-3, 6-2 in the final, while Britain's Alfie Hewett and Gordon Reid won the Gentlemen's Wheelchair Doubles for the third year in a row by beating Joachim Gerard and Stefan Olsson 6-1, 6-4.

Right: British pairing Alfie Hewett and Gordon Reid wrapped up a third consecutive Gentlemen's Wheelchair Doubles title by beating Stefan Olsson and Joachim Gerard

Below: Mike Bryan raises his arms in triumph after winning his fourth gentlemen's doubles title with Jack Sock, his partner in the absence of his injured brother Bob

Thinking of Jana

Delighted Ladies' Doubles Champions Barbora Krejcikova and Katerina Siniakova savour their triumph on No.1 Court

• The brilliant Czech pairing of Barbora Krejcikova and Katerina Siniakova felt it fitting to dedicate their ladies' doubles title to the compatriot who had so inspired them.

On the 20th anniversary of Jana Novotna's Wimbledon singles triumph, Krejcikova threw a kiss to the heavens after they'd beaten Nicole Melichar and Kveta Peschke.

"She really deserves for everyone to think about her in a really good spirit, in a really good way," said Krejcikova of her heroine who had died last year. "I'm really happy that I could meet her. I think she would be really proud, too."

• Our new Ladies' Singles Champion is honest as well as brilliant. Much had been made on social media about Angelique Kerber being a woman of the people after a picture emerged of her standing at a bus stop in Wimbledon seemingly waiting to catch a ride.

Yet after her victory over Serena Williams, she made everyone laugh as she confessed: "I was standing in front of the bus stop, but not taking the bus. I was waiting for my taxi, actually, to be honest!"

• With all four gentlemen's semi-finalists aged over 30 for the first time in the Open era, Anderson tipped his hat to an absent friend for inspiring the rise of the 30-something brigade.

"A while ago, if you looked at some of the guys who've been on the tour for a while and reached 30, their interest and motivation to keep pushing their bodies, keep training, keep travelling the world naturally just gets a little bit less.

"There's been a resurgence where people don't feel that way. When you see one person doing it, it changes the perspective and the mindset as well. Seeing Roger Federer at [nearly] 37 having the results he's had, the success, what he's still striving for, makes me feel at 32 that I've got a lot of years in front of me. It changes the whole dynamic."

• What's it like playing the indefatigable Rafael Nadal? Novak Djokovic sounded tired just answering the question after having covered 3.76 miles at helter-skelter pace to finally outlast a warrior who had scuttled even further – an amazing 3.97 miles – during their semi-final.

The Serbian winner could only come up with one way to describe the toll that playing Nadal – and he's done it 52 times now – takes on the body. "If I show you my feet, you would understand," he smiled.

After their own epic semi-final, this was evidently also a problem for John Isner and Kevin Anderson. "My feet are sore and swollen," said Anderson as he tried to recover for the final while Isner reported that his size 15s were festooned with blisters.

DAY
13

SUNDAY
15 JULY

116 mph

When Novak Djokovic lost first time out at both Indian Wells and Miami earlier in the year, not even his most optimistic supporter could have imagined that the Serb would be preparing less than four months later for his fifth Wimbledon singles final. After going through personal crises, struggling for motivation, dealing with injury and making sweeping changes to his entourage, Djokovic had finally turned to elbow surgery. On his return in March, however, he had seemed as far away as ever from recapturing his former glories. "I'm trying, but it's not working," a downcast Djokovic had said at Indian Wells.

Djokovic's ills could be traced back to the highest point in his career. In winning Roland-Garros in 2016, he had become the first man for 47 years to hold all four Grand Slam singles titles at the same time. However, the first signs of problems came at The Championships four weeks later when he lost to Sam Querrey in the third round. He still made the US Open final that summer, but it was clear that not all was well in his world.

The decline accelerated in 2017. Djokovic lost to Denis Istomin, the world No.117, at the Australian Open, won only nine games in a crushing defeat to Dominic Thiem at Roland-Garros and retired hurt against Tomas Berdych at The Championships. Having been troubled by an elbow injury for 18 months, Djokovic announced that he would be resting for the remainder of the year.

However, the physical issues were only one aspect of Djokovic's woes. Without going into any details he admitted that he had had to deal with personal problems and struggled for motivation in the wake of completing his Grand Slam collection. He had also made sweeping changes to his backroom staff. Boris Becker left at the end of 2016 and five months later Djokovic parted with everyone else in his entire coaching team. Andre Agassi took over as coach but stepped aside 11 months later, saying he and Djokovic had "agreed to disagree" too often.

After making changes to his racket and his service action because of his elbow issues, Djokovic returned after a six-month break to play in the Australian Open in January 2018, only to suffer more pain, which prompted the decision to have surgery. In April, however, he reunited with his long-time coach, Marian Vajda, for the clay court season, at the end of which his form finally started to pick up. He reached the final at The Queen's Club in his first outing on grass and followed that with some increasingly polished performances at The Championships, culminating in his remarkable victory over Rafael Nadal in the semi-finals.

The world No.21 was now one win away from claiming his first Grand Slam title for more than two years, though the imposing 6ft 8in frame of Kevin Anderson stood in his path. The 32-year-old, attempting to become the first South African to win the title, had played in a Grand Slam final at the US Open the previous summer and had shown great resilience in beating Roger Federer and John Isner in the quarter-finals and semi-finals here.

On another glorious afternoon at a Championships blessed with wonderful weather from start to finish, the Royal Box was brimming with former champions. Bjorn Borg, Stefan Edberg, Chris Evert, Neale Fraser, Jan Kodes, Richard Krajicek, Rod Laver, John Newcombe, Manuel Santana and Stan Smith were all present, as were Their Royal Highnesses The Duke and Duchess of Cambridge, Prime Minister Theresa May and a host of celebrities, including Katherine Jenkins, Hugh Grant, Eddie Redmayne and Benedict Cumberbatch.

Left: Kevin Anderson gave everything in his first Wimbledon final but his semi-final heroics undoubtedly contributed to his straight-sets loss

Below: Djokovic was at his athletic best, chasing down every ball on his way to a 6-2, 6-2, 7-6(3) victory

Famous faces

It was perfectly appropriate that the climax of The Championships on Centre Court should attract such a stellar final day courtside cast, headed by Their Royal Highnesses The Duke and Duchess of Cambridge and the Prime Minister, Theresa May.

Among the Hollywood A-listers also enjoying the gentlemen's singles final were Emma Watson (*right*) and (*below, left to right*) Tom Hiddleston, Benedict Cumberbatch, a bespectacled Kate Winslet and Eddie Redmayne.

The actors amongst them would have understood the dangers of stage fright. Anderson, who had received a 'good luck' call from South Africa's President, Cyril Ramaphosa, admitted afterwards that he had felt nervous. However, the bigger question was how much the South African had left in the tank after being on court for nearly 11 hours in his previous two matches. The answer was soon evident. Anderson started poorly, improved by the end but rarely looked capable of denying Djokovic his fourth Wimbledon title. The 31-year-old Serb won 6-2, 6-2, 7-6(3) in two hours and 19 minutes.

Anderson's humility and graciousness, not to mention his resolute tennis, had earned him many supporters and there were big cheers when he won the first point as Djokovic missed a backhand. At 30-30, however, a missed forehand took Djokovic to break point, upon which Anderson double-faulted. After breaking serve again in the fifth game Djokovic served out for the first set. With Anderson continuing to make errors and Djokovic hitting the ball consistently well from the baseline, the second set followed an identical pattern. "They were probably the two best sets I've played in a long time," Djokovic said afterwards.

In the third set, nevertheless, Anderson served better and dictated more of the rallies. Having had his first break point towards the end of the second set, the South African had six more in the third, but failed to take any of them. Five were set points: two at 4-5 as Djokovic hit three double faults, and three more at 5-6, when the Serb got out of trouble with some brilliant serving. Djokovic had appeared to tighten up, but played an almost faultless tie-break. Trailing 6-2, Anderson saved the first match point with a smash but netted a forehand return on the second.

As he had done after past triumphs on Centre Court, Djokovic bent down to pull at some blades of grass and eat them. After all he had gone through in the past two years, the grass had probably never tasted sweeter.

To crown his day, Djokovic saw his three-year-old son, Stefan, join his wife, Jelena, in the players' box before the presentation ceremony. The champion later revealed that the prospect of such a scene had been one of his biggest motivations. "I had been visualising, imagining this moment of him coming to the stands, cherishing this moment with my wife and me and everyone," Djokovic said.

Above: I've done it! Djokovic was overjoyed to add the 2018 title to his Wimbledon wins of 2011, 2014 and 2015

Following pages: The gentlemen's singles final was blessed, as almost the entire duration of The Championships had been, with beautiful weather

The Duke's 50th Championships

Marking his attendance at a 50th Championships as President of the All England Lawn Tennis & Croquet Club, it was a delight to see HRH The Duke of Kent, as ever, presenting the Gentlemen's Singles Trophy to the victor.

His Royal Highness, at 82, is still involved with more than 140 different charities, organisations and professional bodies but has always retained a special affection for Wimbledon and has been at the heart of the Club's activities since becoming its President in 1969.

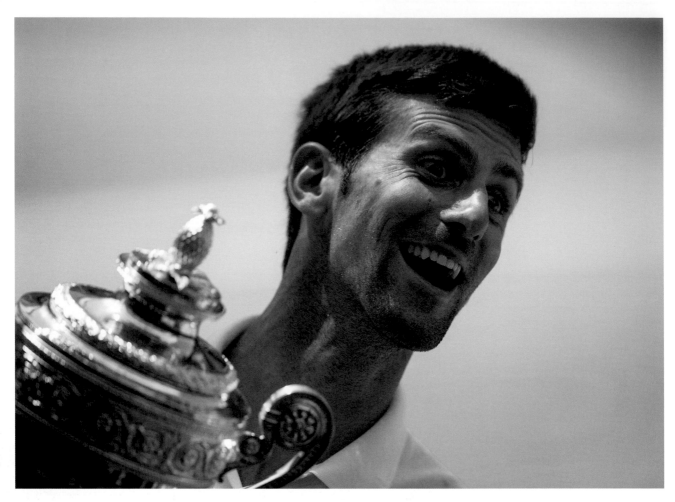

Above: The sheer sense of delight on Novak Djokovic's face when he saw his son, Stefan, in the players' box is one of the enduring images of The Championships

Previous page: Raising the trophy after months of trials and tribulations felt so sweet for Novak Djokovic. "It's in a struggle that you get to know yourself, you get to have an opportunity to rise like a phoenix and evolve and get better," he said

Djokovic admitted that he had not expected to be back at the top so soon after his elbow problems but said there had also been "a part of me that always believes in my own abilities". He added with a grin: "Wimbledon has been always a very special tournament to me. I dreamed of winning it when I was a seven-year-old boy. I made a lot of improvised Wimbledon trophies from different materials. I really always dreamed of winning Wimbledon.

"When that happened back in 2011, when I became No.1 in the world, in just a couple of days all my dreams came true. It's really hard to compare this year's victory and trophy with any of the other three because they're all special. But if I can pick one, that would probably be the first one and this year's because my son was at the trophy ceremony, which made it extra special."

Djokovic also revealed that he and Vajda had agreed to continue working together at least until the end of the year. "We are family," Djokovic said. "We love each other."

Anderson paid credit to Djokovic. "What separates the top guys who have done so well and guys further down is maybe not necessarily just their raw abilities, but their ability to play their best tennis in these sort of matches," Anderson said. "I wasn't able to do that in the beginning. He was."

He added: "Of course, my body didn't feel great. I don't think you're going to expect it to feel great this deep into a tournament when you've played so much tennis."

This was the 16th year in a row that the title was won by one of the 'Big Four' of men's tennis in the shape of Federer, Nadal, Djokovic and Andy Murray. Only three men can better Djokovic's total of 13 Grand Slam singles titles: Federer has won 20, Nadal 17 and Pete Sampras 14. At No.21 in the world, the Serb was also the lowest-ranked Gentlemen's Singles Champion since Goran Ivanisevic won as the world No.125 in 2001.

STEFAN STEALS THE SHOW

After Roger Federer's four children seized the limelight with their Centre Court appearance following their father's 2017 victory, this time it was the turn of three-year-old Stefan Djokovic to upstage his dad during his big moment.

Not that Novak minded a bit. Knowing Stefan was too young to be allowed to watch the match on court, he had rather hoped that if he won the title his little boy would be able to be brought into the box to see the presentation.

And, sure enough, when Stefan appeared, it was difficult to know who was more excited – him or dad! Asked by Sue Barker on court whether his victory felt different to his first three, Djokovic smiled: "It feels amazing because for the first time in my life I have someone screaming 'Daddy, Daddy!' It's the little boy right there! I can't be happier. I'm very emotional for him being there."

The idea that Stefan might see him back to his best was, reckoned

Djokovic, "one of, if not the biggest, motivation I've had for this Wimbledon this year".

He said he had been "visualising, imagining this moment" of his wife Jelena bringing Stefan into the stands. "He was not there until the very moment when I was walking over for the interview. He walked in. So that was just a moment that I will carry inside of my heart forever."

Stefan had inspired Novak but it turns out Djokovic himself may have been something of an inspiration to Their Royal Highnesses The Duke and Duchess of Cambridge, who watched his victory from the Royal Box.

Meeting the Royal couple afterwards, Djokovic asked after their three children and was told by the Duke that he and the Duchess were "trying to get a tennis racket in their hands". Apparently, as the Duchess – the patron of the All England Club – had previously revealed, young

ASIAN INFLUENCES AT SW19

The future of tennis in Asia looked in fine hands after an exciting weekend culminated in 16-year-old Tseng Chun Hsin (*above*) winning the boys' singles title against Britain's Jack Draper, a triumph that made him the first male junior since Frenchman Gael Monfils in 2004 to achieve the Roland-Garros/Wimbledon double in the same year.

The Chinese Taipei youngster's win, the first Wimbledon boys' triumph by an Asian since India's Leander Paes in 1990, came 24 hours after China's Wang Xiyu and Wang Xinyu lifted the girls' doubles title.

Tseng, the world junior No.1, hopes to emulate former winners like Roger Federer, who was born on the same day as him 20 years earlier. He plans to turn professional in 2019 and wants to be a trailblazer for Asian tennis like his hero, Japan's Kei Nishikori.

"I think he's the best Asian player. I play similar to him, so I want to be like him," said Tseng.

The victory of 17-year-old left-hander Wang Xiyu and her 16-year-old friend Wang Xinyu made up for their disappointment in not being able to meet in the girls' singles final after both were knocked out in the semis.

Wimbledon, which is helping develop the game in Asia through the Indian, Japanese and Chinese legs of its international 'Road to Wimbledon' junior event, was also delighted to welcome back Li Na (*right*) to play in the Ladies' Invitation Doubles.

Four years since she played the last match of her career at SW19, the most successful Asian player ever liked what she saw of the new Chinese wave.

At 36, now a mother of two and still one of life's smilers, Li Na laughed: "I saw the Chinese juniors play these past few days. The way they hit the ball is so fast. I'm not strong like them!"

Meanwhile only three other men in the last 100 years can better Djokovic's tally of four Wimbledon singles titles: Federer with eight, Sampras with seven and Borg with five.

Philip Brook, the Chairman of the All England Club, said at the Champions' Dinner that evening that Djokovic had become "one of the most formidable competitors this sport has ever known" and told him: "It has been a privilege to witness you back to your best throughout these Championships."

Interviewed on stage at the Guildhall, Djokovic was asked what his son Stefan had said to him when he showed him the trophy. "He gave me a hug in front of the locker room but then he left to play with his friends," Djokovic said with a smile.

Just as he had when he asked Serena Williams to dance with him at the same event three years ago, Djokovic invited this year's Ladies' Singles Champion, Angelique Kerber, to show her footwork. Djokovic and Kerber danced for a minute or two to 'Be Mine' by Ofenbach to big cheers from the guests.

The dinner celebrated the achievements of all the Fortnight's champions. The last winners had been Austria's Alexander Peya and the American Nicole Melichar, who beat Britain's Jamie Murray and the Belarusian Victoria Azarenka 7-6(1), 6-3 in the mixed doubles final. The champions both said they had dreamed of winning Wimbledon as children, while Melichar said their relaxed attitude as a team had been key. She added: "I joked with him before the tournament that mixed doubles is my happy place, so I call us 'Team Happy Place'. We have fun out there, we support each other. We don't get upset with each other. We just give it our best."

Murray, who had won the title on two previous occasions, with Jelena Jankovic and Martina Hingis, had not planned to enter the mixed event but changed his mind when he had the opportunity to play with Azarenka. "It was a lot of fun to play with Vika," he said. "She's a great player and a great champion."

Philip Brook, the All England Club Chairman, congratulated the new champion as Novak Djokovic enjoyed seeing his name up on the Centre Court honours board for a fourth time

Earlier in the day Tseng Chun Hsin became the first boy to win the Roland-Garros and Wimbledon junior singles titles in the same year since Gael Monfils in 2004. The 16-year-old from Chinese Taipei beat Britain's Jack Draper 6-1, 6-7(2), 6-4. Tseng, who said he would concentrate on playing professional men's tournaments in 2019, was asked how much he would like to follow the example of Federer, who won the boys' title in 1998. "I will just keep doing my best and keep working hard," he said. "Hopefully one day I can come back here again."

Draper, the 16-year-old son of Roger Draper, the former Chief Executive of the Lawn Tennis Association, had been attempting to become the first home player to win the title for 56 years. He said he would take "immense confidence" from his experience here. "It's been an unbelievable week and it's going to give me a lot of inspiration and motivation," he said.

Finland's Otto Virtanen and Turkey's Yanki Erel won the boys' doubles title, beating Nicolas Mejia and Ondrej Styler 7-6(5), 6-4 in the final, while China's Wang Xinyu and Wang Xiyu beat Caty McNally and Whitney Osuigwe 6-2, 6-1 to take the girls' doubles title.

Sweden's Stefan Olsson made a successful defence of his Gentlemen's Wheelchair Singles title, beating Gustavo Fernandez 6-2, 0-6, 6-3 in the final. The Dutchwoman Diede de Groot and Japan's Yui Kamiji won the Ladies' Wheelchair Doubles, beating Britain's Lucy Shuker and Germany's Sabine Ellerbrock 6-1, 6-1.

Tommy Haas and Mark Philippoussis won the Gentlemen's Invitation Doubles, beating Colin Fleming and Xavier Malisse 7-6(4), 6-4 in the final, while Jonas Bjorkman and Todd Woodbridge beat Richard Krajicek and Mark Petchey 6-4, 6-3 to win the Gentlemen's Senior Invitation Doubles. The Ladies' Invitation Doubles, which was as competitive as ever, was won by Kim Clijsters and Rennae Stubbs, who beat Cara Black and Martina Navratilova 6-3, 6-4.

It had been a wonderful Fortnight, highlighted by the remarkable comebacks of Angelique Kerber, Serena Williams and Novak Djokovic and by the enduring excellence of players like Rafael Nadal and Roger Federer. The only sadness was that we would have to wait 50 weeks to enjoy it all again.

The two teams embraced after Alexander Peya and Nicole Melichar ended The Championships with a straight-sets victory in the mixed doubles final over Jamie Murray and Victoria Azarenka

The umpire strides back

 FA/BBC

Umpire James Keothavong steps up to receive his medal having officiated in his second gentlemen's singles final

• Feliciano Lopez may have played in 66 consecutive Grand Slams but one of the game's top umpires, James Keothavong, isn't doing too badly either as he capped his 65th straight Slam with the honour of officiating at his second gentlemen's singles final.

The 36-year-old Briton – whose fine Championships had earlier seen him give Nick Kyrgios a mid-match lesson about the foot fault rule – had previously umpired the 2014 men's final, which saw Novak Djokovic beat Roger Federer across five epic sets. Perhaps Keothavong is something of a lucky charm for the Serbian superstar?

• Djokovic reckoned his three-year-old son Stefan had been the major inspiration behind his Wimbledon triumph, but he also paid tribute to the surgeon who had operated on his elbow in January, surgery which kick-started his road back to the top.

"I saw him yesterday and today before the match. I'm very thankful to him and to his team for doing a great job," explained the beaming champion, who had invited the man in question to the final.

Indeed, after such an obviously fine job one reporter suggested that Novak should perhaps be thinking of splitting his prize money of £2.25 million with the doctor. "Half the prize money?" pondered Novak. "It's a bit unlikely! Maybe something else. We'll see. We'll think about it."

• Djokovic enjoyed the now traditional post-Championship stroll through the All England Club's corridors, which gives the newly crowned champion the chance to be congratulated by royalty, Members and distinguished guests. It concluded with Rod Laver telling him: "Four times. You can have whatever you want!" Rod should know...

• It was the end of an era on Centre Court and in countless homes around Britain as Barry Davies, one of the great voices of British sport, gave the last commentary of his broadcasting career, bowing out at the age of 80 with a few final pearls during the mixed doubles final.

Davies may have been most celebrated for his half-century of memorable football commentaries but he was a superb all-rounder who enjoyed every "interesting, very interesting" moment of the 33 Championships he covered.

"Time comes round and you've got to move on. I wanted to do one more so that I could actually say I covered Wimbledon at the age of 80," explained Davies.

On a documentary about his career screened on the BBC during The Championships, he told Sue Barker: "I shall miss it so I'll be coming to ask you 'any spare tickets, Sue...?' It's been a lot of fun."

Dancing with the Lady in Red

There is no doubt that among his many achievements at Wimbledon, Novak Djokovic can take credit for breathing fresh life into the grand old tradition of the two singles champions dancing together in the post-match evening celebrations.

Three years ago, he invited the Ladies' Singles Champion Serena Williams to join him in a rendition of 'Saturday Night Fever' at the Champions' Dinner in London's Guildhall, a double act which brought the house down.

This time, the new champion asked Ladies' Singles Champion Angelique Kerber to trip the light fantastic with him, suggesting 'Lady in Red' might be appropriate in honour of Angie's scarlet gown.

Instead, after she had gamely accepted his offer, the pair twirled niftily around to the disco beat of Ofenbach's 'Be Mine', much to the appreciation of the assembled throng.

Kerber, though, was rather less keen to pursue another Grand Slam ritual. After she had won the 2016 Australian Open, she jumped into Melbourne's Yarra River in celebration. Asked if she might now jump into the Thames, she laughed: "I thought after that first jump, maybe it's the last one!"

Djokovic, though, had no qualms. "I'll jump in the river, anything you guys want!" beamed the master showman.

A VERY HAPPY ANNIVERSARY

Little more than a fortnight after the conclusion of The Championships 2018, the Wimbledon lawns were once again alive with the sound of tennis.

To mark the 150th anniversary of The All England Lawn Tennis & Croquet Club, tennis clubs from across the globe were invited to help celebrate this milestone by participating in either an International Club Tournament or a UK Club Tournament, both of which were staged on the Grounds of the AELTC.

No fewer than four continents were represented at the international event, with the following 12 clubs – all of whom have long-standing relationships with the AELTC – sending teams to compete: Fitzwilliam LTC (Dublin, Ireland), Grass Court Saga (Saga, Japan), Hellerup IK (Copenhagen, Denmark), Kungl. TK (Stockholm, Sweden), Kooyong LTC (Melbourne, Australia), Longwood Cricket Club (Boston, USA), The Meadow Club of Southampton (New York, USA), Monte Carlo Country Club (Monaco), RCT Barcelona (Barcelona, Spain), TC Weissenhof (Stuttgart, Germany), TC Lido Lugano (Lugano, Switzerland), Villa Primrose (Bordeaux, France) and a series of AELTC teams.

Among those participating were former professionals Albert Montanes and Kenneth Carlsen, both of whom reached the third round of The Championships during their careers, Sally Peers, who reached the ladies' doubles quarter-finals at the 2010 Australian Open, and James Cluskey, who recently broke the Guinness World Record for the longest tennis match alongside three fellow Irish players, after playing for a total of 60 hours, 24 minutes and 14 seconds to raise money for charity.

As such, the international competition was a high-quality affair, involving three separate events that ran simultaneously: men's doubles, ladies' doubles and mixed doubles.

The AELTC pairing of Alistair Felton and Johnny Barr claimed victory in the men's doubles, while the AELTC's Gill Brook and Richard Stoakes were triumphant in the mixed doubles. There was to be no clean sweep on home soil, however, as Laura Pous and Eva Bes of RCT Barcelona won the ladies' doubles. Indeed, RCT Barcelona also came out on top in the overall standings (based on team performance across all three events) with Kooyong LTC in second.

Six more clubs made the journey to Wimbledon for the UK Club Tournament, with Cumberland LTC (London), Edgbaston Priory Club (Birmingham), Roehampton Club (London), The Hurlingham Club (London), The Queen's Club (London) and The Wimbledon Club (London) joining two AELTC teams to make up the field.

Roehampton Club were victorious in both the men's and ladies' doubles, with Oli Golding and Richard Ground and Marta Sirotkina and Joy Tacon their winning pairs. The mixed doubles went to the AELTC duo of Pat Wire and Graham Neale, while Cumberland LTC finished top of the overall standings, with Roehampton Club in second.

Tennis wasn't the only thing on the agenda, however, with the travelling teams invited to enjoy guided tours of the Grounds and try their hands at the Club's original sport of croquet, among a raft of other activities. Proceedings were brought to an end with a gala evening featuring musicians, acrobatics and an 'almost entirely white' dress code, which proved to be a fitting end to a memorable 150th anniversary week.

A week of 150th anniversary celebrations saw two tennis tournaments grace the hallowed Wimbledon turf – an international event featuring clubs from all over the world (above, left) and a UK club tournament for friends of the All England Club a little closer to home (above). Appropriately enough there was also plenty of croquet played (top, right) and, to round the occasion off, a memorable gala dinner with an 'almost entirely white' dress code.

WIMBLEDON 2018

The Gentlemen's Singles

Novak DJOKOVIC

The Ladies' Singles

Angelique KERBER

The Gentlemen's Doubles

Mike BRYAN   **Jack SOCK**

The Ladies' Doubles

Barbora KREJCIKOVA   **Katerina SINIAKOVA**

The Mixed Doubles

Nicole MELICHAR   **Alexander PEYA**

THE CHAMPIONS

The Boys' Singles

**TSENG
Chun Hsin**

The Girls' Singles

Iga SWIATEK

The Boys' Doubles

**Otto VIRTANEN
Yanki EREL**

The Girls' Doubles

**WANG Xiyu
WANG Xinyu**

The Gentlemen's Wheelchair Singles

Stefan OLSSON

The Ladies' Wheelchair Singles

Diede DE GROOT

The Gentlemen's Wheelchair Doubles

**Alfie HEWETT
Gordon REID**

The Ladies' Wheelchair Doubles

**Diede DE GROOT
Yui KAMIJI**

The Gentlemen's Invitation Doubles

**Mark
PHILIPPOUSSIS
Tommy HAAS**

The Ladies' Invitation Doubles

**Rennae STUBBS
Kim CLIJSTERS**

The Senior Gentlemen's Invitation Doubles

**Jonas BJORKMAN
Todd WOODBRIDGE**

EVENT 1 – THE GENTLEMEN'S SINGLES CHAMPIONSHIP 2018

Holder: ROGER FEDERER (SUI)

The Champion will become the holder, for the year only, of the CHALLENGE CUP presented by The All England Lawn Tennis and Croquet Club in 1887. The Champion will receive a silver three-quarter size replica of the Challenge Cup. A Silver Salver will be presented to the Runner-up and a Bronze Medal to each defeated semi-finalist. The matches will be the best of five sets.

First Round

1. **Roger Federer [1]** *(2)* .... (SUI)
2. Dusan Lajovic *(58)* .... (SRB)
3. Lukas Lacko *(73)* .... (SVK)
4. (Q) Benjamin Bonzi *(284)* .... (FRA)
5. Ivo Karlovic *(112)* .... (CRO)
6. Mikhail Youzhny *(102)* .... (RUS)
7. Jan-Lennard Struff *(64)* .... (GER)
8. **Leonardo Mayer [32]** *(36)* .... (ARG)
9. **Adrian Mannarino [22]** *(26)* .... (FRA)
10. (Q) Christian Garin *(167)* .... (CHI)
11. Ryan Harrison *(59)* .... (USA)
12. Roberto Carballes Baena *(79)* .... (ESP)
13. Guillermo Garcia-Lopez *(65)* .... (ESP)
14. Gastao Elias *(118)* .... (POR)
15. Daniil Medvedev *(67)* .... (RUS)
16. **Borna Coric [16]** *(20)* .... (CRO)
17. **Sam Querrey [11]** *(13)* .... (USA)
18. Jordan Thompson *(101)* .... (AUS)
19. (WC) Sergiy Stakhovsky *(109)* .... (UKR)
20. Joao Sousa *(45)* .... (POR)
21. Laslo Djere *(90)* .... (SRB)
22. Paolo Lorenzi *(86)* .... (ITA)
23. Gael Monfils *(44)* .... (FRA)
24. **Richard Gasquet [23]** *(31)* .... (FRA)
25. **Philipp Kohlschreiber [25]** *(27)* .... (GER)
26. Evgeny Donskoy *(83)* .... (RUS)
27. Gilles Muller *(60)* .... (LUX)
28. (LL) Michael Mmoh *(119)* .... (USA)
29. (Q) John-Patrick Smith *(211)* .... (AUS)
30. Andreas Seppi *(50)* .... (ITA)
31. (Q) Norbert Gombos *(190)* .... (SVK)
32. **Kevin Anderson [8]** *(8)* .... (RSA)
33. **Marin Cilic [3]** *(5)* .... (CRO)
34. Yoshihito Nishioka *(66)* .... (JPN)
35. (Q) Jason Kubler *(147)* .... (AUS)
36. Guido Pella *(82)* .... (ARG)
37. Ricardas Berankis *(96)* .... (LTU)
38. Mackenzie McDonald *(103)* .... (USA)
39. Nicolas Jarry *(66)* .... (CHI)
40. **Filip Krajinovic [28]** *(30)* .... (SRB)
41. **Lucas Pouille [17]** *(19)* .... (FRA)
42. (WC) Denis Kudla *(84)* .... (USA)
43. (LL) Peter Polansky *(110)* .... (CAN)
44. (Q) Dennis Novak *(171)* .... (AUT)
45. John Millman *(56)* .... (AUS)
46. (Q) Stefano Travaglia *(137)* .... (ITA)
47. (WC) Liam Broady *(173)* .... (GBR)
48. **Milos Raonic [13]** *(32)* .... (CAN)
49. **John Isner [9]** *(10)* .... (USA)
50. (Q) Yannick Maden *(134)* .... (GER)
51. Steve Johnson *(42)* .... (USA)
52. (Q) Ruben Bemelmans *(104)* .... (BEL)
53. Aljaz Bedene *(71)* .... (SLO)
54. Cameron Norrie *(75)* .... (GBR)
55. Radu Albot *(98)* .... (MDA)
56. **Pablo Carreno Busta [20]** *(12)* .... (ESP)
57. **Stefanos Tsitsipas [31]** *(35)* .... (GRE)
58. (Q) Gregoire Barrere *(188)* .... (FRA)
59. Malek Jaziri *(61)* .... (TUN)
60. Jared Donaldson *(54)* .... (USA)
61. Yuki Bhambri *(85)* .... (IND)
62. (Q) Thomas Fabbiano *(133)* .... (ITA)
63. Stan Wawrinka *(224)* .... (SUI)
64. **Grigor Dimitrov [6]** *(6)* .... (BUL)
65. **Dominic Thiem [7]** *(7)* .... (AUT)
66. Marcos Baghdatis *(95)* .... (CYP)
67. David Ferrer *(37)* .... (ESP)
68. Karen Khachanov *(40)* .... (RUS)
69. Julien Benneteau *(63)* .... (FRA)
70. Marton Fucsovics *(49)* .... (HUN)
71. Frances Tiafoe *(52)* .... (USA)
72. **Fernando Verdasco [30]** *(34)* .... (ESP)
73. **Kyle Edmund [21]** *(17)* .... (GBR)
74. (Q) Alex Bolt *(204)* .... (AUS)
75. Yuichi Sugita *(69)* .... (JPN)
76. (Q) Bradley Klahn *(168)* .... (USA)
77. Guido Andreozzi *(105)* .... (ARG)
78. Horacio Zeballos *(126)* .... (ARG)
79. Tennys Sandgren *(57)* .... (USA)
80. **Novak Djokovic [12]** *(21)* .... (SRB)
81. **Nick Kyrgios [15]** *(18)* .... (AUS)
82. Denis Istomin *(92)* .... (UZB)
83. Marius Copil *(94)* .... (ROU)
84. Robin Haase *(43)* .... (NED)
85. (LL) Bernard Tomic *(184)* .... (AUS)
86. (LL) Hubert Hurkacz *(122)* .... (POL)
87. (Q) Christian Harrison *(198)* .... (USA)
88. **Kei Nishikori [24]** *(28)* .... (JPN)
89. **Damir Dzumhur [27]** *(23)* .... (BIH)
90. Maximilian Marterer *(48)* .... (GER)
91. (Q) Ernests Gulbis *(138)* .... (LAT)
92. (WC) Jay Clarke *(218)* .... (GBR)
93. (LL) Lorenzo Sonego *(121)* .... (ITA)
94. Taylor Fritz *(68)* .... (USA)
95. James Duckworth *(105)* .... (AUS)
96. **Alexander Zverev [4]** *(3)* .... (GER)
97. **Juan Martin Del Potro [5]** *(4)* .... (ARG)
98. Peter Gojowczyk *(39)* .... (GER)
99. Feliciano Lopez *(70)* .... (ESP)
100. Federico Delbonis *(88)* .... (ARG)
101. Benoit Paire *(47)* .... (FRA)
102. (LL) Jason Jung *(155)* .... (TPE)
103. Jeremy Chardy *(46)* .... (FRA)
104. **Denis Shapovalov [26]** *(25)* .... (CAN)
105. **Jack Sock [18]** *(15)* .... (USA)
106. Matteo Berrettini *(81)* .... (ITA)
107. Gilles Simon *(53)* .... (FRA)
108. Nikoloz Basilashvili *(74)* .... (GEO)
109. Albert Ramos-Vinolas *(38)* .... (ESP)
110. (Q) Stephane Robert *(158)* .... (FRA)
111. Matthew Ebden *(51)* .... (AUS)
112. **David Goffin [10]** *(9)* .... (BEL)
113. **Diego Schwartzman [14]** *(11)* .... (ARG)
114. Mirza Basic *(78)* .... (BIH)
115. Jiri Vesely *(93)* .... (CZE)
116. Florian Mayer *(91)* .... (GER)
117. Pablo Cuevas *(76)* .... (URU)
118. (LL) Simone Bolelli *(154)* .... (ITA)
119. Taro Daniel *(87)* .... (JPN)
120. **Fabio Fognini [19]** *(16)* .... (ITA)
121. **Marco Cecchinato [29]** *(29)* .... (ITA)
122. Alex De Minaur *(80)* .... (AUS)
123. Pierre-Hugues Herbert *(72)* .... (FRA)
124. Mischa Zverev *(41)* .... (GER)
125. Vasek Pospisil *(97)* .... (CAN)
126. Mikhail Kukushkin *(77)* .... (KAZ)
127. Dudi Sela *(127)* .... (ISR)
128. **Rafael Nadal [2]** *(1)* .... (ESP)

Second Round

- **Roger Federer [1]** 6/1 6/3 6/4
- Lukas Lacko .... 4/6 6/3 7/6(5) 6/4
- Ivo Karlovic .... 4/6 7/5 7/6(7) 6/3
- Jan-Lennard Struff ... 3/6 6/7(5) 7/6(5) 7/6(5) 6/1
- **Adrian Mannarino [22]** ... 6/3 1/6 7/6(4) 6/2
- Ryan Harrison 6/1 6/4 6/2
- Guillermo Garcia-Lopez 6/2 6/4 6/2
- Daniil Medvedev .... 7/6(6) 6/2 6/2
- **Sam Querrey [11]** 6/2 6/4 6/3
- Sergiy Stakhovsky 6/3 6/3 5/7 1/6 6/4
- Paolo Lorenzi .... 7/6(1) 6/7(3) 6/2 6/4
- Gael Monfils .... 7/6(6) 7/5 6/4
- **Philipp Kohlschreiber [25]** 6/2 6/4 7/5
- Gilles Muller .... 7/5 4/6 7/6(7) 3/6 6/1
- Andreas Seppi 6/2 6/4 6/1
- **Kevin Anderson [8]** 6/3 6/4 6/4
- **Marin Cilic [3]** 6/1 6/4 6/4
- Guido Pella .... 6/4 7/5 4/6 7/6(3)
- Mackenzie McDonald .... 4/6 7/6(6) 6/3 7/6(6)
- Nicolas Jarry .... 6/3 3/6 7/6(5) 6/4
- **Lucas Pouille [17]** 6/3 6/3 2/6 6/3
- Dennis Novak .... 6/2 6/3 7/6(7)
- John Millman .... 6/7(6) 6/3 7/5 6/2
- **Milos Raonic [13]** 7/5 6/0 6/1
- **John Isner [9]** .... 6/2 7/6(4) 7/5
- Ruben Bemelmans ... 7/5 6/3 4/6 6/7(0) 8/6
- Aljaz Bedene .... 4/6 7/6(4) 7/6(4) 6/4
- Radu Albot .... 3/6 6/0 6/7(5) 6/2 6/1
- **Stefanos Tsitsipas [31]** ... 6/3 6/4 6/7(3) 7/5
- Jared Donaldson .... 7/6(5) 6/3 6/1
- Thomas Fabbiano 2/6 6/3 6/3 6/2
- Stan Wawrinka .... 1/6 7/6(3) 7/6(5) 6/4
- Marcos Baghdatis .... 6/4 7/5 2/0 Ret'd
- Karen Khachanov .... 6/1 7/6(3) 3/6 7/5
- Julien Benneteau 7/5 7/5 6/3
- Frances Tiafoe .... 7/6(6) 7/6(5) 3/6 6/3
- **Kyle Edmund [21]** 6/2 6/3 7/5
- Bradley Klahn .... 2/6 7/6(6) 6/2 6/2
- Horacio Zeballos .... 4/6 7/6(1) 6/4 6/4
- **Novak Djokovic [12]** 6/3 6/1 6/2
- **Nick Kyrgios [15]** ... 7/6(3) 7/6(4) 6/7(5) 6/3
- Robin Haase .... 7/6(0) 7/5 4/6 7/6(4)
- Bernard Tomic .... 6/4 6/2 7/6(2)
- **Kei Nishikori [24]** .... 6/2 4/6 7/6(3) 6/2
- **Damir Dzumhur [27]** 6/3 6/2 6/4
- Ernests Gulbis .... 4/6 6/3 7/6(3) 3/6 6/4
- Taylor Fritz 3/6 6/3 6/2 6/2
- **Alexander Zverev [4]** 7/5 6/2 6/0
- **Juan Martin Del Potro [5]** 6/3 6/4 6/3
- Feliciano Lopez 6/3 6/4 6/2
- Benoit Paire .... 7/5 7/6(1) 6/4
- **Denis Shapovalov [26]** 6/3 3/6 7/5 6/4
- Matteo Berrettini ... 6/7(5) 6/7(3) 6/4 7/5 6/2
- Gilles Simon .... 6/1 7/6(5) 6/1
- Stephane Robert .... 7/6(5) 6/2 6/1
- Matthew Ebden 6/4 6/3 6/4
- **Diego Schwartzman [14]** 6/3 6/2 6/1
- Jiri Vesely .... 7/6(3) 6/4 4/6 6/1
- Simone Bolelli .... 7/6(5) 7/6(6) 6/1
- **Fabio Fognini [19]** 3/6 6/3 6/3 6/3
- Alex De Minaur .... 6/4 6/7(6) 7/6(5) 6/4
- Pierre-Hugues Herbert 6/4 6/3 6/4
- Mikhail Kukushkin 6/4 3/6 6/2 6/3
- **Rafael Nadal [2]** 6/3 6/3 6/2

Third Round

- **Roger Federer [1]** 6/4 6/4 6/1
- Jan-Lennard Struff ... 6/7(5) 3/6 7/6(4) 7/6(4) 13/11
- **Adrian Mannarino [22]** .... 7/5 7/5 7/6(4)
- Daniil Medvedev 6/3 6/4 6/2
- **Sam Querrey [11]** .... 7/6(4) 6/3 6/3
- Gael Monfils ... 3/6 6/3 7/6(5) 7/6(3)
- **Philipp Kohlschreiber [25]** ... 7/6(6) 7/6(4) 7/6(3)
- **Kevin Anderson [8]** .... 6/3 6/7(5) 6/3 6/4
- Guido Pella ... 3/6 1/6 6/4 7/6(3) 7/5
- Mackenzie McDonald ... 7/6(5) 5/7 3/6 6/2 11/9
- Dennis Novak ... 6/4 6/2 6/7(8) 3/6 6/2
- **Milos Raonic [13]** ... 7/6(4) 7/6(4) 7/6(4)
- **John Isner [9]** ... 6/1 6/4 6/7(6) 6/7(3) 7/5
- Radu Albot ... 6/2 4/6 7/6(3) 5/7 6/3
- **Stefanos Tsitsipas [31]** ... 6/3 6/2 3/6 4/6 6/3
- Thomas Fabbiano .... 7/6(7) 6/3 7/6(6)
- Karen Khachanov ... 6/3 6/4 3/6 6/7(4) 7/5
- Frances Tiafoe 4/6 6/3 6/4 6/2
- **Kyle Edmund [21]** .... 6/4 7/6(0) 6/2
- **Novak Djokovic [12]** 6/1 6/2 6/3
- **Nick Kyrgios [15]** 6/3 6/4 7/5
- **Kei Nishikori [24]** .... 2/6 6/3 7/6(7) 7/5
- Ernests Gulbis 2/6 6/4 6/3 1/6 6/3
- **Alexander Zverev [4]** ... 6/4 5/7 6/7(0) 6/1 6/2
- **Juan Martin Del Potro [5]** 6/4 6/1 6/2
- Benoit Paire .... 0/6 6/2 6/4 7/6(3)
- Gilles Simon .... 6/3 7/6(4) 6/2
- Matthew Ebden .... 6/3 7/6(5) 4/6 6/1
- Jiri Vesely .... 6/3 6/4 7/6(3)
- **Fabio Fognini [19]** 6/3 6/4 6/1
- Alex De Minaur .... 6/2 6/7(8) 7/5 6/3
- **Rafael Nadal [2]** 6/4 6/3 6/4

Fourth Round

- **Roger Federer [1]** 6/3 7/5 6/2
- **Adrian Mannarino [22]** 6/4 6/3 4/6 5/7 6/3
- Gael Monfils 5/7 6/4 6/4 6/2
- **Kevin Anderson [8]** 6/3 7/5 7/5
- Mackenzie McDonald .... 6/4 6/4 7/6(6)
- **Milos Raonic [13]** .... 7/6(5) 4/6 7/5 6/2
- **John Isner [9]** 6/3 6/3 6/4
- **Stefanos Tsitsipas [31]** 6/2 6/1 6/4
- Karen Khachanov ... 4/6 4/6 7/6(3) 6/2 6/1
- **Novak Djokovic [12]** 4/6 6/3 6/2 6/4
- **Kei Nishikori [24]** .... 6/1 7/6(3) 6/4
- Ernests Gulbis ... 7/6(2) 4/6 5/7 6/3 6/0
- **Juan Martin Del Potro [5]** .... 6/4 7/6(4) 6/3
- Gilles Simon .... 6/1 6/7(3) 6/3 7/6(2)
- Jiri Vesely .... 7/6(4) 3/6 6/3 6/2
- **Rafael Nadal [2]** 6/1 6/2 6/4

Quarter-Finals

- **Roger Federer [1]** 6/0 7/5 6/4
- **Kevin Anderson [8]** .... 7/6(4) 7/6(2) 5/7 7/6(4)
- **Milos Raonic [13]** .... 6/3 6/4 6/7(5) 6/2
- **John Isner [9]** .... 6/4 7/6(8) 7/6(4)
- **Novak Djokovic [12]** 6/4 6/2 6/2
- **Kei Nishikori [24]** ... 4/6 7/6(5) 7/6(10) 6/1
- **Juan Martin Del Potro [5]** .... 7/6(1) 7/6(5) 5/7 7/6(5)
- **Rafael Nadal [2]** 6/3 6/3 6/4

Semi-Finals

- **Kevin Anderson [8]** 2/6 6/7(5) 7/5 6/4 13/11
- **John Isner [9]** 6/7(5) 7/6(7) 6/4 6/3
- **Novak Djokovic [12]** 6/3 3/6 6/2
- **Rafael Nadal [2]** 7/5 6/7(7) 4/6 6/4 6/4

Final

- **Kevin Anderson [8]** 7/6(6) 6/7(5) 6/7(9) 6/4 26/24
- **Novak Djokovic [12]** 6/4 3/6 7/6(9) 3/6 10/8

Novak Djokovic [12] 6/2 6/2 7/6(3)

Heavy type denotes seeded players. The figure in brackets against names denotes the order in which they have been seeded. The figure in italics denotes ATP World Tour Ranking – 02.07.2018.
(WC)=Wild card. (Q)=Qualifier. (LL)=Lucky loser.

EVENT 2 – THE GENTLEMEN'S DOUBLES CHAMPIONSHIP 2018
Holders: LUKASZ KUBOT (POL) & MARCELO MELO (BRA)

The Champions will become the holders, for the year only, of the CHALLENGE CUPS presented by the OXFORD UNIVERSITY LAWN TENNIS CLUB in 1884 and the late SIR HERBERT WILBERFORCE in 1937.
The Champions will each receive a silver three-quarter size replica of the Challenge Cup. A Silver Salver will be presented to each of the Runners-up, and a Bronze Medal to each defeated semi-finalist. The matches will be the best of five sets.

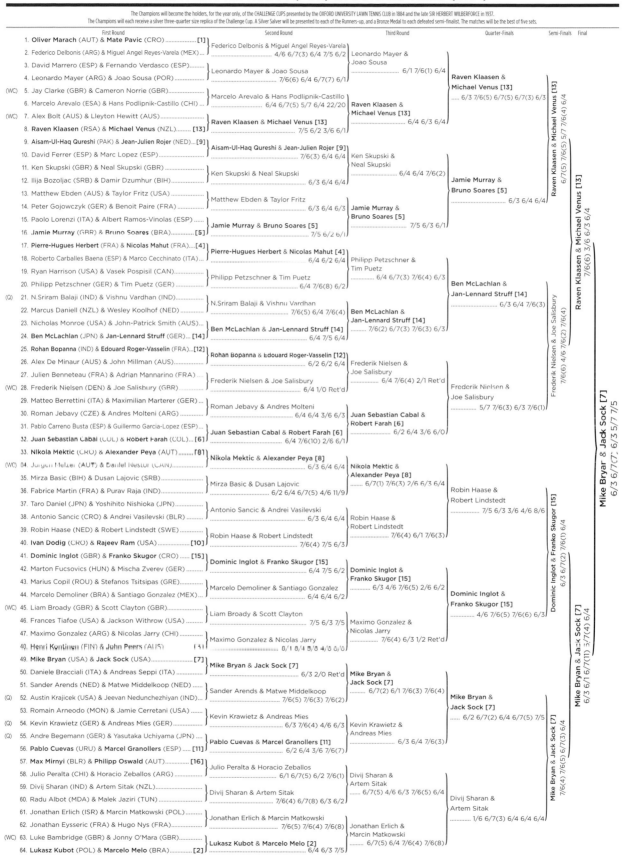

First Round	Second Round	Third Round	Quarter-Finals	Semi-Finals	Final

1. **Oliver Marach** (AUT) & **Mate Pavic** (CRO) .... [1]
2. Federico Delbonis (ARG) & Miguel Angel Reyes-Varela (MEX) ...
  Federico Delbonis & Miguel Angel Reyes-Varela — 4/6 6/7(3) 6/4 7/5 6/2
3. David Marrero (ESP) & Fernando Verdasco (ESP) ...
4. Leonardo Mayer (ARG) & Joao Sousa (POR) ...
  Leonardo Mayer & Joao Sousa — 7/6(6) 6/4 6/7(7) 6/1
  Leonardo Mayer & Joao Sousa — 6/1 7/6(1) 6/4
(WC) 5. Jay Clarke (GBR) & Cameron Norrie (GBR) ...
6. Marcelo Arevalo (ESA) & Hans Podlipnik-Castillo (CHI) ...
  Marcelo Arevalo & Hans Podlipnik-Castillo — 6/4 6/7(5) 5/7 6/4 22/20
  Raven Klaasen & Michael Venus [13] — 6/4 6/3 6/4
(WC) 7. Alex Bolt (AUS) & Lleyton Hewitt (AUS) ...
8. **Raven Klaasen** (RSA) & **Michael Venus** (NZL) ... [13]
  Raven Klaasen & Michael Venus [13] — 7/5 6/2 3/6 6/1
  Raven Klaasen & Michael Venus [13] — 6/3 7/6(5) 6/7(5) 6/7(3) 6/3
9. **Aisam-Ul-Haq Qureshi** (PAK) & **Jean-Julien Rojer** (NED) ... [9]
10. David Ferrer (ESP) & Marc Lopez (ESP) ...
  Aisam-Ul-Haq Qureshi & Jean-Julien Rojer [9] — 7/6(3) 6/4 6/4
11. Ken Skupski (GBR) & Neal Skupski (GBR) ...
12. Ilija Bozoljac (SRB) & Damir Dzumhur (BIH) ...
  Ken Skupski & Neal Skupski — 6/3 6/4 6/4
  Ken Skupski & Neal Skupski — 6/4 6/4 7/6(2)
13. Matthew Ebden (AUS) & Taylor Fritz (USA) ...
14. Peter Gojowczyk (GER) & Benoit Paire (FRA) ...
  Matthew Ebden & Taylor Fritz — 6/3 6/4 6/3
  Jamie Murray & Bruno Soares [5] — 7/5 6/3 6/1
15. Paolo Lorenzi (ITA) & Albert Ramos-Vinolas (ESP) ...
16. **Jamie Murray** (GBR) & **Bruno Soares** (BRA) ... [5]
  Jamie Murray & Bruno Soares [5] — 7/5 6/2 6/1
17. **Pierre-Hugues Herbert** (FRA) & **Nicolas Mahut** (FRA) ... [4]
18. Roberto Carballes Baena (ESP) & Marco Cecchinato (ITA) ...
  Pierre-Hugues Herbert & Nicolas Mahut [4] — 6/4 6/2 6/4
19. Ryan Harrison (USA) & Vasek Pospisil (CAN) ...
20. Philipp Petzschner (GER) & Tim Puetz (GER) ...
  Philipp Petzschner & Tim Puetz — 6/4 7/6(8) 6/2
  Philipp Petzschner & Tim Puetz — 6/4 6/7(3) 7/6(4) 6/3
(Q) 21. N.Sriram Balaji (IND) & Vishnu Vardhan (IND) ...
22. Marcus Daniell (NZL) & Wesley Koolhof (NED) ...
  N.Sriram Balaji & Vishnu Vardhan — 7/6(5) 6/4 7/6(4)
  Ben McLachlan & Jan-Lennard Struff [14] — 7/6(2) 6/7(3) 6/3
23. Nicholas Monroe (USA) & John-Patrick Smith (AUS) ...
24. **Ben McLachlan** (JPN) & **Jan-Lennard Struff** (GER) ... [14]
  Ben McLachlan & Jan-Lennard Struff [14] — 6/4 7/5 6/4
  Ben McLachlan & Jan-Lennard Struff [14] — 6/3 6/4 7/6(3)
25. **Rohan Bopanna** (IND) & **Edouard Roger-Vasselin** (FRA) ... [12]
26. Alex De Minaur (AUS) & John Millman (AUS) ...
  Rohan Bopanna & Edouard Roger-Vasselin [12] — 6/2 6/2 6/4
27. Julien Benneteau (FRA) & Adrian Mannarino (FRA) ...
(WC) 28. Frederik Nielsen (DEN) & Joe Salisbury (GBR) ...
  Frederik Nielsen & Joe Salisbury — 6/4 1/0 Ret'd
  Frederik Nielsen & Joe Salisbury — 6/4 7/6(4) 2/1 Ret'd
  Frederik Nielsen & Joe Salisbury — 5/7 7/6(6) 4/6 7/6(2) 7/6(4)
29. Matteo Berrettini (ITA) & Maximilian Marterer (GER) ...
30. Roman Jebavy (CZE) & Andres Molteni (ARG) ...
  Roman Jebavy & Andres Molteni — 6/4 6/3 6/6 3/6
  Juan Sebastian Cabal & Robert Farah [6] — 6/2 6/4 3/6 6/0
31. Pablo Carreno Busta (ESP) & Guillermo Garcia-Lopez (ESP) ...
32. **Juan Sebastian Cabal** (COL) & **Robert Farah** (COL) ... [6]
  Juan Sebastian Cabal & Robert Farah [6] — 6/4 7/6(10) 2/6 6/1
  Frederik Nielsen & Joe Salisbury — 5/7 7/6(6) 3/6 3/7 6/1(1)
33. **Nikola Mektic** (CRO) & **Alexander Peya** (AUT) ... [8]
(WC) 34. Jurgen Melzer (AUT) & Daniel Nestor (CAN) ...
  Nikola Mektic & Alexander Peya [8] — 6/3 6/4 6/4
35. Mirza Basic (BIH) & Dusan Lajovic (SRB) ...
36. Fabrice Martin (FRA) & Purav Raja (IND) ...
  Mirza Basic & Dusan Lajovic — 6/2 6/4 6/7(5) 4/6 11/9
  Nikola Mektic & Alexander Peya [8] — 6/7(1) 7/6(3) 2/6 6/3 6/4
37. Taro Daniel (JPN) & Yoshihito Nishioka (JPN) ...
38. Antonio Sancic (CRO) & Andrei Vasilevski (BLR) ...
  Antonio Sancic & Andrei Vasilevski — 6/3 6/4 6/4
  Robin Haase & Robert Lindstedt — 7/6(4) 6/1 7/6(3)
39. Robin Haase (NED) & Robert Lindstedt (SWE) ...
40. **Ivan Dodig** (CRO) & **Rajeev Ram** (USA) ... [10]
  Robin Haase & Robert Lindstedt — 7/6(4) 7/5 6/3
  Robin Haase & Robert Lindstedt — 7/5 6/3 3/6 4/6 8/6
41. **Dominic Inglot** (GBR) & **Franko Skugor** (CRO) ... [15]
42. Marton Fucsovics (HUN) & Mischa Zverev (GER) ...
  Dominic Inglot & Franko Skugor [15] — 6/4 7/5 6/2
43. Marius Copil (ROU) & Stefanos Tsitsipas (GRE) ...
44. Marcelo Demoliner (BRA) & Santiago Gonzalez (MEX) ...
  Marcelo Demoliner & Santiago Gonzalez — 6/4 6/4 6/2
  Dominic Inglot & Franko Skugor [15] — 6/3 4/6 7/6(5) 2/6 6/2
(WC) 45. Liam Broady (GBR) & Scott Clayton (GBR) ...
46. Frances Tiafoe (USA) & Jackson Withrow (USA) ...
  Liam Broady & Scott Clayton — 7/5 6/3 7/5
  Dominic Inglot & Franko Skugor [15] — 4/6 7/6(5) 7/6(6) 6/3
47. Maximo Gonzalez (ARG) & Nicolas Jarry (CHI) ...
48. Henri Kontinen (FIN) & John Peers (AUS) ... [3]
  Maximo Gonzalez & Nicolas Jarry — 6/1 6/4 6/3 4/6 6/3
  Maximo Gonzalez & Nicolas Jarry — 7/6(4) 6/3 1/2 Ret'd
49. **Mike Bryan** (USA) & **Jack Sock** (USA) ... [7]
50. Daniele Bracciali (ITA) & Andreas Seppi (ITA) ...
  Mike Bryan & Jack Sock [7] — 6/3 2/0 Ret'd
51. Sander Arends (NED) & Matwe Middelkoop (NED) ...
(Q) 52. Austin Krajicek (USA) & Jeevan Nedunchezhiyan (IND) ...
  Sander Arends & Matwe Middelkoop — 7/6(5) 7/6(3) 7/6(2)
  Mike Bryan & Jack Sock [7] — 6/7(2) 6/1 7/6(3) 7/6(4)
53. Romain Arneodo (MON) & Jamie Cerretani (USA) ...
(Q) 54. Kevin Krawietz (GER) & Andreas Mies (GER) ...
  Kevin Krawietz & Andreas Mies — 6/3 7/6(4) 4/6 6/3
  Kevin Krawietz & Andreas Mies — 6/3 6/4 7/6(3)
(Q) 55. Andre Begemann (GER) & Yasutaka Uchiyama (JPN) ...
56. **Pablo Cuevas** (URU) & **Marcel Granollers** (ESP) ... [11]
  Pablo Cuevas & Marcel Granollers [11] — 6/2 6/4 3/6 7/6(7)
  Mike Bryan & Jack Sock [7] — 6/2 6/7(2) 6/4 6/7(5) 7/5
57. **Max Mirnyi** (BLR) & **Philipp Oswald** (AUT) ... [16]
58. Julio Peralta (CHI) & Horacio Zeballos (ARG) ...
  Julio Peralta & Horacio Zeballos — 6/1 6/7(5) 6/2 7/6(1)
59. Divij Sharan (IND) & Artem Sitak (NZL) ...
60. Radu Albot (MDA) & Malek Jaziri (TUN) ...
  Divij Sharan & Artem Sitak — 7/6(4) 6/7(8) 6/3 6/2
  Divij Sharan & Artem Sitak — 6/7(5) 4/6 6/3 7/6(5) 6/4
61. Jonathan Erlich (ISR) & Marcin Matkowski (POL) ...
62. Jonathan Eysseric (FRA) & Hugo Nys (FRA) ...
  Jonathan Erlich & Marcin Matkowski — 7/6(5) 7/6(4) 7/6(8)
  Jonathan Erlich & Marcin Matkowski — 6/7(5) 6/4 7/6(4) 7/6(8)
  Divij Sharan & Artem Sitak — 1/6 6/7(3) 6/4 6/4 6/4
(WC) 63. Luke Bambridge (GBR) & Jonny O'Mara (GBR) ...
64. **Lukasz Kubot** (POL) & **Marcelo Melo** (BRA) ... [2]
  Lukasz Kubot & Marcelo Melo [2] — 6/4 6/3 7/5

Raven Klaasen & Michael Venus [13] — 7/6(5) 5/7 7/6(4) 6/4

Jamie Murray & Bruno Soares [5] — 6/3 6/4 6/4

Raven Klaasen & Michael Venus [13] — 6/3 7/6(5) 6/7(5) 6/7(3) 6/3

Ben McLachlan & Jan-Lennard Struff [14] — 6/3 6/4 7/6(3)

Frederik Nielsen & Joe Salisbury — 7/6(5) 4/6 7/6(2) 7/6(4)

Raven Klaasen & Michael Venus [13] — 7/6(6) 3/6 6/3 6/4

Robin Haase & Robert Lindstedt — 7/5 6/3 3/6 4/6 8/6

Dominic Inglot & Franko Skugor [15] — 6/3 6/7(2) 7/6(1) 6/4

Mike Bryan & Jack Sock [7] — 6/2 6/7(2) 6/4 6/7(5) 7/5

Divij Sharan & Artem Sitak — 7/6(4) 7/6(5) 6/7(3) 6/4

Mike Bryan & Jack Sock [7] — 6/3 6/7(7) 6/3 5/7(4) 6/4

Mike Bryan & Jack Sock [7] — 6/3 6/7(7) 6/3 5/7 7/5

Heavy type denotes seeded players. The figure in brackets against names denotes the order in which they have been seeded.
(WC)=Wild cards. (Q)=Qualifiers. (LL)=Lucky losers.

WIMBLEDON 2018

EVENT 3 – THE LADIES' SINGLES CHAMPIONSHIP 2018
Holder: GARBIÑE MUGURUZA (ESP)

The Champion will become the holder, for the year only, of the CHALLENGE TROPHY presented by The All England Lawn Tennis and Croquet Club in 1886. The Champion will receive a silver three-quarter size replica of the Challenge Trophy.
A Silver Salver will be presented to the Runner-up and a Bronze Medal to each defeated semi-finalist. The matches will be the best of three sets.

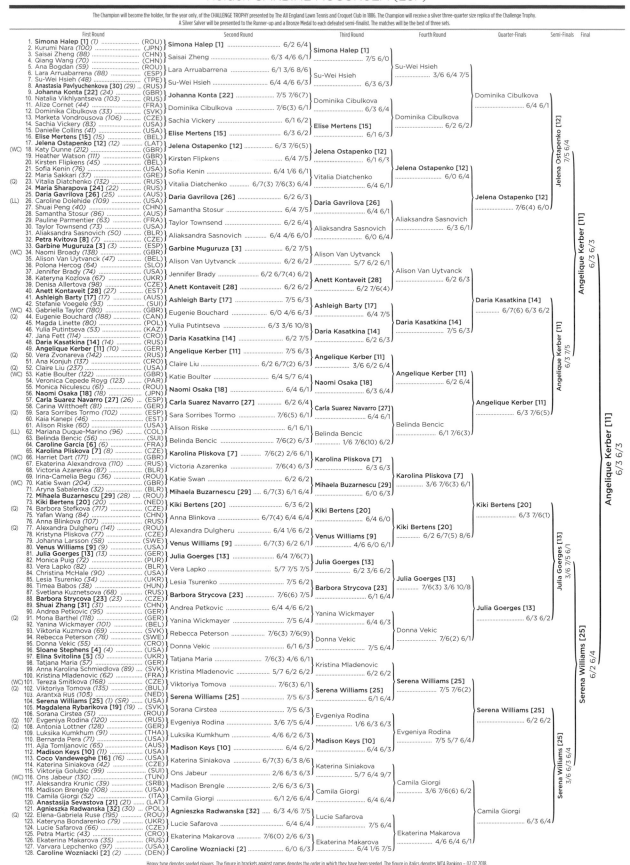

	First Round		Second Round	Third Round	Fourth Round	Quarter-Finals	Semi-Finals	Final
	1. **Simona Halep [1]** *(1)*	(ROU)	Simona Halep [1] 6/2 6/4	Simona Halep [1]				
	2. Kurumi Nara *(100)*	(JPN)		.... 7/5 6/0				
	3. Saisai Zheng *(88)*	(CHN)	Saisai Zheng 6/3 4/6 6/1		Su-Wei Hsieh			
	4. Qiang Wang *(70)*	(CHN)			.... 3/6 6/4 7/5			
	5. Ana Bogdan *(59)*	(ROU)	Lara Arruabarrena 6/1 3/6 8/6	Su-Wei Hsieh				
	6. Lara Arruabarrena *(88)*	(ESP)		.... 6/3 6/3				
	7. Su-Wei Hsieh *(48)*	(TPE)	Su-Wei Hsieh 6/4 4/6 6/3					
	8. **Anastasia Pavlyuchenkova [30]** *(29)*	(RUS)				Dominika Cibulkova		
	9. **Johanna Konta [22]** *(24)*	(GBR)	Johanna Konta [22] ...... 7/5 7/6(7)	Dominika Cibulkova		.... 6/4 6/1		
	10. Natalia Vikhlyantseva *(103)*	(RUS)		.... 6/3 6/4				
	11. Alize Cornet *(44)*	(FRA)	Dominika Cibulkova .... 7/6(3) 6/1		Dominika Cibulkova			
	12. **Dominika Cibulkova [33]**	(SVK)			.... 6/2 6/2			
	13. Marketa Vondrousova *(106)*	(CZE)	Sachia Vickery 6/1 6/2	Elise Mertens [15]				
	14. Sachia Vickery *(83)*	(USA)		.... 6/1 6/3				
	15. Danielle Collins *(41)*	(USA)	Elise Mertens [15] 6/3 6/2					
	16. **Elise Mertens [15]** *(15)*	(BEL)					Jelena Ostapenko [12]	
	17. **Jelena Ostapenko [12]** *(12)*	(LAT)	Jelena Ostapenko [12] ...... 6/3 7/6(5)	Jelena Ostapenko [12]			.... 7/5 6/4	
(WC)	18. Katy Dunne *(212)*	(GBR)		.... 6/1 6/3				
	19. Heather Watson *(111)*	(GBR)	Kirsten Flipkens 6/4 7/5		Jelena Ostapenko [12]			
	20. Kirsten Flipkens *(45)*	(BEL)			.... 6/0 6/4			
	21. Sofia Kenin *(76)*	(USA)	Sofia Kenin 6/4 1/6 6/1	Vitalia Diatchenko				
	22. Maria Sakkari *(37)*	(GRE)		.... 6/4 6/1				
(Q)	23. Vitalia Diatchenko *(132)*	(RUS)	Vitalia Diatchenko .... 6/7(3) 7/6(3) 6/4			Jelena Ostapenko [12]		
	24. **Maria Sharapova [24]** *(22)*	(RUS)				.... 7/6(4) 6/0		
	25. **Daria Gavrilova [26]** *(25)*	(AUS)	Daria Gavrilova [26] 6/2 6/3	Daria Gavrilova [26]				
(LL)	26. Caroline Dolehide *(109)*	(USA)		.... 6/4 6/1				
	27. Shuai Peng *(40)*	(CHN)	Samantha Stosur 6/4 7/5		Aliaksandra Sasnovich			
	28. Samantha Stosur *(86)*	(AUS)			.... 6/3 6/1			
	29. Pauline Parmentier *(63)*	(FRA)	Taylor Townsend 6/2 6/4	Aliaksandra Sasnovich				
	30. Taylor Townsend *(73)*	(USA)		.... 6/0 6/4				
	31. Aliaksandra Sasnovich *(50)*	(BLR)	Aliaksandra Sasnovich 6/4 4/6 6/0					
	32. **Petra Kvitova [8]** *(7)*	(CZE)				Alison Van Uytvanck		
	33. **Garbine Muguruza [3]** *(3)*	(ESP)	Garbine Muguruza [3] 6/2 7/5	Alison Van Uytvanck		.... 5/7 6/2 6/1		
(WC)	34. Naomi Broady *(138)*	(GBR)		.... 5/7 6/2 6/1				
	35. Alison Van Uytvanck *(47)*	(BEL)	Alison Van Uytvanck 6/2 6/2		Alison Van Uytvanck			
	36. Polona Hercog *(64)*	(SLO)			.... 6/2 6/3			
	37. Jennifer Brady *(74)*	(USA)	Jennifer Brady .... 6/2 6/7(4) 6/2	Anett Kontaveit [28]				
	38. Kateryna Kozlova *(67)*	(UKR)		.... 6/2 7/6(4)				
	39. Denisa Allertova *(98)*	(CZE)	Anett Kontaveit [28] 6/2 6/2					
	40. **Anett Kontaveit [28]** *(27)*	(EST)					Daria Kasatkina [14]	
	41. **Ashleigh Barty [17]** *(17)*	(AUS)	Ashleigh Barty [17] 7/5 6/3	Ashleigh Barty [17]			.... 6/7(6) 6/3 6/2	
	42. Stefanie Voegele *(93)*	(SUI)		.... 6/4 7/5				
(WC)	43. Gabriella Taylor *(180)*	(GBR)	Eugenie Bouchard 6/0 4/6 6/3		Daria Kasatkina [14]			
(Q)	44. Eugenie Bouchard *(188)*	(CAN)			.... 7/5 6/3			
	45. Magda Linette *(80)*	(POL)	Yulia Putintseva 6/3 3/6 10/8	Daria Kasatkina [14]				
	46. Yulia Putintseva *(53)*	(KAZ)		.... 6/2 6/3				
	47. Jana Fett *(114)*	(CRO)	Daria Kasatkina [14] 6/2 7/5					
	48. **Daria Kasatkina [14]** *(14)*	(RUS)				Angelique Kerber [11]		
	49. **Angelique Kerber [11]** *(10)*	(GER)	Angelique Kerber [11] 7/5 6/3	Angelique Kerber [11]		.... 6/2 6/4		
(Q)	50. Vera Zvonareva *(142)*	(RUS)		.... 3/6 6/2 6/4				
	51. Ana Konjuh *(137)*	(CRO)	Claire Liu .... 6/2 6/7(2) 6/3		Naomi Osaka [18]			
(Q)	52. Claire Liu *(237)*	(USA)			.... 6/2 6/4			
(WC)	53. Katie Boulter *(122)*	(GBR)	Katie Boulter 6/4 5/7 6/4	Naomi Osaka [18]				
	54. Veronica Cepede Royg *(123)*	(PAR)		.... 6/3 6/4				
	55. Monica Niculescu *(61)*	(ROU)	Naomi Osaka [18] 6/4 6/1					
	56. **Naomi Osaka [18]** *(18)*	(JPN)					Angelique Kerber [11]	
	57. **Carla Suarez Navarro [27]** *(26)*	(ESP)	Carla Suarez Navarro [27] .. 6/2 6/4	Carla Suarez Navarro [27]			.... 6/3 7/6(5)	
	58. Carina Witthoeft *(81)*	(GER)		.... 6/4 6/1				
(Q)	59. Sara Sorribes Tormo *(102)*	(ESP)	Sara Sorribes Tormo .... 7/6(5) 6/1		Belinda Bencic			
	60. Kaia Kanepi *(46)*	(EST)			.... 6/1 7/6(3)			
	61. Alison Riske *(60)*	(USA)	Alison Riske 6/1 6/1	Belinda Bencic				
(LL)	62. Mariana Duque-Marino *(96)*	(COL)		.... 1/6 7/6(10) 6/2				
	63. Belinda Bencic *(56)*	(SUI)	Belinda Bencic .... 7/6(2) 6/3					
	64. **Caroline Garcia [6]** *(6)*	(FRA)				Kiki Bertens [20]		
	65. **Karolina Pliskova [7]** *(8)*	(CZE)	Karolina Pliskova [7] ...... 7/6(2) 2/6 6/1	Karolina Pliskova [7]		.... 6/3 7/6(1)		
(WC)	66. Harriet Dart *(171)*	(GBR)		.... 6/3 6/3				
	67. Ekaterina Alexandrova *(110)*	(RUS)	Victoria Azarenka .... 7/6(4) 6/3		Karolina Pliskova [7]			
	68. Victoria Azarenka *(87)*	(BLR)			.... 3/6 7/6(3) 6/1			
	69. Irina-Camelia Begu *(36)*	(ROU)	Katie Swan 6/2 6/2	Mihaela Buzarnescu [29]				
(WC)	70. Katie Swan *(204)*	(GBR)		.... 6/0 6/1				
	71. Aryna Sabalenka *(32)*	(BLR)	Mihaela Buzarnescu [29] .. 6/7(3) 6/1 6/4					
	72. **Mihaela Buzarnescu [29]** *(28)*	(ROU)					Kiki Bertens [20]	
	73. **Kiki Bertens [20]** *(20)*	(NED)	Kiki Bertens [20] 6/3 6/2	Kiki Bertens [20]			.... 6/3 7/6(1)	
(Q)	74. Barbora Stefkova *(717)*	(CZE)		.... 6/4 6/0				
	75. Yafan Wang *(84)*	(CHN)	Anna Blinkova ...... 6/7(4) 6/4 6/4		Kiki Bertens [20]			
	76. Anna Blinkova *(107)*	(RUS)			.... 6/2 6/7(5) 8/6			
(Q)	77. Alexandra Dulgheru *(141)*	(ROU)	Alexandra Dulgheru 6/4 1/6 6/2	Venus Williams [9]				
	78. Kristyna Pliskova *(77)*	(CZE)		.... 4/6 6/0 6/1				
	79. Johanna Larsson *(58)*	(SWE)	Venus Williams [9] .... 6/7(3) 6/2 6/1					
	80. **Venus Williams [9]** *(9)*	(USA)				Julia Goerges [13]		
	81. **Julia Goerges [13]** *(13)*	(GER)	Julia Goerges [13] .... 6/4 7/6(7)	Julia Goerges [13]		.... 7/6(3) 3/6 10/8		
	82. Monica Puig *(72)*	(PUR)		.... 6/2 3/6 6/2				
	83. Vera Lapko *(82)*	(BLR)	Vera Lapko 5/7 7/5 7/5		Julia Goerges [13]			
	84. Christina McHale *(90)*	(USA)			.... 6/3 6/2			
	85. Lesia Tsurenko *(34)*	(UKR)	Lesia Tsurenko 7/5 6/2	Barbora Strycova [23]				
	86. Timea Babos *(38)*	(HUN)		.... 6/1 6/4				
	87. Svetlana Kuznetsova *(68)*	(RUS)	Barbora Strycova [23] ...... 7/6(6) 7/5					
	88. **Barbora Strycova [23]** *(23)*	(CZE)					Serena Williams [25]	
	89. **Shuai Zhang [31]** *(31)*	(CHN)	Andrea Petkovic 6/4 4/6 6/2	Yanina Wickmayer			.... 6/2 6/4	
	90. Andrea Petkovic *(95)*	(GER)		.... 6/4 6/3				
(Q)	91. Mona Barthel *(118)*	(GER)	Yanina Wickmayer 7/5 6/4		Donna Vekic			
	92. Yanina Wickmayer *(101)*	(BEL)			.... 7/6(2) 6/1			
	93. Viktoria Kuzmova *(69)*	(SVK)	Rebecca Peterson ..... 7/6(3) 7/6(9)	Donna Vekic				
	94. Rebecca Peterson *(78)*	(SWE)		.... 7/5 6/2				
	95. Donna Vekic *(55)*	(CRO)	Donna Vekic 6/1 6/3					
	96. **Sloane Stephens [4]** *(4)*	(USA)				Serena Williams [25]		
	97. **Elina Svitolina [5]** *(5)*	(UKR)	Tatjana Maria .... 7/6(3) 4/6 6/1	Kristina Mladenovic		.... 7/5 7/6(2)		
	98. Tatjana Maria *(57)*	(GER)		.... 6/2 6/2				
	99. Anna Karolina Schmiedlova *(89)*	(SVK)	Kristina Mladenovic 5/7 6/2 6/2		Serena Williams [25]			
	100. Kristina Mladenovic *(62)*	(FRA)			.... 7/5 6/1			
(WC)	101. Tereza Smitkova *(168)*	(CZE)	Viktoriya Tomova .... 7/6(3) 6/1	Serena Williams [25]				
(Q)	102. Viktoriya Tomova *(135)*	(BUL)		.... 6/1 6/4				
	103. Arantxa Rus *(105)*	(NED)	Serena Williams [25] 7/5 6/3					
	104. **Serena Williams [25]** *(1) (SR)*	(USA)				Serena Williams [25]		
	105. **Magdalena Rybarikova [19]** *(19)*	(SVK)	Sorana Cirstea 7/5 6/3	Evgeniya Rodina		.... 6/2 6/2		
	106. Sorana Cirstea *(51)*	(ROU)		.... 1/6 6/3 6/3				
(Q)	107. Evgeniya Rodina *(120)*	(RUS)	Evgeniya Rodina 3/6 7/5 6/4		Evgeniya Rodina			
(Q)	108. Antonia Lottner *(128)*	(GER)			.... 7/5 5/7 6/4			
	109. Luksika Kumkhum *(91)*	(THA)	Luksika Kumkhum 4/6 6/2 6/3	Madison Keys [10]				
	110. Bernarda Pera *(71)*	(USA)		.... 6/4 6/3				
	111. Ajla Tomljanovic *(65)*	(AUS)	Madison Keys [10] 6/4 6/2					
	112. **Madison Keys [10]** *(11)*	(USA)				Camila Giorgi		
	113. **Coco Vandeweghe [16]** *(16)*	(USA)	Katerina Siniakova ..... 6/7(3) 6/3 8/6	Katerina Siniakova		.... 3/6 7/6(6) 6/2		
	114. Katerina Siniakova *(42)*	(CZE)		.... 5/7 6/4 9/7				
	115. Viktorija Golubic *(99)*	(SUI)	Ons Jabeur 2/6 6/3 6/3		Camila Giorgi			
(WC)	116. Ons Jabeur *(130)*	(TUN)			.... 3/6 7/6(6) 6/2			
	117. Aleksandra Krunic *(39)*	(SRB)	Madison Brengle 2/6 6/3 6/3	Camila Giorgi				
	118. Madison Brengle *(108)*	(USA)		.... 6/4 6/4				
	119. Camila Giorgi *(52)*	(ITA)	Camila Giorgi 6/1 2/6 6/4					
	120. **Anastasija Sevastova [21]** *(21)*	(LAT)				Camila Giorgi		
	121. **Agnieszka Radwanska [32]** *(30)*	(POL)	Agnieszka Radwanska [32] .. 6/3 4/6 7/5	Lucie Safarova		.... 6/3 6/4		
(Q)	122. Elena-Gabriela Ruse *(195)*	(ROU)		.... 7/5 6/2				
	123. Kateryna Bondarenko *(79)*	(UKR)	Lucie Safarova 6/4 6/4		Ekaterina Makarova			
	124. Lucie Safarova *(66)*	(CZE)			.... 4/6 6/4 6/1			
	125. Petra Martic *(43)*	(CRO)	Ekaterina Makarova ..... 7/6(0) 2/6 6/3	Ekaterina Makarova				
	126. Ekaterina Makarova *(35)*	(RUS)		.... 6/4 1/6 7/5				
	127. Varvara Lepchenko *(97)*	(USA)	Caroline Wozniacki [2] 6/0 6/4					
	128. **Caroline Wozniacki [2]** *(2)*	(DEN)						

Heavy type denotes seeded players. The figure in brackets against names denotes the order in which they have been seeded. The figure in italics denotes WTA Ranking – 02.07.2018.
(WC)=Wild card. (Q)=Qualifier. (LL)=Lucky loser.

EVENT 4 – THE LADIES' DOUBLES CHAMPIONSHIP 2018
Holders: EKATERINA MAKAROVA (RUS) & ELENA VESNINA (RUS)

The Champions will become the holders, for the year only, of the CHALLENGE CUPS presented by H.R.H. PRINCESS MARINA, DUCHESS OF KENT, the late President of The All England Lawn Tennis and Croquet Club in 1949 and The All England Lawn Tennis and Croquet Club in 2001. The Champions will each receive a silver three-quarter size replica of the Challenge Cup. A Silver Salver will be presented to each of the Runners-up and a Bronze Medal to each defeated semi-finalist. The matches will be the best of three sets.

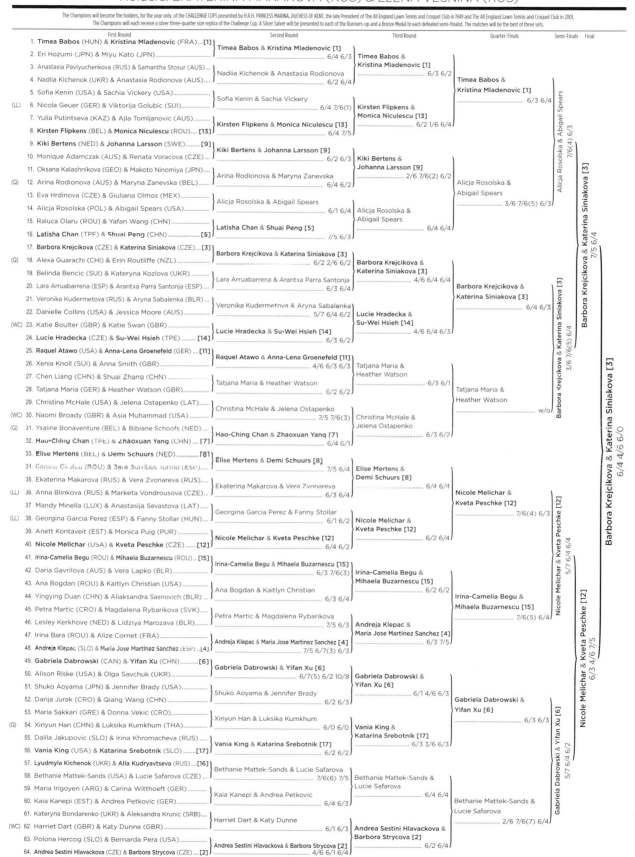

First Round	Second Round	Third Round	Quarter-Finals	Semi-Finals	Final

1. **Timea Babos** (HUN) & **Kristina Mladenovic** (FRA).... [1]
2. Eri Hozumi (JPN) & Miyu Kato (JPN) ....
3. Anastasia Pavlyuchenkova (RUS) & Samantha Stosur (AUS)...
4. Nadiia Kichenok (UKR) & Anastasia Rodionova (AUS)....
5. Sofia Kenin (USA) & Sachia Vickery (USA)....................
(LL) 6. Nicola Geuer (GER) & Viktorija Golubic (SUI)..............
7. Yulia Putintseva (KAZ) & Ajla Tomljanovic (AUS)..........
8. **Kirsten Flipkens** (BEL) & **Monica Niculescu** (ROU) .. [13]
9. **Kiki Bertens** (NED) & **Johanna Larsson** (SWE)....[9]
10. Monique Adamczak (AUS) & Renata Voracova (CZE)...
11. Oksana Kalashnikova (GEO) & Makoto Ninomiya (JPN)...
(Q) 12. Arina Rodionova (AUS) & Maryna Zanevska (BEL)......
13. Eva Hrdinova (CZE) & Giuliana Olmos (MEX)...............
14. Alicja Rosolska (POL) & Abigail Spears (USA).............
15. Raluca Olaru (ROU) & Yafan Wang (CHN).................
16. **Latisha Chan** (TPE) & **Shuai Peng** (CHN).............. [5]
17. **Barbora Krejcikova** (CZE) & **Katerina Siniakova** (CZE).... [3]
(Q) 18. Alexa Guarachi (CHI) & Erin Routliffe (NZL).............
19. Belinda Bencic (SUI) & Kateryna Kozlova (UKR)..............
20. Lara Arruabarrena (ESP) & Arantxa Parra Santonja (ESP)....
21. Veronika Kudermetova (RUS) & Aryna Sabalenka (BLR)...
22. Danielle Collins (USA) & Jessica Moore (AUS)...............
(WC) 23. Katie Boulter (GBR) & Katie Swan (GBR)....................
24. **Lucie Hradecka** (CZE) & **Su-Wei Hsieh** (TPE) .... [14]
25. **Raquel Atawo** (USA) & **Anna-Lena Groenefeld** (GER) .... [11]
26. Xenia Knoll (SUI) & Anna Smith (GBR)......................
27. Chen Liang (CHN) & Shuai Zhang (CHN).................
28. Tatjana Maria (GER) & Heather Watson (GBR)............
29. Christina McHale (USA) & Jelena Ostapenko (LAT)......
(WC) 30. Naomi Broady (GBR) & Asia Muhammad (USA) ....
(Q) 31. Ysaline Bonaventure (BEL) & Bibiane Schoofs (NED)......
32. **Hao-Ching Chan** (TPE) & **Zhaoxuan Yang** (CHN) .. [7]
33. **Elise Mertens** (BEL) & **Demi Schuurs** (NED).............. [8]
34. Garana Cristea (ROU) & Sara Sorribes Tormo (ESP)....
35. Ekaterina Makarova (RUS) & Vera Zvonareva (RUS)......
(LL) 36. Anna Blinkova (RUS) & Marketa Vondrousova (CZE)...
37. Mandy Minella (LUX) & Anastasija Sevastova (LAT)...
(LL) 38. Georgina Garcia Perez (ESP) & Fanny Stollar (HUN)....
39. Anett Kontaveit (EST) & Monica Puig (PUR)............
40. **Nicole Melichar** (USA) & **Kveta Peschke** (CZE)......[12]
41. **Irina-Camelia Begu** (ROU) & **Mihaela Buzarnescu** (ROU) .. [15]
42. Daria Gavrilova (AUS) & Vera Lapko (BLR)..................
43. Ana Bogdan (ROU) & Kaitlyn Christian (USA)................
44. Yingying Duan (CHN) & Aliaksandra Sasnovich (BLR)...
45. Petra Martic (CRO) & Magdalena Rybarikova (SVK)...
46. Lesley Kerkhove (NED) & Lidziya Marozava (BLR)........
47. Irina Bara (ROU) & Alize Cornet (FRA) ....
48. **Andreja Klepac** (SLO) & **Maria Jose Martinez Sanchez** (ESP) .. [4]
49. **Gabriela Dabrowski** (CAN) & **Yifan Xu** (CHN) ....[6]
50. Alison Riske (USA) & Olga Savchuk (UKR)....................
51. Shuko Aoyama (JPN) & Jennifer Brady (USA)..............
52. Darija Jurak (CRO) & Qiang Wang (CHN)..................
53. Maria Sakkari (GRE) & Donna Vekic (CRO)................
(Q) 54. Xinyun Han (CHN) & Luksika Kumkhum (THA)..........
55. Dalila Jakupovic (SLO) & Irina Khromacheva (RUS)....
56. **Vania King** (USA) & **Katarina Srebotnik** (SLO)......[17]
57. Lyudmyla Kichenok (UKR) & Alla Kudryavtseva (RUS)..[16]
58. Bethanie Mattek-Sands (USA) & Lucie Safarova (CZE)...
59. Maria Irigoyen (ARG) & Carina Witthoeft (GER)............
60. Kaia Kanepi (EST) & Andrea Petkovic (GER)..............
61. Kateryna Bondarenko (UKR) & Aleksandra Krunic (SRB)....
(WC) 62. Harriet Dart (GBR) & Katy Dunne (GBR)...................
63. Polona Hercog (SLO) & Bernarda Pera (USA)..............
64. **Andrea Sestini Hlavackova** (CZE) & **Barbora Strycova** (CZE) .. [2]

Second Round
Timea Babos & Kristina Mladenovic [1] — 6/4 6/3
Nadiia Kichenok & Anastasia Rodionova — 6/2 6/4
Sofia Kenin & Sachia Vickery — 6/4 7/6(1)
Kirsten Flipkens & Monica Niculescu [13] — 6/4 7/5
Kiki Bertens & Johanna Larsson [9] — 6/2 6/3
Arina Rodionova & Maryna Zanevska — 6/4 6/2
Alicja Rosolska & Abigail Spears — 6/1 6/4
Latisha Chan & Shuai Peng [5] — //5 6/3
Barbora Krejcikova & Katerina Siniakova [3] — 6/2 2/6 6/2
Lara Arruabarrena & Arantxa Parra Santonja — 6/3 6/4
Veronika Kudermetova & Aryna Sabalenka — 5/7 6/4 6/2
Lucie Hradecka & Su-Wei Hsieh [14] — 6/3 6/2
Raquel Atawo & Anna-Lena Groenefeld [11] — 4/6 6/3 6/3
Tatjana Maria & Heather Watson — 6/2 6/2
Christina McHale & Jelena Ostapenko — 7/5 7/6(3)
Hao-Ching Chan & Zhaoxuan Yang [7] — 6/4 6/1
Elise Mertens & Demi Schuurs [8] — 7/5 6/4
Ekaterina Makarova & Vera Zvonareva — 6/3 6/4
Georgina Garcia Perez & Fanny Stollar — 6/1 6/2
Nicole Melichar & Kveta Peschke [12] — 6/4 6/2
Irina-Camelia Begu & Mihaela Buzarnescu [15] — 6/3 7/6(3)
Ana Bogdan & Kaitlyn Christian — 6/3 6/4
Petra Martic & Magdalena Rybarikova — 7/5 6/3
Andreja Klepac & Maria Jose Martinez Sanchez [4] — 7/5 6/7(3) 6/3
Gabriela Dabrowski & Yifan Xu [6] — 6/7(5) 6/2 10/8
Shuko Aoyama & Jennifer Brady — 6/2 6/3
Xinyun Han & Luksika Kumkhum — 6/0 6/0
Vania King & Katarina Srebotnik [17] — 6/2 6/2
Bethanie Mattek-Sands & Lucie Safarova — 7/6(6) 7/5
Kaia Kanepi & Andrea Petkovic — 6/4 6/3
Harriet Dart & Katy Dunne — 6/1 6/3
Andrea Sestini Hlavackova & Barbora Strycova [2] — 4/6 6/1 6/4

Third Round
Timea Babos & Kristina Mladenovic [1] — 6/3 6/2
Kirsten Flipkens & Monica Niculescu [13] — 6/2 1/6 6/4
Kiki Bertens & Johanna Larsson [9] — 2/6 7/6(2) 6/2
Alicja Rosolska & Abigail Spears — 6/4 6/4
Barbora Krejcikova & Katerina Siniakova [3] — 4/6 6/4 6/4
Lucie Hradecka & Su-Wei Hsieh [14] — 4/6 6/4 6/3
Tatjana Maria & Heather Watson — 6/3 6/1
Christina McHale & Jelena Ostapenko — 6/3 6/2
Elise Mertens & Demi Schuurs [8] — 6/4 6/4
Nicole Melichar & Kveta Peschke [12] — 6/2 6/4
Irina-Camelia Begu & Mihaela Buzarnescu [15] — 6/2 6/2
Andreja Klepac & Maria Jose Martinez Sanchez [4] — 6/3 7/5
Gabriela Dabrowski & Yifan Xu [6] — 6/1 4/6 6/2
Vania King & Katarina Srebotnik [17] — 6/3 3/6 6/3
Bethanie Mattek-Sands & Lucie Safarova — 6/4 6/4
Andrea Sestini Hlavackova & Barbora Strycova [2] — 6/2 6/4

Quarter-Finals
Timea Babos & Kristina Mladenovic [1] — 6/3 6/4
Alicja Rosolska & Abigail Spears — 3/6 7/6(5) 6/3
Barbora Krejcikova & Katerina Siniakova [3] — 6/4 6/4
Tatjana Maria & Heather Watson — w/o
Nicole Melichar & Kveta Peschke [12] — 7/6(4) 6/3
Irina-Camelia Begu & Mihaela Buzarnescu [15] — 7/6(5) 6/4
Gabriela Dabrowski & Yifan Xu [6] — 6/3 6/3
Bethanie Mattek-Sands & Lucie Safarova — 2/6 7/6(7) 6/4

Semi-Finals
Alicja Rosolska & Abigail Spears [3] — 7/6(4) 6/3
Barbora Krejcikova & Katerina Siniakova [3] — 3/6 7/6(5) 6/4
Nicole Melichar & Kveta Peschke [12] — 5/7 6/4 6/4
Gabriela Dabrowski & Yifan Xu [6] — 5/7 6/4 6/2

Barbora Krejcikova & Katerina Siniakova [3] — 7/5 6/4
Nicole Melichar & Kveta Peschke [12] — 6/3 4/6 7/5

Final
Barbora Krejcikova & Katerina Siniakova [3] — 6/4 4/6 6/0

Heavy type denotes seeded players. The figure in brackets against names denotes the order in which they have been seeded.
(WC)=Wild cards. (Q)=Qualifiers. (LL)=Lucky Losers.

EVENT 5 – THE MIXED DOUBLES CHAMPIONSHIP 2018
Holders: JAMIE MURRAY (GBR) & MARTINA HINGIS (SUI)

The Champions will become the holders, for the year only, of the CHALLENGE CUPS presented by members of the family of the late Mr. S. H. SMITH in 1949 and The All England Lawn Tennis and Croquet Club in 2001.
The Champions will each receive a silver three-quarter size replica of the Challenge Cup. A Silver Salver will be presented to each of the Runners-up and a Bronze Medal to each defeated semi-finalist. The matches will be the best of three sets.

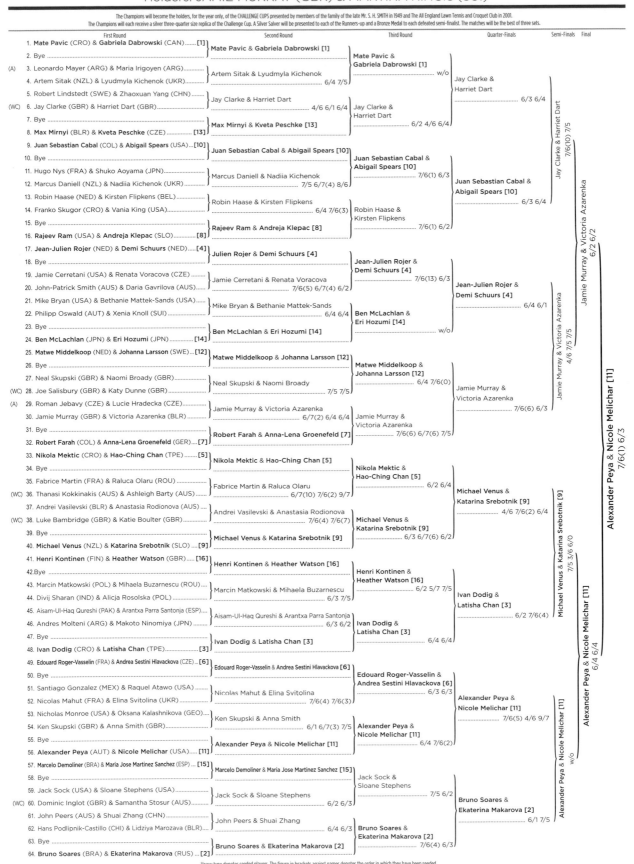

First Round	Second Round	Third Round	Quarter-Finals	Semi-Finals	Final

1. **Mate Pavic** (CRO) & **Gabriela Dabrowski** (CAN) .... [1] — Mate Pavic & Gabriela Dabrowski [1]
2. Bye
   - Mate Pavic & Gabriela Dabrowski [1] — w/o
(A) 3. Leonardo Mayer (ARG) & Maria Irigoyen (ARG)
4. Artem Sitak (NZL) & Lyudmyla Kichenok (UKR) — Artem Sitak & Lyudmyla Kichenok — 6/4 7/5
   - Jay Clarke & Harriet Dart
5. Robert Lindstedt (SWE) & Zhaoxuan Yang (CHN) — Jay Clarke & Harriet Dart — 4/6 6/1 6/4
(WC) 6. Jay Clarke (GBR) & Harriet Dart (GBR)
   - Jay Clarke & Harriet Dart — 6/2 4/6 6/4
   - Jay Clarke & Harriet Dart — 6/3 6/4
7. Bye
8. **Max Mirnyi** (BLR) & **Kveta Peschke** (CZE) ...... [13] — Max Mirnyi & Kveta Peschke [13]
9. **Juan Sebastian Cabal** (COL) & **Abigail Spears** (USA) ... [10] — Juan Sebastian Cabal & Abigail Spears [10]
10. Bye
   - Juan Sebastian Cabal & Abigail Spears [10] — 7/6(1) 6/3
11. Hugo Nys (FRA) & Shuko Aoyama (JPN) — Marcus Daniell & Nadiia Kichenok — 7/5 6/7(4) 8/6
12. Marcus Daniell (NZL) & Nadiia Kichenok (UKR)
   - Juan Sebastian Cabal & Abigail Spears [10] — 6/3 6/4
13. Robin Haase (NED) & Kirsten Flipkens (BEL) — Robin Haase & Kirsten Flipkens — 6/4 7/6(3)
14. Franko Skugor (CRO) & Vania King (USA)
   - Robin Haase & Kirsten Flipkens — 7/6(1) 6/2
15. Bye
16. **Rajeev Ram** (USA) & **Andreja Klepac** (SLO) .... [8] — Rajeev Ram & Andreja Klepac [8]

   - Jay Clarke & Harriet Dart — 7/6(10) 7/5

17. **Jean-Julien Rojer** (NED) & **Demi Schuurs** (NED) ..... [4] — Julien Rojer & Demi Schuurs [4]
18. Bye
   - Jean-Julien Rojer & Demi Schuurs [4] — 7/6(13) 6/3
19. Jamie Cerretani (USA) & Renata Voracova (CZE) — Jamie Cerretani & Renata Voracova — 7/6(5) 6/7(4) 6/2
20. John-Patrick Smith (AUS) & Daria Gavrilova (AUS)
   - Jean-Julien Rojer & Demi Schuurs [4] — 6/4 6/1
21. Mike Bryan (USA) & Bethanie Mattek-Sands (USA) — Mike Bryan & Bethanie Mattek-Sands — 6/4 6/4
22. Philipp Oswald (AUT) & Xenia Knoll (SUI)
   - Ben McLachlan & Eri Hozumi [14] — w/o
23. Bye
24. **Ben McLachlan** (JPN) & **Eri Hozumi** (JPN) ...... [14] — Ben McLachlan & Eri Hozumi [14]
25. **Matwe Middelkoop** (NED) & **Johanna Larsson** (SWE) ... [12] — Matwe Middelkoop & Johanna Larsson [12]
26. Bye
   - Matwe Middelkoop & Johanna Larsson [12] — 6/4 7/6(0)
27. Neal Skupski (GBR) & Naomi Broady (GBR) — Neal Skupski & Naomi Broady — 7/5 7/5
   - Jamie Murray & Victoria Azarenka — 7/6(6) 6/3
(WC) 28. Joe Salisbury (GBR) & Katy Dunne (GBR)
(A) 29. Roman Jebavy (CZE) & Lucie Hradecka (CZE) — Jamie Murray & Victoria Azarenka — 6/7(2) 6/4 6/4
30. Jamie Murray (GBR) & Victoria Azarenka (BLR)
   - Jamie Murray & Victoria Azarenka — 7/6(6) 6/7(6) 7/5
31. Bye
32. **Robert Farah** (COL) & **Anna-Lena Groenefeld** (GER) .... [7] — Robert Farah & Anna-Lena Groenefeld [7]

   - Jamie Murray & Victoria Azarenka — 4/6 7/5 7/5

33. **Nikola Mektic** (CRO) & **Hao-Ching Chan** (TPE) ...... [5] — Nikola Mektic & Hao-Ching Chan [5]
34. Bye
   - Nikola Mektic & Hao-Ching Chan [5] — 6/2 6/4
35. Fabrice Martin (FRA) & Raluca Olaru (ROU) — Fabrice Martin & Raluca Olaru — 6/7(10) 7/6(2) 9/7
(WC) 36. Thanasi Kokkinakis (AUS) & Ashleigh Barty (AUS)
   - Michael Venus & Katarina Srebotnik [9] — 4/6 7/6(2) 6/4
37. Andrei Vasilevski (BLR) & Anastasia Rodionova (AUS) — Andrei Vasilevski & Anastasia Rodionova — 7/6(4) 7/6(7)
(WC) 38. Luke Bambridge (GBR) & Katie Boulter (GBR)
   - Michael Venus & Katarina Srebotnik [9] — 6/3 6/7(6) 6/2
39. Bye
40. **Michael Venus** (NZL) & **Katarina Srebotnik** (SLO) .... [9] — Michael Venus & Katarina Srebotnik [9]

   - Michael Venus & Katarina Srebotnik [9] — 7/5 3/6 6/0

41. **Henri Kontinen** (FIN) & **Heather Watson** (GBR) ..... [16] — Henri Kontinen & Heather Watson [16]
42. Bye
   - Henri Kontinen & Heather Watson [16] — 6/2 5/7 7/5
43. Marcin Matkowski (POL) & Mihaela Buzarnescu (ROU) — Marcin Matkowski & Mihaela Buzarnescu — 6/3 7/5
44. Divij Sharan (IND) & Alicja Rosolska (POL)
   - Ivan Dodig & Latisha Chan [3] — 6/2 7/6(4)
45. Aisam-Ul-Haq Qureshi (PAK) & Arantxa Parra Santonja (ESP) — Aisam-Ul-Haq Qureshi & Arantxa Parra Santonja — 6/3 6/2
46. Andres Molteni (ARG) & Makoto Ninomiya (JPN)
   - Ivan Dodig & Latisha Chan [3] — 6/4 6/4
47. Bye
48. **Ivan Dodig** (CRO) & **Latisha Chan** (TPE) ...... [3] — Ivan Dodig & Latisha Chan [3]

   - Michael Venus & Katarina Srebotnik [9] — 6/4 6/4

49. **Edouard Roger-Vasselin** (FRA) & **Andrea Sestini Hlavackova** (CZE) ... [6] — Edouard Roger-Vasselin & Andrea Sestini Hlavackova [6]
50. Bye
   - Edouard Roger-Vasselin & Andrea Sestini Hlavackova [6] — 6/3 6/3
51. Santiago Gonzalez (MEX) & Raquel Atawo (USA) — Nicolas Mahut & Elina Svitolina — 7/6(4) 7/6(3)
52. Nicolas Mahut (FRA) & Elina Svitolina (UKR)
   - Alexander Peya & Nicole Melichar [11] — 7/6(5) 4/6 9/7
53. Nicholas Monroe (USA) & Oksana Kalashnikova (GEO) — Ken Skupski & Anna Smith — 6/1 6/7(3) 7/5
54. Ken Skupski (GBR) & Anna Smith (GBR)
   - Alexander Peya & Nicole Melichar [11] — 6/4 7/6(2)
55. Bye
56. **Alexander Peya** (AUT) & **Nicole Melichar** (USA) .... [11] — Alexander Peya & Nicole Melichar [11]

   - Alexander Peya & Nicole Melichar [11] — w/o

57. **Marcelo Demoliner** (BRA) & **Maria Jose Martinez Sanchez** (ESP) ... [15] — Marcelo Demoliner & Maria Jose Martinez Sanchez [15]
58. Bye
   - Jack Sock & Sloane Stephens — 7/5 6/2
59. Jack Sock (USA) & Sloane Stephens (USA) — Jack Sock & Sloane Stephens — 6/2 6/3
(WC) 60. Dominic Inglot (GBR) & Samantha Stosur (AUS)
   - Bruno Soares & Ekaterina Makarova [2] — 6/1 7/5
61. John Peers (AUS) & Shuai Zhang (CHN) — John Peers & Shuai Zhang — 6/4 6/3
62. Hans Podlipnik-Castillo (CHI) & Lidziya Marozava (BLR)
   - Bruno Soares & Ekaterina Makarova [2] — 6/1 7/5
63. Bye
64. **Bruno Soares** (BRA) & **Ekaterina Makarova** (RUS) ... [2] — Bruno Soares & Ekaterina Makarova [2] — 7/6(4) 6/3

Jamie Murray & Victoria Azarenka — 6/2 6/2

Alexander Peya & Nicole Melichar [11] — Michael Venus & Katarina Srebotnik [11] — 6/4 6/4

Alexander Peya & Nicole Melichar [11] — 7/6(1) 6/3

Heavy type denotes seeded players. The figure in brackets against names denotes the order in which they have been seeded.
(A)=Alternates. (WC)=Wild cards.

EVENT 6 – THE BOYS' SINGLES CHAMPIONSHIP 2018
Holder: ALEJANDRO DAVIDOVICH FOKINA (ESP)

The Champion will become the holder, for the year only, of a Cup presented by The All England Lawn Tennis and Croquet Club.
The Champion will receive a three-quarter size Cup and the Runner-up will receive a Silver Salver. The matches will be the best of three sets.

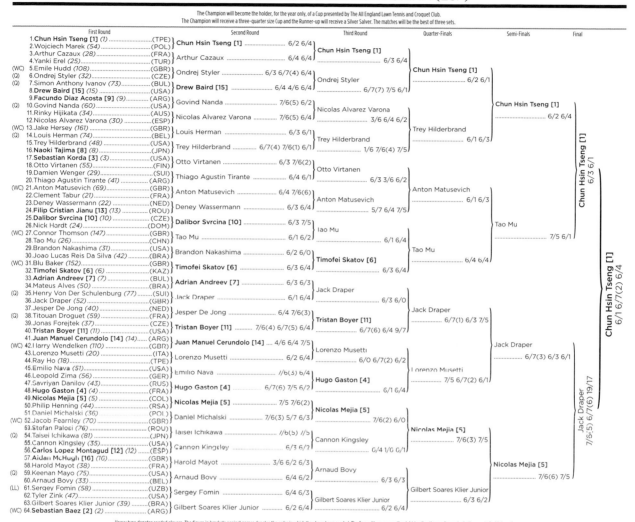

Heavy type denotes seeded players. The figure in brackets against names denotes the order in which they have been seeded. The Committee reserves the right to alter the seeding order in the event of withdrawals.
(WC)=Wild card. (Q)=Qualifier. (LL)=Lucky loser.

EVENT 7 – THE BOYS' DOUBLES CHAMPIONSHIP 2018
Holders: AXEL GELLER (ARG) & YU HSIOU HSU (TPE)

The Champions will become the holders, for the year only, of a Cup presented by The All England Lawn Tennis and Croquet Club.
The Champions will receive a three-quarter size Cup and the Runners-up will receive Silver Salvers. The matches will be the best of three sets.

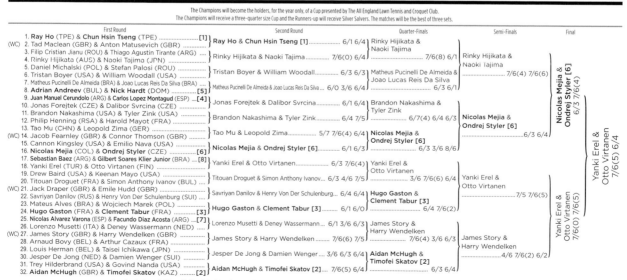

Heavy type denotes seeded players. The figure in brackets against names denotes the order in which they have been seeded. The Committee reserves the right to alter the seeding order in the event of withdrawals.
(WC)=Wild cards. (A)=Alternates.

EVENT 8 – THE GIRLS' SINGLES CHAMPIONSHIP 2018
Holder: CLAIRE LIU (USA)

The Champion will become the holder, for the year only, of a Cup presented by The All England Lawn Tennis and Croquet Club.
The Champion will receive a three-quarter size Cup and the Runner-up will receive a Silver Salver. The matches will be the best of three sets.

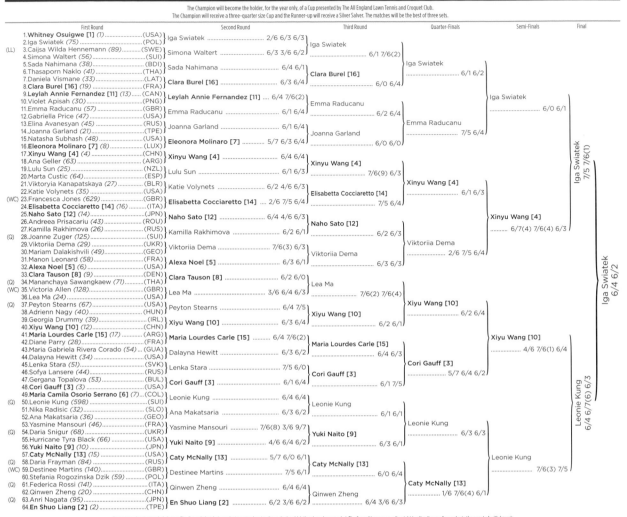

First Round	Second Round	Third Round	Quarter-Finals	Semi-Finals	Final
1.**Whitney Osuigwe [1]** *(1)* ....(USA)	Iga Swiatek 2/6 6/3 6/3	Iga Swiatek			
2.Iga Swiatek *(75)* ....(POL)			Iga Swiatek		
(LL) 3.Caijsa Wilda Hennemann *(89)* ...(SWE)	Simona Waltert 6/3 3/6 6/2	6/1 7/6(2)			
4.Simona Waltert *(56)* ....(SUI)				Iga Swiatek	
5.Sada Nahimana *(38)* ....(BDI)	Sada Nahimana 6/4 6/1	Clara Burel [16]		6/0 6/1	
6.Thasaporn Naklo *(41)* ....(THA)					
7.Daniela Vismane *(33)* ....(LAT)	Clara Burel [16] 6/3 6/4	6/0 6/4			
8.**Clara Burel [16]** *(19)* ....(FRA)					
9.**Leylah Annie Fernandez [11]** *(13)*..(CAN)	Leylah Annie Fernandez [11] .... 6/4 7/6(2)	Emma Raducanu			
10.Violet Apisah *(30)* ....(PNG)			Emma Raducanu		
11.Emma Raducanu *(57)* ....(GBR)	Emma Raducanu 6/1 6/4	6/2 6/4			
12.Gabriella Price *(47)* ....(USA)					Iga Swiatek
13.Elina Avanesyan *(45)* ....(RUS)	Joanna Garland 6/1 6/4	Joanna Garland	7/5 6/4		7/5 7/6(1)
14.Joanna Garland *(21)* ....(TPE)					
15.Natasha Subhash *(48)* ....(USA)	Eleonora Molinaro [7] 5/7 6/3 6/4	6/0 6/0			
16.**Eleonora Molinaro [7]** *(8)* ....(LUX)					
17.**Xinyu Wang [4]** *(4)* ....(CHN)	Xinyu Wang [4] 6/4 6/4	Xinyu Wang [4]			
18.Ana Geller *(63)* ....(ARG)			Xinyu Wang [4]		
19.Lulu Sun *(25)* ....(NZL)	Lulu Sun 6/1 6/3	7/6(9) 6/3			
20.Marta Custic *(64)* ....(ESP)					
21.Viktoryia Kanapatskaya *(27)* ....(BLR)	Katie Volynets 6/2 4/6 6/3	Elisabetta Cocciaretto [14]	6/1 6/3		
22.Katie Volynets *(35)* ....(USA)					
(WC) 23.Francesca Jones *(629)* ....(GBR)	Elisabetta Cocciaretto [14] 2/6 7/5 6/4	7/5 6/4			
24.**Elisabetta Cocciaretto [14]** *(16)* ....(ITA)				Xinyu Wang [4]	
25.**Naho Sato [12]** *(14)* ....(JPN)	Naho Sato [12] 6/4 4/6 6/3	Naho Sato [12]		6/7(4) 7/6(4) 6/3	
26.Andreea Prisacariu *(43)* ....(ROU)					
27.Kamilla Rakhimova *(26)* ....(RUS)	Kamilla Rakhimova 6/2 6/1	6/2 6/3			
(Q) 28.Joanne Zuger *(125)* ....(SUI)			Viktoriia Dema		
29.Viktoriia Dema *(29)* ....(UKR)	Viktoriia Dema ...... 7/6(3) 6/3	Viktoriia Dema	2/6 7/5 6/4		
30.Mariam Dalakishvili *(49)* ....(GEO)					
31.Manon Leonard *(58)* ....(FRA)	Alexa Noel [5] 6/3 6/1	6/3 6/3			
32.**Alexa Noel [5]** *(6)* ....(USA)					
33.Clara Tauson [8] *(9)* ....(DEN)	Clara Tauson [8] 6/2 6/0	Lea Ma			
(Q) 34.Mananchaya Sawangkaew *(71)* ......(THA)					
(WC) 35.Victoria Allen *(128)* ....(GBR)	Lea Ma 3/6 6/4 6/3	7/6(2) 7/6(4)	Xiyu Wang [10]		
36.Lea Ma *(24)* ....(USA)					
(Q) 37.Peyton Stearns *(67)* ....(USA)	Peyton Stearns 6/4 7/5	Xiyu Wang [10]	6/2 6/4		
38.Adrienn Nagy *(40)* ....(HUN)					
39.Georgia Drummy *(39)* ....(IRL)	Xiyu Wang [10] 6/3 6/4	6/2 6/1		Xiyu Wang [10]	
40.**Xiyu Wang [10]** *(12)* ....(CHN)				4/6 7/6(1) 6/4	
41.**Maria Lourdes Carle [15]** *(17)*...(ARG)	Maria Lourdes Carle [15] .... 6/4 7/6(2)	Maria Lourdes Carle [15]			
42.Diane Parry *(28)* ....(FRA)					
43.Maria Gabriela Rivera Corado *(54)*..(GUA)	Dalayna Hewitt 6/3 6/2	6/4 6/4			
44.Dalayna Hewitt *(34)* ....(USA)				Cori Gauff [3]	
45.Lenka Stara *(51)* ....(SVK)	Lenka Stara 7/5 6/0	Cori Gauff [3]	5/7 6/4 6/2		
46.Sofya Lansere *(44)* ....(RUS)					
47.Gergana Topalova *(53)* ....(BUL)	Cori Gauff [3] 6/1 6/4	6/1 7/5			
48.**Cori Gauff [3]** *(3)* ....(USA)					Leonie Kung
49.**Maria Camila Osorio Serrano [6]** *(7)*..(COL)	Leonie Kung 6/4 6/4	Leonie Kung			6/4 6/7(6) 6/3
(Q) 50.Leonie Kung *(598)* ....(SUI)			Leonie Kung		
51.Nika Radisic *(32)* ....(SLO)	Ana Makatsaria 6/3 6/2	6/1 6/1			
52.Ana Makatsaria *(36)* ....(GEO)				Leonie Kung	
53.Yasmine Mansouri *(46)* ....(FRA)	Yasmine Mansouri ...... 7/6(8) 3/6 9/7	Yuki Naito [9]	6/3 6/3		
(Q) 54.Daria Snigur *(68)* ....(UKR)					
55.Hurricane Tyra Black *(66)* ....(USA)	Yuki Naito [9] 4/6 6/4 6/2	6/3 6/1			
56.**Yuki Naito [9]** *(10)* ....(JPN)					Leonie Kung
57.**Caty McNally [13]** *(15)* ....(USA)	Caty McNally [13] 5/7 6/0 6/4	Caty McNally [13]			7/6(3) 7/5
(Q) 58.Daria Frayman *(84)* ....(RUS)					
(WC) 59.Destinee Martins *(140)* ....(GBR)	Destinee Martins 7/5 6/1	6/0 6/4	Caty McNally [13]		
60.Stefania Rogozinska Dzik *(59)* ....(POL)					
(Q) 61.Federica Rossi *(141)* ....(ITA)	Qinwen Zheng 6/4 6/4	Qinwen Zheng	1/6 7/6(4) 6/1		
62.Qinwen Zheng *(20)* ....(CHN)					
(Q) 63.Anri Nagata *(95)* ....(JPN)	En Shuo Liang [2] 6/2 3/6 6/2	6/4 3/6 6/3			
64.**En Shuo Liang [2]** *(2)* ....(TPE)					

Heavy type denotes seeded players. The figure in brackets against names denotes the order in which they have been seeded. The Committee reserves the right to alter the seeding order in the event of withdrawals.
(WC)=Wild card. (Q)=Qualifier. (LL)=Lucky loser.

EVENT 9 – THE GIRLS' DOUBLES CHAMPIONSHIP 2018
Holders: OLGA DANILOVIC (SRB) & KAJA JUVAN (SLO)

The Champions will become the holders, for the year only, of a Cup presented by The All England Lawn Tennis and Croquet Club. The Champions will receive a three-quarter size Cup and the Runners-up will receive Silver Salvers.
The matches will be the best of three sets.

First Round	Second Round	Quarter-Finals	Semi-Finals	Final
1. **Xinyu Wang** (CHN) & **Xiyu Wang** (CHN) ....[1]	Xinyu Wang & Xiyu Wang [1].............. 6/2 6/2	Xinyu Wang & Xiyu Wang [1]		
2. Natasha Subhash (USA) & Katie Volynets (USA)				
3. Leonie Kung (SUI) & Joanne Zuger (SUI)	Leonie Kung & Joanne Zuger...... 6/4 6/4	6/2 6/0	Xinyu Wang & Xiyu Wang [1]	
4. Ana Makatsaria (GEO) & Lea Ma (USA)				
(WC) 5. Sonay Kartal (GBR) & Erin Richardson (GBR)	Sonay Kartal & Erin Richardson........ 7/5 5/7 6/4	Joanna Garland & En Shuo Liang [5]	6/4 6/2	
6. Loudmilla Bencheikh (FRA) & Manon Leonard (FRA)				
7. Mariam Dalakishvili (GEO) & Sada Nahimana (BDI)	Joanna Garland & En Shuo Liang [5] 6/2 6/4	7/5 7/5		
8. **Joanna Garland** (TPE) & **En Shuo Liang** (TPE) .....[5]				
9. **Maria Lourdes Carle** (ARG) & **Cori Gauff** (USA) ....[4]	Maria Lourdes Carle & Cori Gauff [4].... 6/3 6/1	Maria Lourdes Carle & Cori Gauff [4]		Xinyu Wang & Xiyu Wang [1]
10. Maria Camila Osorio Serrano (COL) & Maria Gabriela Rivera Corado (GUA)				6/4 6/2
11. Hurricane Tyra Black (USA) & Ana Geller (ARG)	Sofya Lansere & Kamilla Rakhimova...... 6/4 6/2	7/6(4) 6/1	Maria Lourdes Carle & Cori Gauff [4]	
12. Sofya Lansere (RUS) & Kamilla Rakhimova (RUS)				
(WC) 13. Victoria Allen (GBR) & Destinee Martins (GBR)	Victoria Allen & Destinee Martins.............. 6/1 7/5	Victoria Allen & Destinee Martins	7/5 6/3	
14. Violet Apisah (PNG) & Lulu Sun (NZL)				
15. Elina Avanesyan (RUS) & Caijsa Wilda Hennemann (SWE) ...	Yuki Naito & Naho Sato [6] .... 6/0 7/6(5)	4/6 6/4 6/2		
16. **Yuki Naito** (JPN) & **Naho Sato** (JPN) ....[6]				
17. **Clara Burel** (FRA) & **Diane Parry** (FRA) ....[8]	Clara Burel & Diane Parry [8] 6/4 6/4	Clara Burel & Diane Parry [8]		Xinyu Wang & Xiyu Wang [1]
18. Marta Custic (ESP) & Qinwen Zheng (CHN)				6/2 6/1
(WC) 19. Danielle Daley (GBR) & Tanysha Dissanayake (GBR) ...	Leylah Annie Fernandez & Gabriella Price 6/2 6/2	6/4 6/4	Dalayna Hewitt & Peyton Stearns	
20. Leylah Annie Fernandez (CAN) & Gabriella Price (USA) ...				
21. Daria Frayman (RUS) & Federica Rossi (ITA)	Dalayna Hewitt & Peyton Stearns....... 7/6(9) 6/0	Dalayna Hewitt & Peyton Stearns	6/3 7/5	
22. Dalayna Hewitt (USA) & Peyton Stearns (USA)				
23. Thasaporn Naklo (THA) & Mananchaya Sawangkaew (THA) ...	Thasaporn Naklo & Mananchaya Sawangkaew... 2/6 7/6(4) 6/3	7/5 7/6(4)		
24. **Eleonora Molinaro** (LUX) & **Clara Tauson** (DEN) .....[3]				
25. **Georgia Drummy** (IRL) & **Alexa Noel** (USA) ....[7]	Georgia Drummy & Alexa Noel [7]........ 6/3 6/2	Georgia Drummy & Alexa Noel [7]		Caty McNally & Whitney Osuigwe [2]
26. Viktoryia Kanapatskaya (BLR) & Lenka Stara (SVK) ...				6/2 7/5
27. Elisabetta Cocciaretto (ITA) & Nika Radisic (SLO)	Amelia Bissett & Morgan Cross ...... 6/3 7/6(5)	6/2 6/3	Caty McNally & Whitney Osuigwe [2]	
(WC) 28. Amelia Bissett (GBR) & Morgan Cross (GBR)				
29. Adrienn Nagy (HUN) & Stefania Rogozinska Dzik (POL) ...	Francesca Curmi & Viktoriia Dema............. 7/5 6/2	Caty McNally & Whitney Osuigwe [2]	7/5 7/5	
30. Francesca Curmi (MLT) & Viktoriia Dema (UKR)				
31. Gergana Topalova (BUL) & Daniela Vismane (LAT)	Caty McNally & Whitney Osuigwe [2].... 6/1 6/2	6/4 6/1		
32. **Caty McNally** (USA) & **Whitney Osuigwe** (USA) ......[2]				

Heavy type denotes seeded players. The figure in brackets against names denotes the order in which they have been seeded. The Committee reserves the right to alter the seeding order in the event of withdrawals.
(WC)=Wild cards. (A)=Alternates.

EVENT 10 – THE GENTLEMEN'S WHEELCHAIR SINGLES 2018
Holder: STEFAN OLSSON (SWE)

The Champion will become the holder, for the year only, of a Cup presented by The All England Lawn Tennis and Croquet Club. The Champion will receive a Silver Salver. A Silver Medal will be presented to the Runner-up.
The matches will be the best of three tie-break sets.

First Round	Semi-final	Final
1. **Shingo Kunieda [1]** *(1)* .... (JPN)		
	Gustavo Fernandez	
2. Gustavo Fernandez *(3)* .... (ARG)	.... 6/4 3/6 7/5	
		Gustavo Fernandez
3. Gordon Reid *(5)* .... (GBR)		.... 6/1 4/6 6/2
	Joachim Gerard	
(WC) 4. Joachim Gerard *(7)* .... (BEL)	.... 6/3 6/3	
5. Nicolas Peifer *(9)* .... (FRA)		
	Stefan Olsson	
6. Stefan Olsson *(6)* .... (SWE)	.... 6/2 6/3	
		Stefan Olsson
7. Stephane Houdet *(4)* .... (FRA)		.... 6/2 6/4
	Alfie Hewett [2]	
8. **Alfie Hewett [2]** *(2)* .... (GBR)	.... 7/6(3) 6/4	

Stefan Olsson
6/2 0/6 6/3

Heavy type denotes seeded players. The figure in brackets against names denotes the order in which they have been seeded. The Committee reserves the right to alter the seeding order in the event of withdrawals.
(WC)=Wild cards. (A)=Alternates.

EVENT 11 – THE GENTLEMEN'S WHEELCHAIR DOUBLES 2018
Holders: ALFIE HEWETT (GBR) & GORDON REID (GBR)

The Champions will become the holders, for the year only, of a Cup presented by The All England Lawn Tennis and Croquet Club. The Champions will receive a Silver Salver. A Silver Medal will be presented to each of the Runners-up.
The matches will be the best of three tie-break sets.

First Round	Final
1. **Stephane Houdet** (FRA) & **Nicolas Peifer** (FRA) .... [1]	Joachim Gerard &
	Stefan Olsson
2. Joachim Gerard (BEL) & Stefan Olsson (SWE)	.... 6/1 3/6 7/5
3. Gustavo Fernandez (ARG) & Shingo Kunieda (JPN)	**Alfie Hewett** &
	Gordon Reid [2]
4. **Alfie Hewett** (GBR) & **Gordon Reid** (GBR) .... [2]	.... 6/1 3/6 7/6(3)

Alfie Hewett
&
Gordon Reid [2]
6/1 6/4

Heavy type denotes seeded players. The figure in brackets against names denotes the order in which they have been seeded. The Committee reserves the right to alter the seeding order in the event of withdrawals.
(WC)=Wild cards. (A)=Alternates.

EVENT 12 – THE LADIES' WHEELCHAIR SINGLES 2018
Holder: DIEDE DE GROOT (NED)

The Champion will become the holder, for the year only, of a Cup presented by The All England Lawn Tennis and Croquet Club. The Champion will receive a Silver Salver. A Silver Medal will be presented to the Runner-up.
The matches will be the best of three tie-break sets.

First Round	Semi-final	Final
1. **Diede De Groot [1]** *(1)* .... (NED)		
	Diede De Groot [1]	
2. Sabine Ellerbrock *(4)* .... (GER)	.... 6/4 6/3	
		Diede De Groot [1]
3. Katharina Kruger *(6)* .... (GER)		.... 6/1 7/5
	Kgothatso Montjane	
(WC) 4. Kgothatso Montjane *(8)* .... (RSA)	.... 6/3 2/6 6/1	
5. Lucy Shuker *(7)* .... (GBR)		
	Aniek Van Koot	
6. Aniek Van Koot *(3)* .... (NED)	.... 6/2 6/1	
		Aniek Van Koot
7. Marjolein Buis *(5)* .... (NED)		.... 1/6 6/4 7/6(11)
	Yui Kamiji [2]	
8. **Yui Kamiji [2]** *(2)* .... (JPN)	.... 6/4 6/4	

Diede De Groot [1]
6/3 6/2

Heavy type denotes seeded players. The figure in brackets against names denotes the order in which they have been seeded. The Committee reserves the right to alter the seeding order in the event of withdrawals.
(WC)=Wild cards. (A)=Alternates.

EVENT 13 – THE LADIES' WHEELCHAIR DOUBLES 2018
Holders: YUI KAMIJI (JPN) & JORDANNE WHILEY (GBR)

The Champions will become the holders, for the year only, of a Cup presented by The All England Lawn Tennis and Croquet Club. The Champions will receive a Silver Salver. A Silver Medal will be presented to each of the Runners-up.
The matches will be the best of three tie-break sets.

First Round	Final
1. Diede De Groot (NED) & Yui Kamiji (JPN) .... [1]	**Diede De Groot** &
	Yui Kamiji [1]
2. Katharina Kruger (GER) & Kgothatso Montjane (RSA)	.... 6/0 6/0
3. Sabine Ellerbrock (GER) & Lucy Shuker (GBR)	Sabine Ellerbrock &
	Lucy Shuker
4. Marjolein Buis (NED) & Aniek Van Koot (NED) .... [2]	.... 3/6 6/4 6/4

Diede De Groot
&
Yui Kamiji [1]
6/1 6/1

Heavy type denotes seeded players. The figure in brackets against names denotes the order in which they have been seeded. The Committee reserves the right to alter the seeding order in the event of withdrawals.
(WC)=Wild cards. (A)=Alternates.

EVENT 14 – THE GENTLEMEN'S INVITATION DOUBLES 2018
Holders: LLEYTON HEWITT (AUS) & MARK PHILIPPOUSSIS (AUS)

The Champions will become the holders, for the year only, of a Cup presented by The All England Lawn Tennis and Croquet Club. The Champions will receive a silver three-quarter size Cup. A Silver Medal will be presented to each of the Runners-up.
The matches will be the best of three sets. If a match should reach one set all a 10-point tie-break will replace the third set.

GROUP A	Arnaud Clement (FRA) & Miles Maclagan (GBR)	Colin Fleming (GBR) & Xavier Malisse (BEL)	Justin Gimelstob (USA) & Ross Hutchins (GBR)	Greg Rusedski (GBR) & Fabrice Santoro (FRA)	Wins	Losses	Final
Arnaud Clement (FRA) & Miles Maclagan (GBR)		6/7(9) 6/3 [3-10] L	2/6 5/7 L	7/5 6/3 W	1	2	
Colin Fleming (GBR) & Xavier Malisse (BEL)	7/6(9) 3/6 [10-3] W		7/5 7/6(3) W	6/4 7/5 W	3	0	Colin Fleming & Xavier Malisse
Justin Gimelstob (USA) & Ross Hutchins (GBR)	6/2 7/5 W	5/7 6/7(3) L		1/6 4/6 L	1	2	
Greg Rusedski (GBR) & Fabrice Santoro (FRA)	5/7 3/6 L	4/6 5/7 L	6/1 6/4 W		1	2	

GROUP B	Jamie Delgado (GBR) & Jonathan Marray (GBR)	Thomas Enqvist (SWE) & Thomas Johansson (SWE)	Fernando Gonzalez (CHI) & Sebastien Grosjean (FRA)	Tommy Haas (GER) & Mark Philippoussis (AUS)	Wins	Losses	Final
Jamie Delgado (GBR) & Jonathan Marray (GBR)		6/7(3) 3/6 L	6/4 3/6 [7-10] L	3/6 4/6 L	0	3	
Thomas Enqvist (SWE) & Thomas Johansson (SWE)	7/6(3) 6/3 W		5/7 6/4 [10-4] W	2/6 7/6(3) [8-10] L	2	1	Tommy Haas & Mark Philippoussis
Fernando Gonzalez (CHI) & Sebastien Grosjean (FRA)	4/6 6/3 [10-7] W	7/5 4/6 [4-10] L		3/6 4/6 L	1	2	
Tommy Haas (GER) & Mark Philippoussis (AUS)	6/3 6/4 W	6/2 6/7(3) [10-8] W	6/3 6/4 W		3	0	

Final: Tommy Haas & Mark Philippoussis 7/6(4) 6/4

This event consists of eight invited pairs divided into two groups, playing each other within their group on a 'round robin' basis. The group winner is the pair with the highest number of wins.
In the case of a tie the winning pair may be determined by head to head results or a formula based on percentage of sets/games won to those played.

EVENT 15 – THE GENTLEMEN'S SENIOR INVITATION DOUBLES 2018
Holders: JACCO ELTINGH (NED) & PAUL HAARHUIS (NED)

The Champions will become the holders, for the year only, of a Cup presented by The All England Lawn Tennis and Croquet Club. The Champions will receive a silver half-size Cup. A Silver Medal will be presented to each of the Runners-up.
The matches will be the best of three sets. If a match should reach one set all a 10-point tie-break will replace the third set.

GROUP A	Mansour Bahrami (FRA) & Goran Ivanisevic (CRO)	Jeremy Bates (GBR) & Andrew Castle (GBR)	Jonas Bjorkman (SWE) & Todd Woodbridge (AUS)	Jacco Eltingh (NED) & Paul Haarhuis (NED)	Wins	Losses	Final
Mansour Bahrami (FRA) & Goran Ivanisevic (CRO)		4/6 6/7(4) L	4/6 6/4 [7-10] L	4/6 3/6 L	0	3	
Jeremy Bates (GBR) & Andrew Castle (GBR)	6/4 7/6(4) W		6/7(6) 2/6 L	4/6 3/6 L	1	2	Jonas Bjorkman & Todd Woodbridge
Jonas Bjorkman (SWE) & Todd Woodbridge (AUS)	6/4 4/6 [10-7] W	7/6(6) 6/2 W		w/o W	3	0	
Jacco Eltingh (NED) & Paul Haarhuis (NED)	6/4 6/3 W	6/4 6/3 W	w/o L		2	1	

GROUP B	Wayne Ferreira (RSA) & Mark Woodforde (AUS)	Richard Krajicek (NED) & Mark Petchey (GBR)	Henri Leconte (FRA) & Cedric Pioline (FRA)	Patrick McEnroe (USA) & Jeff Tarango (USA)	Wins	Losses	Final
Wayne Ferreira (RSA) & Mark Woodforde (AUS)		6/7(6) 4/6 L	7/6(12) 6/3 W	6/2 6/3 W	2	1	
Richard Krajicek (NED) & Mark Petchey (GBR)	7/6(6) 6/4 W		6/3 6/3 W	6/4 6/2 W	3	0	Richard Krajicek & Mark Petchey
Henri Leconte (FRA) & Cedric Pioline (FRA)	6/7(12) 3/6 L	3/6 3/6 L		6/4 7/5 W	1	2	
Patrick McEnroe (USA) & Jeff Tarango (USA)	2/6 3/6 L	4/6 2/6 L	4/6 5/7 L		0	3	

Final: Jonas Bjorkman & Todd Woodbridge 6/4 6/3

This event consists of eight invited pairs divided into two groups, playing each other within their group on a 'round robin' basis. The group winner is the pair with the highest number of wins.
In the case of a tie the winning pair may be determined by head to head results or a formula based on percentage of sets/games won to those played.

EVENT 16 – THE LADIES' INVITATION DOUBLES 2018
Holders: CARA BLACK (ZIM) & MARTINA NAVRATILOVA (USA)

The Champions will become the holders, for the year only, of a Cup presented by The All England Lawn Tennis and Croquet Club. The Champions will receive a silver three-quarter size Cup. A Silver Medal will be presented to each of the Runners-up.
The matches will be the best of three sets. If a match should reach one set all a 10-point tie-break will replace the third set.

GROUP A	Marion Bartoli (FRA) & Daniela Hantuchova (SVK)	Cara Black (ZIM) & Martina Navratilova (USA)	Lindsay Davenport (USA) & Mary Joe Fernandez (USA)	Conchita Martinez (ESP) & Barbara Schett (AUT)	Wins	Losses	Final
Marion Bartoli (FRA) & Daniela Hantuchova (SVK)		1/6 3/6 L	6/4 6/3 W	7/5 3/6 [10-8] W	2	1	
Cara Black (ZIM) & Martina Navratilova (USA)	6/1 6/3 W		6/3 6/3 W	6/4 6/3 W	3	0	Cara Black & Martina Navratilova
Lindsay Davenport (USA) & Mary Joe Fernandez (USA)	4/6 3/6 L	3/6 3/6 L		4/6 6/4 [6-10] L	0	3	
Conchita Martinez (ESP) & Barbara Schett (AUT)	5/7 6/3 [8-10] L	4/6 3/6 L	6/4 4/6 [10-6] W		1	2	

GROUP B	Tracy Austin (USA) & Anne Keothavong (GBR)	Kim Clijsters (BEL) & Rennae Stubbs (AUS)	Na Li (CHN) & Ai Sugiyama (JPN)	Iva Majoli (CRO) & Selima Sfar (TUN)	Wins	Losses	
Tracy Austin (USA) & Anne Keothavong (GBR)		3/6 3/6 L	1/6 4/6 L	7/5 3/6 [7-10] L	0	3	Kim Clijsters & Rennae Stubbs 6/3 6/4
Kim Clijsters (BEL) & Rennae Stubbs (AUS)	6/3 6/3 W		6/1 6/4 W	6/2 6/2 W	3	0	Kim Clijsters & Rennae Stubbs
Na Li (CHN) & Ai Sugiyama (JPN)	6/1 6/4 W	1/6 4/6 L		6/4 4/6 [10-8] W	2	1	
Iva Majoli (CRO) & Selima Sfar (TUN)	5/7 6/3 [10-7] W	2/6 2/6 L	4/6 6/4 [8-10] L		1	2	

This event consists of eight invited pairs divided into two groups, playing each other within their group on a 'round robin' basis. The group winner is the pair with the highest number of wins.
In the case of a tie the winning pair may be determined by head to head results or a formula based on percentage of sets/games won to those played.

QUAD WHEELCHAIR DOUBLES EXHIBITION 2018

1. Andy Lapthorne (GBR) &
   David Wagner (USA) ....

   Andy Lapthorne &
   David Wagner
   .... 6/2 6/3

2. Dylan Alcott (AUS) &
   Lucas Sithole (RSA) ....

COUNTRIES IN THE CHAMPIONSHIPS 2018 – ABBREVIATIONS

ARG .... Argentina	DOM .... Dominican Republic	JPN .... Japan	ROU .... Romania
AUS .... Australia	ESA .... El Salvador	KAZ .... Kazakhstan	RSA .... South Africa
AUT .... Austria	ESP .... Spain	LAT .... Latvia	RUS .... Russia
BDI .... Burundi	EST .... Estonia	LTU .... Lithuania	SLO .... Slovenia
BEL .... Belgium	FIN .... Finland	LUX .... Luxembourg	SRB .... Serbia
BIH .... Bosnia-Herzegovina	FRA .... France	MDA .... Moldova	SUI .... Switzerland
BLR .... Belarus	GBR .... Great Britain	MEX .... Mexico	SVK .... Slovakia
BRA .... Brazil	GEO .... Georgia	MLT .... Malta	SWE .... Sweden
BUL .... Bulgaria	GER .... Germany	MON .... Monaco	THA .... Thailand
CAN .... Canada	GRE .... Greece	NED .... Netherlands	TPE .... Chinese Taipei
CHI .... Chile	GUA .... Guatemala	NZL .... New Zealand	TUN .... Tunisia
CHN .... China	HUN .... Hungary	PAK .... Pakistan	TUR .... Turkey
COL .... Colombia	IND .... India	PAR .... Paraguay	UKR .... Ukraine
CRO .... Croatia	IRL .... Ireland	PNG .... Papua New Guinea	URU .... Uruguay
CYP .... Cyprus	ISR .... Israel	POL .... Poland	USA .... USA
CZE .... Czech Republic	ITA .... Italy	POR .... Portugal	UZB .... Uzbekistan
DEN .... Denmark		PUR .... Puerto Rico	ZIM .... Zimbabwe

THE ROLLS OF HONOUR
GENTLEMEN'S SINGLES CHAMPIONS & RUNNERS-UP

1877 S.W.Gore *W.C.Marshall*	1904 H.L.Doherty *F.L.Riseley*	1935 F.J.Perry *G.von Cramm*	1968 R.G.Laver *A.D.Roche*	1995 P.Sampras *B.F.Becker*
1878 P.F.Hadow *S.W.Gore*	1905 H.L.Doherty *N.E.Brookes*	1936 F.J.Perry *G.von Cramm*	1969 R.G.Laver *J.D.Newcombe*	1996 R.P.S.Krajicek *M.O.Washington*
*1879 J.T.Hartley *V.T.St.L.Goold*	1906 H.L.Doherty *F.L.Riseley*	*1937 J.D.Budge *G.von Cramm*	1970 J.D.Newcombe *K.R.Rosewall*	1997 P.Sampras *C.A.Pioline*
1880 J.T.Hartley *H.F.Lawford*	*1907 N.E.Brookes *A.W.Gore*	1938 J.D.Budge *H.W.Austin*	1971 J.D.Newcombe *S.R.Smith*	1998 P.Sampras *G.S.Ivanisevic*
1881 W.C.Renshaw *J.T.Hartley*	*1908 A.W.Gore *H.R.Barrett*	*1939 R.L.Riggs *E.T.Cooke*	*1972 S.R.Smith *I.Nastase*	1999 P.Sampras *A.K.Agassi*
1882 W.C.Renshaw *J.E.Renshaw*	1909 A.W.Gore *M.J.G.Ritchie*	*1946 Y.F.M.Petra *G.E.Brown*	*1973 J.Kodes *A.Metreveli*	2000 P.Sampras *P.M.Rafter*
1883 W.C.Renshaw *J.E.Renshaw*	1910 A.F.Wilding *A.W.Gore*	1947 J.A.Kramer *T.P.Brown*	1974 J.S.Connors *K.R.Rosewall*	2001 G.Ivanisevic *P.M.Rafter*
1884 W.C.Renshaw *H.F.Lawford*	1911 A.F.Wilding *H.R.Barrett*	*1948 R.Falkenburg *J.E.Bromwich*	1975 A.R.Ashe *J.S.Connors*	2002 L.G.Hewitt *D.P.Nalbandian*
1885 W.C.Renshaw *H.F.Lawford*	1912 A.F.Wilding *A.W.Gore*	1949 F.R.Schroeder *J.Drobny*	1976 B.R.Borg *I.Nastase*	2003 R.Federer *M.A.Philippoussis*
1886 W.C.Renshaw *H.F.Lawford*	1913 A.F.Wilding *M.E.McLoughlin*	*1950 J.E.Patty *F.A.Sedgman*	1977 B.R.Borg *J.S.Connors*	2004 R.Federer *A.S.Roddick*
*1887 H.F.Lawford *J.E.Renshaw*	1914 N.E.Brookes *A.F.Wilding*	1951 R.Savitt *K.B.McGregor*	1978 B.R.Borg *J.S.Connors*	2005 R.Federer *A.S.Roddick*
1888 J.E.Renshaw *H.F.Lawford*	1919 G.L.Patterson *N.E.Brookes*	1952 F.A.Sedgman *J.Drobny*	1979 B.R.Borg *L.R.Tanner*	2006 R.Federer *R.Nadal*
1889 W.C.Renshaw *J.E.Renshaw*	1920 W.T.Tilden *G.L.Patterson*	*1953 E.V.Seixas *K.Nielsen*	1980 B.Borg *J.P.McEnroe*	2007 R.Federer *R.Nadal*
1890 W.J.Hamilton *W.C.Renshaw*	1921 W.T.Tilden *B.I.C.Norton*	1954 J.Drobny *K.R.Rosewall*	1981 J.P.McEnroe *B.R.Borg*	2008 R.Nadal *R.Federer*
*1891 W.Baddeley *J.Pim*	*†1922 G.L.Patterson *R.Lycett*	1955 M.A.Trabert *K.Nielsen*	1982 J.S.Connors *J.P.McEnroe*	2009 R.Federer *A.S.Roddick*
1892 W.Baddeley *J.Pim*	*1923 W.M.Johnston *F.T.Hunter*	*1956 L.A.Hoad *K.R.Rosewall*	1983 J.P.McEnroe *C.J.Lewis*	2010 R.Nadal *T.Berdych*
1893 J.Pim *W.Baddeley*	*1924 J.R.Borotra *J.R.Lacoste*	1957 L.A.Hoad *A.J.Cooper*	1984 J.P.McEnroe *J.S.Connors*	2011 N.Djokovic *R.Nadal*
1894 J.Pim *W.Baddeley*	1925 J.R.Lacoste *J.R.Borotra*	*1958 A.J.Cooper *N.A.Fraser*	1985 B.F.Becker *K.M.Curren*	2012 R.Federer *A.B.Murray*
*1895 W.Baddeley *W.V.Eaves*	*1926 J.R.Borotra *H.O.Kinsey*	*1959 A.R.Olmedo *R.G.Laver*	1986 B.F.Becker *I.Lendl*	2013 A.B.Murray *N.Djokovic*
1896 H.S.Mahony *W.Baddeley*	1927 H.J.Cochet *J.R.Borotra*	*1960 N.A.Fraser *R.G.Laver*	1987 P.H.Cash *I.Lendl*	2014 N.Djokovic *R.Federer*
1897 R.F.Doherty *H.S.Mahony*	1928 J.R.Lacoste *H.J.Cochet*	1961 R.G.Laver *C.R.McKinley*	1988 S.B.Edberg *B.F.Becker*	2015 N.Djokovic *R.Federer*
1898 R.F.Doherty *H.L.Doherty*	*1929 H.J.Cochet *J.R.Borotra*	1962 R.G.Laver *M.F.Mulligan*	1989 B.F.Becker *S.B.Edberg*	2016 A.B.Murray *M.Raonic*
1899 R.F.Doherty *A.W.Gore*	1930 W.T.Tilden *W.L.Allison*	*1963 C.R.McKinley *F.S.Stolle*	1990 S.B.Edberg *B.F.Becker*	2017 R.Federer *M.Cilic*
1900 R.F.Doherty *S.H.Smith*	*1931 S.B.B.Wood *F.X.Shields*	1964 R.S.Emerson *F.S.Stolle*	1991 M.D.Stich *B.F.Becker*	2018 N.Djokovic *K.Anderson*
1901 A.W.Gore *R.F.Doherty*	1932 H.E.Vines *H.W.Austin*	1965 R.S.Emerson *F.S.Stolle*	1992 A.K.Agassi *G.S.Ivanisevic*	
1902 H.L.Doherty *A.W.Gore*	1933 J.H.Crawford *H.E.Vines*	1966 M.M.Santana *R.D.Ralston*	1993 P.Sampras *J.S.Courier*	
1903 H.L.Doherty *F.L.Riseley*	1934 F.J.Perry *J.H.Crawford*	1967 J.D.Newcombe *W.P.Bungert*	1994 P.Sampras *G.S.Ivanisevic*	

For the years 1913, 1914 and 1919-1923 inclusive the above records include the "World's Championships on Grass" granted to The Lawn Tennis Association by The International Lawn Tennis Federation. This title was then abolished and commencing in 1924 they became The Official Lawn Tennis Championships recognised by The International Lawn Tennis Federation.
Prior to 1922 the holders in the Singles Events and Gentlemen's Doubles did not compete in The Championships but met the winners of these events in the Challenge Rounds.
† Challenge Round abolished: holders subsequently played through.
* The holder did not defend the title.

LADIES' SINGLES CHAMPIONS & RUNNERS-UP

Year	Champion	Runner-up
1884	Miss M.E.E.Watson	Miss L.M.Watson
1885	Miss M.E.E.Watson	Miss B.Bingley
1886	Miss B.Bingley	Miss M.E.E.Watson
1887	Miss C.Dod	Miss B.Bingley
1888	Miss C.Dod	Mrs.G.W.Hillyard
*1889	Mrs.G.W.Hillyard	Miss H.G.B.Rice
*1890	Miss H.G.B.Rice	Miss M.Jacks
*1891	Miss C.Dod	Mrs.G.W.Hillyard
1892	Miss C.Dod	Mrs.G.W.Hillyard
1893	Miss C.Dod	Mrs.G.W.Hillyard
*1894	Mrs.G.W.Hillyard	Miss E.L.Austin
*1895	Miss C.R.Cooper	Miss H.Jackson
1896	Miss C.R.Cooper	Mrs.W.H.Pickering
1897	Mrs.G.W.Hillyard	Miss C.R.Cooper
*1898	Miss C.R.Cooper	Miss M.L.Martin
1899	Mrs.G.W.Hillyard	Miss C.R.Cooper
1900	Mrs.G.W.Hillyard	Miss C.R.Cooper
1901	Mrs.A.Sterry	Mrs.G.W.Hillyard
1902	Miss M.E.Robb	Mrs.A.Sterry
*1903	Miss D.K.Douglass	Miss E.W.Thomson
1904	Miss D.K.Douglass	Mrs.A.Sterry
1905	Miss M.G.Sutton	Miss D.K.Douglass
1906	Miss D.K.Douglass	Miss M.G.Sutton
1907	Miss M.G.Sutton	Mrs.R.L.Chambers
*1908	Mrs.A.Sterry	Miss A.M.Morton
*1909	Miss P.D.H.Boothby	Miss A.M.Morton
1910	Mrs.R.L.Chambers	Miss P.D.H.Boothby
1911	Mrs.R.L.Chambers	Miss P.D.H.Boothby
*1912	Mrs.D.T.R.Larcombe	Mrs.A.Sterry
*1913	Mrs.R.L.Chambers	Mrs.R.J.McNair
1914	Mrs.R.L.Chambers	Mrs.D.T.R.Larcombe
1919	Miss S.R.F.Lenglen	Mrs.R.L.Chambers
1920	Miss S.R.F.Lenglen	Mrs.R.L.Chambers
1921	Miss S.R.F.Lenglen	Miss E.M.Ryan
†1922	Miss S.R.F.Lenglen	Mrs.F.I.Mallory
1923	Miss S.R.F.Lenglen	Miss K.McKane
1924	Miss K.McKane	Miss H.N.Wills
1925	Miss S.R.F.Lenglen	Miss J.C.Fry
1926	Mrs.L.A.Godfree	Miss E.M.de Alvarez
1927	Miss H.Wills	Miss E.M.de Alvarez
1928	Miss H.N.Wills	Miss E.M.de Alvarez
1929	Miss H.N.Wills	Miss H.H.Jacobs
1930	Mrs.F.S.Moody	Miss E.M.Ryan
*1931	Miss C.Aussem	Miss H.Krahwinkel
*1932	Mrs.F.S.Moody	Miss H.H.Jacobs
1933	Mrs.F.S.Moody	Miss D.E.Round
*1934	Miss D.E.Round	Miss H.H.Jacobs
1935	Mrs.F.S.Moody	Miss H.H.Jacobs
*1936	Miss H.H.Jacobs	Miss S.Sperling
1937	Mrs.D.E.Round	Miss J.Jedrzejowska
*1938	Mrs.F.S.Moody	Miss H.H.Jacobs
*1939	Miss A.Marble	Miss K.E.Stammers
*1946	Miss P.M.Betz	Miss A.L.Brough
*1947	Miss M.E.Osborne	Miss D.J.Hart
1948	Miss A.L.Brough	Miss D.J.Hart
1949	Miss A.L.Brough	Mrs.W.du Pont
1950	Miss A.L.Brough	Mrs.W.du Pont
1951	Miss D.J.Hart	Miss S.J.Fry
1952	Miss M.C.Connolly	Miss A.L.Brough
1953	Miss M.C.Connolly	Miss D.J.Hart
1954	Miss M.C.Connolly	Miss A.L.Brough
*1955	Miss A.L.Brough	Mrs.J.G.Fleitz
1956	Miss S.J.Fry	Miss A.Buxton
*1957	Miss A.Gibson	Miss D.R.Hard
1958	Miss A.Gibson	Miss F.A.M.Mortimer
*1959	Miss M.E.A.Bueno	Miss D.R.Hard
1960	Miss M.E.A.Bueno	Miss S.Reynolds
*1961	Miss F.A.M.Mortimer	Miss C.C.Truman
1962	Mrs.J.R.Susman	Mrs.C.Sukova
*1963	Miss M.Smith	Miss B.J.Moffitt
1964	Miss M.E.A.Bueno	Miss M.Smith
1965	Miss M.Smith	Miss M.E.A.Bueno
1966	Mrs.L.W.King	Miss M.E.A.Bueno
1967	Mrs.L.W.King	Mrs.P.F.Jones
1968	Mrs.L.W.King	Miss J.A.M.Tegart
1969	Mrs.P.F.Jones	Mrs.L.W.King
*1970	Mrs.B.M.Court	Mrs.L.W.King
1971	Miss E.F.Goolagong	Mrs.B.M.Court
1972	Mrs.L.W.King	Miss E.F.Goolagong
1973	Mrs.L.W.King	Miss C.M.Evert
1974	Miss C.M.Evert	Mrs.O.V.Morozova
1975	Mrs.L.W.King	Mrs.R.A.Cawley
*1976	Miss C.M.Evert	Mrs.R.A.Cawley
1977	Miss S.V.Wade	Miss B.F.Stove
1978	Miss M.Navratilova	Miss C.M.Evert
1979	Miss M.Navratilova	Mrs.J.M.Lloyd
1980	Mrs.R.A.Cawley	Mrs.J.M.Lloyd
*1981	Mrs.J.M.Lloyd	Miss H.Mandlikova
1982	Miss M.Navratilova	Mrs.J.M.Lloyd
1983	Miss M.Navratilova	Miss A.Jaeger
1984	Miss M.Navratilova	Mrs.J.M.Lloyd
1985	Miss M.Navratilova	Mrs.J.M.Lloyd
1986	Miss M.Navratilova	Miss H.Mandlikova
1987	Miss M.Navratilova	Miss S.M.Graf
1988	Miss S.M.Graf	Miss M.Navratilova
1989	Miss S.M.Graf	Miss M.Navratilova
1990	Miss M.Navratilova	Miss Z.L.Garrison
1991	Miss S.M.Graf	Miss G.B.Sabatini
1992	Miss S.M.Graf	Miss M.Seles
1993	Miss S.M.Graf	Miss J.Novotna
1994	Miss I.C.Martinez	Miss M.Navratilova
1995	Miss S.M.Graf	Miss A.I.M.Sanchez Vicario
1996	Miss S.M.Graf	Miss A.I.M.Sanchez Vicario
*1997	Miss M.Hingis	Miss J.Novotna
1998	Miss J.Novotna	Miss N.Tauziat
1999	Miss L.A.Davenport	Miss S.M.Graf
2000	Miss V.E.S.Williams	Miss L.A.Davenport
2001	Miss V.E.S.Williams	Miss J.Henin
2002	Miss S.J.Williams	Miss V.E.S.Williams
2003	Miss S.J.Williams	Miss V.E.S.Williams
2004	Miss M.Sharapova	Miss S.J.Williams
2005	Miss V.E.S.Williams	Miss L.A.Davenport
2006	Miss A.Mauresmo	Mrs.J.Henin-Hardenne
2007	Miss V.E.S.Williams	Miss M.S.Bartoli
2008	Miss V.E.S.Williams	Miss S.J.Williams
2009	Miss S.J.Williams	Miss V.E.S.Williams
2010	Miss S.J.Williams	Miss V.Zvonareva
2011	Miss P.Kvitova	Miss M.Sharapova
2012	Miss S.J.Williams	Miss A.R.Radwanska
2013	Miss M.S.Bartoli	Miss S.Lisicki
2014	Miss P.Kvitova	Miss E.C.M.Bouchard
2015	Miss S.J.Williams	Miss G.Muguruza
2016	Miss S.J.Williams	Miss A.Kerber
2017	Miss G.Muguruza	Miss V.E.S.Williams
2018	Miss A.Kerber	Mrs.S.J.Williams

MAIDEN NAMES OF LADIES' CHAMPIONS (In the tables the following have been recorded in both married and single identities)

Mrs. R. Cawley...................Miss E. F. Goolagong	Mrs. G. W. Hillyard...................Miss B. Bingley	Mrs. G. E. Reid...................Miss K. Melville
Mrs. R. L. Chambers...................Miss D. K. Douglass	Mrs. P. F. Jones...................Miss A. S. Haydon	Mrs. P. D. Smylie...................Miss E. M. Sayers
Mrs. B. M. Court...................Miss M. Smith	Mrs. L. W. King...................Miss B. J. Moffitt	Mrs. S. Sperling...................Fräulein H. Krahwinkel
Mrs. B. C. Covell...................Miss P. L. Howkins	Mrs. M. R. King...................Miss P. E. Mudford	Mrs. A. Sterry...................Miss C.R. Cooper
Mrs. D. E. Dalton...................Miss J. A. M. Tegart	Mrs. D. R. Larcombe...................Miss E. W. Thomson	Mrs. J. R. Susman...................Miss K. Hantze
Mrs. W. du Pont...................Miss M.E. Osborne	Mrs. J. M. Lloyd...................Miss C. M. Evert	
Mrs. L. A. Godfree...................Miss K. McKane	Mrs. F. S. Moody...................Miss H.N. Wills	
Mrs. R.L. Cawley...................Miss H. F. Gourlay	Mrs. O.V. Morozova...................Miss O.V. Morozova	
Mrs. J. Henin-Hardenne...................Miss J. Henin	Mrs. L. E. G. Price...................Miss S. Reynolds	

WIMBLEDON 2018

GENTLEMEN'S DOUBLES CHAMPIONS & RUNNERS-UP

1879	L.R.Erskine and H.F.Lawford *F.Durant and G.E.Tabor*	1913	H.R.Barrett and C.P.Dixon *F.W.Rahe and H.Kleinschroth*	1957	G.P.Mulloy and J.E.Patty *N.A.Fraser and L.A.Hoad*	1991	J.B.Fitzgerald and A.P.Jarryd *J.A.Frana and L.Lavalle*

1879   L.R.Erskine and H.F.Lawford
F.Durant and G.E.Tabor

1880   W.C.Renshaw and J.E.Renshaw
O.E.Woodhouse and C.J.Cole

1881   W.C.Renshaw and J.E.Renshaw
W.J.Down and H.Vaughan

1882   J.T.Hartley and R.T.Richardson
J.G.Horn and C.B.Russell

1883   C.W.Grinstead and C.E.Welldon
C.B.Russell and R.T.Milford

1884   W.C.Renshaw and J.E.Renshaw
E.W.Lewis and E.L.Williams

1885   W.C.Renshaw and J.E.Renshaw
C.E.Farrer and A.J.Stanley

1886   W.C.Renshaw and J.E.Renshaw
C.E.Farrer and A.J.Stanley

1887   P.B.Lyon and
H.W.W.Wilberforce
J.H.Crispe and E.Barratt-Smith

1888   W.C.Renshaw and J.E.Renshaw
*P B.Lyon and
H.W.W.Wilberforce*

1889   W.C.Renshaw and J.E.Renshaw
E.W.Lewis and G.W.Hillyard

1890   J.Pim and F.O.Stoker
E.W.Lewis and G.W.Hillyard

1891   W.Baddeley and H.Baddeley
J.Pim and F.O.Stoker

1892   H.S.Barlow and E.W.Lewis
W.Baddeley and H.Baddeley

1893   J.Pim and F.O.Stoker
E.W.Lewis and H.S.Barlow

1894   W.Baddeley and H.Baddeley
H.S.Barlow and C.H.Martin

1895   W.Baddeley and H.Baddeley
E.W.Lewis and W.V.Eaves

1896   W.Baddeley and H.Baddeley
R.F.Doherty and H.A.Nisbet

1897   R.F.Doherty and H.L.Doherty
W.Baddeley and H.Baddeley

1898   R.F.Doherty and H.L.Doherty
H.A.Nisbet and C.Hobart

1899   R.F.Doherty and H.L.Doherty
H.A.Nisbet and C.Hobart

1900   R.F.Doherty and H.L.Doherty
H.R.Barrett and H.A.Nisbet

1901   R.F.Doherty and H.L.Doherty
D.Davis and H.Ward

1902   S.H.Smith and F.L.Riseley
R.F.Doherty and H.L.Doherty

1903   R.F.Doherty and H.L.Doherty
S.H.Smith and F.L.Riseley

1904   R.F.Doherty and H.L.Doherty
S.H.Smith and F.L.Riseley

1905   R.F.Doherty and H.L.Doherty
S.H.Smith and F.L.Riseley

1906   S.H.Smith and F.L.Riseley
R.F.Doherty and H.L.Doherty

1907   N.E.Brookes and A.F.Wilding
B.C.Wright and K.Behr

1908   A.F.Wilding and M.J.G.Ritchie
A.W.Gore and H.R.Barrett

1909   A.W.Gore and H.R.Barrett
S.N.Doust and H.A.Parker

1910   A.F.Wilding and M.J.G.Ritchie
A.W.Gore and H.R.Barrett

1911   M.O.M.Decugis and A.H.Gobert
M.J.G.Ritchie and A.F.Wilding

1912   H.R.Barrett and C.P.Dixon
M.O.Decugis and A.H.Gobert

1913   H.R.Barrett and C.P.Dixon
F.W.Rahe and H.Kleinschroth

1914   N.E.Brookes and A.F.Wilding
H.R.Barrett and C.P.Dixon

1919   R.V.Thomas and P.O.Wood
R.Lycett and R.W.Heath

1920   R.N.Williams and C.S.Garland
A.R.F.Kingscote and J.C.Parke

1921   R.Lycett and M.Woosnam
F.G.Lowe and A.H.Lowe

1922   R.Lycett and J.O.Anderson
G.L.Patterson and P.O.Wood

1923   R.Lycett and L.A.Godfree
*Count M.de Gomar and
E.Flaquer*

1924   F.T.Hunter and V.Richards
*R.N.Williams and
W.M.Washburn*

1925   J.R.Borotra and R.Lacoste
J.F.Hennessey and R.J.Casey

1926   H.J.Cochet and J.Brugnon
V.Richards and H.O.Kinsey

1927   F.T.Hunter and W.T.Tilden
J.Brugnon and H.J.Cochet

1928   H.J.Cochet and J.Brugnon
G.L.Patterson and J.B.Hawkes

1929   W.L.Allison and J.W.Van Ryn
J.C.Gregory and I.G.Collins

1930   W.L.Allison and J.W.Van Ryn
J.T.G.H.Doeg and G.M.Lott

1931   G.M Lott and J.W.Van Ryn
H.J.Cochet and J.Brugnon

1932   J.R.Borotra and J.Brugnon
G.P.Hughes and F.J.Perry

1933   J.R.Borotra and J.Brugnon
R.Nunoi and J.Satoh

1934   G.M.Lott and L.R.Stoefen
J.R.Borotra and J.Brugnon

1935   J.H.Crawford and A.K.Quist
W.L.Allison and J.W.Van Ryn

1936   G.P.Hughes and C.R.D.Tuckey
C.E.Hare and F.H.D.Wilde

1937   J.D.Budge and G.C.Mako
G.P.Hughes and C.R.D.Tuckey

1938   J.D.Budge and G.C.Mako
H.E.O.Henkel and G.von Metaxa

1939   R.L.Riggs and E.T.Cooke
C.E.Hare and F.H.D.Wilde

1946   T.P.Brown and J.A.Kramer
G.E.Brown and D.R.Pails

1947   R.Falkenburg and J.A.Kramer
A.J.Mottram and O.W.T.Sidwell

1948   J.E.Bromwich and F.A.Sedgman
T.P.Brown and G.P.Mulloy

1949   R.A.Gonzales and F.A.Parker
G.P.Mulloy and F.R.Schroeder

1950   J.E.Bromwich and A.K.Quist
G.E.Brown and O.W.T.Sidwell

1951   K.B.McGregor and F.A.Sedgman
J.Drobny and E.W.Sturgess

1952   K.B.McGregor and F.A.Sedgman
E.V.Seixas and E.W.Sturgess

1953   L.A.Hoad and K.R.Rosewall
R.N.Hartwig and M.G.Rose

1954   R.N.Hartwig and M.G.Rose
E.V.Seixas and M.A.Trabert

1955   R.N.Hartwig and L.A.Hoad
N.A.Fraser and K.R.Rosewall

1956   L.A.Hoad and K.R.Rosewall
N.Pietrangeli and O.Sirola

1957   G.P.Mulloy and J.E.Patty
N.A.Fraser and L.A.Hoad

1958   S.V.Davidson and U.C.J.Schmidt
A.J.Cooper and N.A.Fraser

1959   R.S.Emerson and N.A.Fraser
R.G.Laver and R.Mark

1960   R.H.Osuna and R.D.Ralston
M.G.Davies and R.K.Wilson

1961   R.S.Emerson and N.A.Fraser
R.A.J.Hewitt and F.S.Stolle

1962   R.A.J.Hewitt and F.S.Stolle
B.Jovanovic and N.Pilic

1963   R.H.Osuna and A.Palafox
J.C.Barclay and P.Darmon

1964   R.A.J.Hewitt and F.S.Stolle
R.S.Emerson and K.N.Fletcher

1965   J.D.Newcombe and A.D.Roche
K.N.Fletcher and R.A.J.Hewitt

1966   K.N.Fletcher and J.D.Newcombe
W.W.Bowrey and O.K.Davidson

1967   R.A.J.Hewitt and F.D.McMillan
R.S.Emerson and K.N.Fletcher

1968   J.D.Newcombe and A.D.Roche
K.R.Rosewall and F.S.Stolle

1969   J.D.Newcombe and A.D.Roche
T.S.Okker and M.C.Reissen

1970   J.D.Newcombe and A.D.Roche
K.R.Rosewall and F.S.Stolle

1971   R.S.Emerson and R.G.Laver
A.R.Ashe and R.D.Ralston

1972   R.A.J.Hewitt and F.D.McMillan
S.R.Smith and E.J.van Dillen

1973   J.S.Connors and I.Nastase
J.R.Cooper and N.A.Fraser

1974   J.D.Newcombe and A.D.Roche
R.C.Lutz and S.R.Smith

1975   V.K.Gerulaitis and A.Mayer
C.Dowdeswell and A.J.Stone

1976   B.E.Gottfried and R.C.Ramirez
R.L.Case and G.Masters

1977   R.L.Case and G.Masters
J.G.Alexander and P.C.Dent

1978   R.A.J.Hewitt and F.D.McMillan
P.B.Fleming and J.P.McEnroe

1979   P.B.Fleming and J.P.McEnroe
B.E.Gottfried and R.C.Ramirez

1980   P.McNamara and P.F.McNamee
R.C.Lutz and S.R.Smith

1981   P.B.Fleming and J.P.McEnroe
R.C.Lutz and S.R.Smith

1982   P.McNamara and P.F.McNamee
P.B.Fleming and J.P.McEnroe

1983   P.B.Fleming and J.P.McEnroe
T.E.Gullikson and T.R.Gullikson

1984   P.B.Fleming and J.P.McEnroe
P.Cash and P.McNamee

1985   H.P.Guenthardt and B.Taroczy
P.H.Cash and J.B.Fitzgerald

1986   T.K.Nystrom and
M.A.O.Wilander
G.W.Donnelly and P.B.Fleming

1987   K.E.Flach and R.A.Seguso
S.Casal and E.Sanchez

1988   K.E.Flach and R.A.Seguso
J.B.Fitzgerald and A.P.Jarryd

1989   J.B.Fitzgerald and A.P.Jarryd
R.D.Leach and J.R.Pugh

1990   R.D.Leach and J.R.Pugh
P.Aldrich and D.T.Visser

1991   J.B.Fitzgerald and A.P.Jarryd
J.A.Frana and L.Lavalle

1992   J.P.McEnroe and M.D.Stich
J.F.Grabb and R.A.Reneberg

1993   T.A.Woodbridge and
M.R.Woodforde
G.D.Connell and P.J.Galbraith

1994   T.A.Woodbridge and
M.R.Woodforde
G.D.Connell and P.J.Galbraith

1995   T.A.Woodbridge and
M.R.Woodforde
R.D.Leach and S.D.Melville

1996   T.A.Woodbridge and
M.R.Woodforde
B.H.Black and G.D.Connell

1997   T.A.Woodbridge and
M.R.Woodforde
J.F.Eltingh and P.V.N.Haarhuis

1998   J.F.Eltingh and P.V.N.Haarhuis
*T.A.Woodbridge and
M.R.Woodforde*

1999   M.S.Bhupathi and L.A.Paes
P.V.N.Haarhuis and J.E.Palmer

2000   T.A.Woodbridge and
M.R.Woodforde
P.V.N.Haarhuis and S.F.Stolle

2001   D.J.Johnson and J.E.Palmer
J.Novak and D.Rikl

2002   J.L.Bjorkman and T.A.
Woodbridge
M.S.Knowles and D.M.Nestor

2003   J.L.Bjorkman and T.A.
Woodbridge
M.S.Bhupathi and M.N.Mirnyi

2004   J.L.Bjorkman and T.A.
Woodbridge
J.Knowle and N.Zimonjic

2005   S.W.I.Huss and W.A.Moodie
R.C.Bryan and M.C.Bryan

2006   R.C.Bryan and M.C.Bryan
F.V.Santoro and N.Zimonjic

2007   A.Clement and M.Llodra
R.C.Bryan and M.C.Bryan

2008   D.M.Nestor and N.Zimonjic
J.L.Bjorkman and K.R.Ullyett

2009   D.M.Nestor and N.Zimonjic
R.C.Bryan and M.C.Bryan

2010   J.Melzer and P.Petzschner
R.S.Lindstedt and H.V.Tecau

2011   R.C.Bryan and M.C.Bryan
R.S.Lindstedt and H.V.Tecau

2012   J.F.Marray and F.L.Nielsen
R.S.Lindstedt and H.V.Tecau

2013   R.C.Bryan and M.C.Bryan
I.Dodig and M.P.D.Melo

2014   V.Pospisil and J.E.Sock
R.C.Bryan and M.C.Bryan

2015   J.J.Rojer and H.Tecau
J.R.Murray and J.Peers

2016   P-H.Herbert and N.P.A.Mahut
*J.Benneteau and E.Roger-
Vasselin*

2017   L.Kubot and M.P.D.Melo
O.Marach and M.Pavic

2018   M.C.Bryan and J.Sock
R.Klaasen and M.Venus

LADIES' DOUBLES CHAMPIONS & RUNNERS-UP

1913	Mrs.R.J.McNair and Miss P.D.H.Boothby *Mrs.A.Sterry and Mrs.R.L.Chambers*	
1914	Miss E.M.Ryan and Miss A.M.Morton *Mrs.D.T.R.Larcombe and Mrs.F.J.Hannam*	
1919	Miss S.R.F.Lenglen and Miss E.M.Ryan *Mrs.R.L.Chambers and Mrs.D.T.R.Larcombe*	
1920	Miss S.R.F.Lenglen and Miss E.M.Ryan *Mrs.R.L.Chambers and Mrs.D.T.R.Larcombe*	
1921	Miss S.R.F.Lenglen and Miss E.M.Ryan *Mrs.A.E.Beamish and Mrs.G.E.Peacock*	
1922	Miss S.R.F.Lenglen and Miss E.M.Ryan *Mrs.A.D.Stocks and Miss K.McKane*	
1923	Miss S.R.F.Lenglen and Miss E.M.Ryan *Miss J.W.Austin and Miss E.L.Colyer*	
1924	Mrs.G.Wightman and Miss H.Wills *Mrs.B.C.Covell and Miss K.McKane*	
1925	Miss S.Lenglen and Miss E.Ryan *Mrs.A.V.Bridge and Mrs.C.G.McIlquham*	
1926	Miss E.M.Ryan and Miss M.K.Browne *Mrs.L.A.Godfree and Miss E.L.Colyer*	
1927	Miss H.N.Wills and Miss E.M.Ryan *Miss E.L.Heine and Mrs.G.E.Peacock*	
1928	Mrs.M.R.Watson and Miss M.A.Saunders *Miss E.H.Harvey and Miss E.Bennett*	
1929	Mrs.M.R.Watson and Mrs.L.R.C.Michell *Mrs.B.C.Covell and Mrs.W.P.Barron*	
1930	Mrs.F.S.Moody and Miss E.M.Ryan *Miss E.A.Cross and Miss S.H.Palfrey*	
1931	Mrs.D.C.Shepherd-Barron and Miss P.E.Mudford *Miss D.E.Metaxa and Miss J.Sigart*	
1932	Miss D.E.Metaxa and Miss J.Sigart *Miss E.M.Ryan and Miss H.H.Jacobs*	
1933	Mrs.R.Mathieu and Miss E.M.Ryan *Miss W.A.James and Miss A.M.Yorke*	
1934	Mrs.R.Mathieu and Miss E.M.Ryan *Mrs.D.B.Andrus and Mrs.C.F.Henrotin*	
1935	Miss W.A.James and Miss K.E.Stammers *Mrs.R.Mathieu and Mrs.S.Sperling*	
1936	Miss W.A.James and Miss K.E.Stammers *Mrs.M.Fabyan and Miss H.H.Jacobs*	
1937	Mrs.R.Mathieu and Miss A.M.Yorke *Mrs.M.R.King and Mrs.J.B.Pittman*	
1938	Mrs.M.Fabyan and Miss A.Marble *Mrs.R.Mathieu and Miss A.M.Yorke*	
1939	Mrs.M.Fabyan and Miss A.Marble *Miss H.H.Jacobs and Miss A.M.Yorke*	
1946	Miss A.L.Brough and Miss M.E.Osborne *Miss P.M.Betz and Miss D.J.Hart*	
1947	Miss D.J.Hart and Mrs.R.B.Todd *Miss A.L.Brough and Miss M.E.Osborne*	
1948	Miss A.L.Brough and Mrs.W.du Pont *Miss D.J.Hart and Mrs.R.B.Todd*	
1949	Miss A.L.Brough and Mrs.W.du Pont *Miss G.Moran and Mrs.R.B.Todd*	
1950	Miss A.L.Brough and Mrs.W.du Pont *Miss S.J.Fry and Miss D.J.Hart*	
1951	Miss S.J.Fry and Miss D.J.Hart *Miss A.L.Brough and Mrs.W.du Pont*	
1952	Miss S.J.Fry and Miss D.J.Hart *Miss A.L.Brough and Miss M.C.Connolly*	
1953	Miss S.J.Fry and Miss D.J.Hart *Miss M.C.Connolly and Miss J.A.Sampson*	
1954	Miss A.L.Brough and Mrs.W.du Pont *Miss S.J.Fry and Miss D.J.Hart*	
1955	Miss F.A.Mortimer and Miss J.A.Shilcock *Miss S.J.Bloomer and Miss P.E.Ward*	
1956	Miss A.Buxton and Miss A.Gibson *Miss E.F.Muller and Miss D.G.Seeney*	
1957	Miss A.Gibson and Miss D.R.Hard *Mrs.K.Hawton and Mrs.M.N.Long*	
1958	Miss M.E.A.Bueno and Miss A.Gibson *Mrs.W.du Pont and Miss M.Varner*	
1959	Miss J.M.Arth and Miss D.R.Hard *Mrs.J.G.Fleitz and Miss C.C.Truman*	
1960	Miss M.E.A.Bueno and Miss D.R.Hard *Miss S.Reynolds and Miss R.Schuurman*	
1961	Miss K.J.Hantze and Miss B.J.Moffitt *Miss J.P.Lehane and Miss M.Smith*	
1962	Miss B.J.Moffitt and Mrs.J.R.Susman *Mrs.L.E.G.Price and Miss R.Schuurman*	
1963	Miss M.E.A.Bueno and Miss D.R.Hard *Miss R.A.Ebbern and Miss M.Smith*	
1964	Miss M.Smith and Miss L.R.Turner *Miss B.J.Moffitt and Mrs.J.R.Susman*	
1965	Miss M.E.A.Bueno and Miss B.J.Moffitt *Miss F.G.Durr and Miss J.P.Lieffrig*	
1966	Miss M.E.A.Bueno and Miss N.A.Richey *Miss M.Smith and Miss J.A.M.Tegart*	
1967	Miss R.Casals and Mrs.L.W.King *Miss M.E.A.Bueno and Miss N.A.Richey*	
1968	Miss R.Casals and Mrs.L.W.King *Miss F.G.Durr and Mrs.P.F.Jones*	
1969	Mrs.B.M.Court and Miss J.A.M.Tegart *Miss P.S.A.Hogan and Miss M.Michel*	
1970	Miss R.Casals and Mrs.L.W.King *Miss F.G.Durr and Miss S.V.Wade*	
1971	Miss R.Casals and Mrs.L.W.King *Mrs.B.M.Court and Miss E.F.Goolagong*	
1972	Mrs.L.W.King and Miss B.F.Stove *Mrs.D.E.Dalton and Miss F.G.Durr*	
1973	Miss R.Casals and Mrs.L.W.King *Miss F.G.Durr and Miss B.F.Stove*	
1974	Miss E.F.Goolagong and Miss M.Michel *Miss H.F.Gourlay and Miss K.M.Krantzcke*	
1975	Miss A.K.Kiyomura and Miss K.Sawamatsu *Miss F.G.Durr and Miss B.F.Stove*	
1976	Miss C.M.Evert and Miss M.Navratilova *Mrs.L.W.King and Miss B.F.Stove*	
1977	Mrs.R.L.Cawley and Miss J.C.Russell *Miss M.Navratilova and Miss B.F.Stove*	
1978	Mrs.G.E.Reid and Miss W.M.Turnbull *Miss M.Jausovec and Miss V.Ruzici*	
1979	Mrs.L.W.King and Miss M.Navratilova *Miss B.F.Stove and Miss W.M.Turnbull*	
1980	Miss K.Jordan and Miss A.E.Smith *Miss R.Casals and Miss W.M.Turnbull*	
1981	Miss M.Navratilova and Miss P.H.Shriver *Miss K.Jordan and Miss A.E.Smith*	
1982	Miss M.Navratilova and Miss P.H.Shriver *Miss K.Jordan and Miss A.E.Smith*	
1983	Miss M.Navratilova and Miss P.H.Shriver *Miss R.Casals and Miss W.M.Turnbull*	
1984	Miss M.Navratilova and Miss P.H.Shriver *Miss K.Jordan and Miss A.E.Smith*	
1985	Miss K.Jordan and Mrs.P.D.Smylie *Miss M.Navratilova and Miss P.H.Shriver*	
1986	Miss M.Navratilova and Miss P.H.Shriver *Miss H.Mandlikova and Miss W.M.Turnbull*	
1987	Miss C.G.Kohde-Kilsch and Miss H.Sukova *Miss H.E.Nagelsen and Mrs.P.D.Smylie*	
1988	Miss S.M.Graf and Miss G.B.Sabatini *Miss L.I.Savchenko and Miss N.M.Zvereva*	
1989	Miss J.Novotna and Miss H.Sukova *Miss L.I.Savchenko and Miss N.M.Zvereva*	
1990	Miss J.Novotna and Miss H.Sukova *Miss K.Jordan and Mrs.P.D.Smylie*	
1991	Miss L.I.Savchenko and Miss N.M.Zvereva *Miss B.C.Fernandez and Miss J.Novotna*	
1992	Miss B.C.Fernandez and Miss N.M.Zvereva *Miss J.Novotna and Mrs.A.Neiland*	
1993	Miss B.C.Fernandez and Miss N.M.Zvereva *Mrs.A.Neiland and Miss J.Novotna*	
1994	Miss B.C.Fernandez and Miss N.M.Zvereva *Miss J.Novotna and Miss A.I.M.Sanchez Vicario*	
1995	Miss J.Novotna and Miss A.I.M.Sanchez Vicario *Miss B.C.Fernandez and Miss N.M.Zvereva*	
1996	Miss M.Hingis and Miss H.Sukova *Miss M.J.McGrath and Mrs.A.Neiland*	
1997	Miss B.C.Fernandez and Miss N.M.Zvereva *Miss N.J.Arendt and Miss M.M.Bollegraf*	
1998	Miss M.Hingis and Miss J.Novotna *Miss L.A.Davenport and Miss N.M.Zvereva*	
1999	Miss L.A.Davenport and Miss C.M.Morariu *Miss M.de Swardt and Miss E.Tatarkova*	
2000	Miss S.J.Williams and Miss V.E.S.Williams *Mrs.A.Decugis and Miss A.Sugiyama*	
2001	Miss L.M.Raymond and Miss R.P.Stubbs *Miss K.Clijsters and Miss A.Sugiyama*	
2002	Miss S.J.Williams and Miss V.E.S.Williams *Miss V.Ruano Pascual and Miss P.L.Suarez*	
2003	Miss K.Clijsters and Miss A.Sugiyama *Miss V.Ruano Pascual and Miss P.L.Suarez*	
2004	Miss C.C.Black and Miss R.P.Stubbs *Mrs.A.Huber and Miss A.Sugiyama*	
2005	Miss C.C.Black and Mrs.L.Huber *Miss S.Kuznetsova and Miss A.Muresmo*	
2006	Miss Z.Yan and Miss J.Zheng *Miss V.Ruano Pascual and Miss P.L.Suarez*	
2007	Miss C.C.Black and Mrs.L.Huber *Miss K.Srebotnik and Miss A.Sugiyama*	
2008	Miss S.J.Williams and Miss V.E.S.Williams *Miss L.M.Raymond and Miss S.J.Stosur*	
2009	Miss S.J.Williams and Miss V.E.S.Williams *Miss S.J.Stosur and Miss R.P.Stubbs*	
2010	Miss V.King and Miss Y.V.Shvedova *Miss E.S.Vesnina and Miss V.Zvonareva*	
2011	Mrs.K.Peschke and Miss K.Srebotnik *Miss S.Lisicki and Miss S.J.Stosur*	
2012	Miss S.J.Williams and Miss V.E.S.Williams *Miss A.Hlavackova and Miss L.Hradecka*	
2013	Miss S-W.Hsieh and Miss S.Peng *Miss A.Barty and Miss C.Dellacqua*	
2014	Miss S.Errani and Miss R.Vinci *Miss T.Babos and Miss K.Mladenovic*	
2015	Miss M.Hingis and Miss S.Mirza *Miss E.Makarova and Mrs E.S.Vesnina*	
2016	Miss S.J.Williams and Miss V.E.S.Williams *Miss T.Babos and Miss Y.Shvedova*	
2017	Miss E.Makarova and Mrs.E.S.Vesnina *Miss H-C.Chan and Miss M.Niculescu*	
2018	Miss B.Krejcikova and Miss K.Siniakova *Miss N.Melichar and Mrs.K.Peschke*	

MIXED DOUBLES CHAMPIONS & RUNNERS-UP

1913 H.Crisp and Mrs.C.O.Tuckey
J.C.Parke and Mrs.D.T.R.Larcombe

1914 J.C.Parke and Mrs.D.T.R.Larcombe
A.F.Wilding and Miss M.Broquedis

1919 R.Lycett and Miss E.M.Ryan
A.D.Prebble and Mrs.R.L.Chambers

1920 G.L.Patterson and Miss S.R.F.Lenglen
R.Lycett and Miss E.M.Ryan

1921 R.Lycett and Miss E.M.Ryan
M.Woosnam and Miss P.L.Howkins

1922 P.O.Wood and Miss S.R.F.Lenglen
R.Lycett and Miss E.M.Ryan

1923 R.Lycett and Miss E.M.Ryan
L.S.Deane and Mrs.W.P.Barron

1924 J.B.Gilbert and Miss K.McKane
L.A.Godfree and Mrs.W.P.Barron

1925 J.Borotra and Miss S.R.F.Lenglen
U.L.de Morpurgo and Miss E.M.Ryan

1926 L.A.Godfree and Mrs.L.A.Godfree
H.O.Kinsey and Miss M.K.Browne

1927 F.T.Hunter and Miss E.M.Ryan
L.A.Godfree and Mrs.L.A.Godfree

1928 P.D.B.Spence and Miss E.M.Ryan
J.H.Crawford and Miss D.J.Akhurst

1929 F.T.Hunter and Miss H.N.Wills
I.G.Collins and Miss J.C.Fry

1930 J.H.Crawford and Miss E.M.Ryan
D.D.Prenn and Miss H.Krahwinkel

1931 G.M.Lott and Mrs.L.A.Harper
I.G.Collins and Miss J.C.Ridley

1932 E.G.Maier and Miss E.M.Ryan
H.C.Hopman and Miss J.Sigart

1933 G.von Cramm and Miss H.Krahwinkel
N.G.Farquharson and Miss G.M.Heeley

1934 R.Miki and Miss D.E.Round
H.W.Austin and Mrs.W.P.Barron

1935 F.J.Perry and Miss D.E.Round
H.C.Hopman and Mrs.H.C.Hopman

1936 F.J.Perry and Miss D.E.Round
J.D.Budge and Mrs.M.Fabyan

1937 J.D.Budge and Miss A.Marble
Y.F.M.Petra and Mrs.R.Mathieu

1938 J.D.Budge and Miss A.Marble
H.E.O.Henkel and Mrs.M.Fabyan

1939 R.L.Riggs and Miss A.Marble
F.H.D.Wilde and Miss N.B.Brown

1946 T.P.Brown and Miss A.L.Brough
G.E.Brown and Miss D.M.Bundy

1947 J.E.Bromwich and Miss A.L.Brough
C.F.Long and Mrs.G.F.Bolton

1948 J.E.Bromwich and Miss A.L.Brough
F.A.Sedgman and Miss D.J.Hart

1949 E.W.Sturgess and Mrs.R.A.Summers
J.E.Bromwich and Miss A.L.Brough

1950 E.W.Sturgess and Miss A.L.Brough
G.E.Brown and Mrs.R.B.Todd

1951 F.A.Sedgman and Miss D.J.Hart
M.G.Rose and Mrs.G.F.Bolton

1952 F.A.Sedgman and Miss D.J.Hart
E.J.Morea and Mrs.M.N.Long

1953 E.V.Seixas and Miss D.J.Hart
E.J.Morea and Miss S.J.Fry

1954 E.V.Seixas and Miss D.J.Hart
K.R.Rosewall and Mrs.W.du Pont

1955 E.V.Seixas and Miss D.J.Hart
E.J.Morea and Miss A.L.Brough

1956 E.V.Seixas and Miss S.J.Fry
G.P.Mulloy and Miss A.Gibson

1957 M.G.Rose and Miss D.R.Hard
N.A.Fraser and Miss A.Gibson

1958 R.N.Howe and Miss L.Coghlan
K.Nielsen and Miss A.Gibson

1959 R.G.Laver and Miss D.R.Hard
N.A.Fraser and Miss M.E.A.Bueno

1960 R.G.Laver and Miss D.R.Hard
R.N.Howe and Miss M.E.A.Bueno

1961 F.S.Stolle and Miss L.R.Turner
R.N.Howe and Miss E.Buding

1962 N.A.Fraser and Mrs.W.du Pont
R.D.Ralston and Miss A.S.Haydon

1963 K.N.Fletcher and Miss M.Smith
R.A.J.Hewitt and Miss D.R.Hard

1964 F.S.Stolle and Miss L.R.Turner
K.N.Fletcher and Miss M.Smith

1965 K.N.Fletcher and Miss M.Smith
A.D.Roche and Miss J.A.M.Tegart

1966 K.N.Fletcher and Miss M.Smith
R.D.Ralston and Mrs.L.W.King

1967 O.K.Davidson and Mrs.L.W.King
K.N.Fletcher and Miss M.E.A.Bueno

1968 K.N.Fletcher and Mrs.B.M.Court
A.Metreveli and Miss O.V.Morozova

1969 F.S.Stolle and Mrs.P.F.Jones
A.D.Roche and Miss J.A.M.Tegart

1970 I.Nastase and Miss R.Casals
A.Metreveli and Miss O.V.Morozova

1971 O.K.Davidson and Mrs.L.W.King
M.C.Riessen and Mrs.B.M.Court

1972 I.Nastase and Miss R.Casals
K.G.Warwick and Miss E.F.Goolagong

1973 O.K.Davidson and Mrs.L.W.King
R.C.Ramirez and Miss J.S.Newberry

1974 O.K.Davidson and Mrs.L.W.King
M.J.Farrell and Miss L.J.Charles

1975 M.C.Riessen and Mrs.B.M.Court
A.J.Stone and Miss B.F.Stove

1976 A.D.Roche and Miss F.G.Durr
R.L.Stockton and Miss R.Casals

1977 R.A.J.Hewitt and Miss G.R.Stevens
F.D.McMillan and Miss B.F.Stove

1978 F.D.McMillan and Miss B.F.Stove
R.O.Ruffels and Mrs.L.W.King

1979 R.A.J.Hewitt and Miss G.R.Stevens
F.D.McMillan and Miss B.F.Stove

1980 J.R.Austin and Miss T.A.Austin
M.R.Edmondson and Miss D.L.Fromholtz

1981 F.D.McMillan and Miss B.F.Stove
J.R.Austin and Miss T.A.Austin

1982 K.M.Curren and Miss A.E.Smith
J.M.Lloyd and Miss W.M.Turnbull

1983 J.M.Lloyd and Miss W.M.Turnbull
S.B.Denton and Mrs.L.W.King

1984 J.M.Lloyd and Miss W.M.Turnbull
S.B.Denton and Miss K.Jordan

1985 P.F.McNamee and Miss M.Navratilova
J.B.Fitzgerald and Mrs.P.D.Smylie

1986 K.E.Flach and Miss K.Jordan
H.P.Guenthardt and Miss M.Navratilova

1987 M.J.Bates and Miss J.M.Durie
D.A.Cahill and Miss N.A-L.Provis

1988 S.E.Stewart and Miss Z.L.Garrison
K.L.Jones and Mrs.S.W.Magers

1989 J.R.Pugh and Miss J.Novotna
M.Kratzmann and Miss J.M.Byrne

1990 R.D.Leach and Miss Z.L.Garrison
J.B.Fitzgerald and Mrs.P.D.Smylie

1991 J.B.Fitzgerald and Mrs.P.D.Smylie
J.R.Pugh and Miss N.M.Zvereva

1992 C.Suk and Mrs.A.Neiland
J.F.Eltingh and Miss M.J.M.M.Oremans

1993 M.R.Woodforde and Miss M.Navratilova
T.J.C.M.Nijssen and Miss M.M.Bollegraf

1994 T.A.Woodbridge and Miss H.Sukova
T.J.Middleton and Miss L.M.McNeil

1995 J.A.Stark and Miss M.Navratilova
C.Suk and Miss B.C.Fernandez

1996 C.Suk and Miss H.Sukova
M.R.Woodforde and Mrs.A.Neiland

1997 C.Suk and Miss H.Sukova
A.Olhovskiy and Mrs.A.Neiland

1998 M.N.Mirnyi and Miss S.J.Williams
M.S.Bhupathi and Miss M.Lucic

1999 L.A.Paes and Miss L.M.Raymond
J.L.Bjorkman and Miss A.S.Kournikova

2000 D.J.Johnson and Miss K.Y.Po
L.G.Hewitt and Miss K.Clijsters

2001 L.Friedl and Miss D.Hantuchova
M.C.Bryan and Mrs.L.Huber

2002 M.S.Bhupathi and Miss E.A.Likhovtseva
K.R.Ullyett and Miss D.Hantuchova

2003 L.A.Paes and Miss M.Navratilova
A.Ram and Miss A.Rodionova

2004 W.Black and Miss C.C.Black
T.A.Woodbridge and Miss A.H.Molik

2005 M.S.Bhupathi and Miss M.C.Pierce
P.Hanley and Miss T.Perebiynis

2006 A.Ram and Miss V.Zvonareva
R.C.Bryan and Miss V.E.S.Williams

2007 J.R.Murray and Miss J.Jankovic
J.L.Bjorkman and Miss A.H.Molik

2008 R.C.Bryan and Miss S.J.Stosur
M.C.Bryan and Miss K.Srebotnik

2009 M.S.Knowles and Miss A-L.Groenefeld
L.A.Paes and Miss C.C.Black

2010 L.A.Paes and Miss C.C.Black
W.A.Moodie and Miss L.M.Raymond

2011 J.Melzer and Miss I.Benesova
M.S.Bhupathi and Miss E.S.Vesnina

2012 M.Bryan and Miss L.M.Raymond
L.A.Paes and Miss E.S.Vesnina

2013 D.M.Nestor and Miss K.Mladenovic
B.Soares and Miss L.M.Raymond

2014 N.Zimonjic and Miss S.J.Stosur
M.N.Mirnyi and Miss H-C.Chan

2015 L.A.Paes and Miss M.Hingis
A.Peya and Miss T.Babos

2016 H.Kontinen and Miss H.M.Watson
R.F.Farah and Miss A-L.Groenefeld

2017 J.R.Murray and Miss M.Hingis
H.Kontinen and Miss H.M.Watson

2018 A.Peya and Miss N.Melichar
J.R.Murray and Miss V.A.Azarenka

BOYS' SINGLES CHAMPIONS & RUNNERS-UP

1947 K.Nielsen *S.V.Davidson*	1965 V.Korotkov *G.Goven*	1983 S.B.Edberg *J.Frawley*	2001 R.Valent *G.Muller*
1948 S.O.Stockenberg *D.Vad*	1966 V.Korotkov *B.E.Fairlie*	1984 M.Kratzmann *S.Kruger*	2002 T.C.Reid *L.Quahab*
1949 S.O.Stockenberg *J.A.T.Horn*	1967 M.Orantes *M.S.Estep*	1985 L.Lavalle *E.Velez*	2003 F.Mergea *C.Guccione*
1950 J.A.T.Horn *K.Mobarek*	1968 J.G.Alexander *J.Thamin*	1986 E.Velez *J.Sanchez*	2004 G.Monfils *M.Kasiri*
1951 J.Kupferburger *K.Mobarek*	1969 B.M.Bertram *J.G.Alexander*	1987 D.Nargiso *J.R.Stoltenberg*	2005 J.Chardy *R.Haase*
1952 R.K.Wilson *T.T.Fancutt*	1970 B.M.Bertram *F.Gebert*	1988 N.Pereira *G.Raoux*	2006 T.De Bakker *M.Gawron*
1953 W.A.Knight *R.Krishnan*	1971 R.I.Kreiss *S.A.Warboys*	1989 L.J.N.Kulti *T.A.Woodbridge*	2007 D.Young *V.Ignatic*
1954 R.Krishnan *A.J.Cooper*	1972 B.R.Borg *C.J.Mottram*	1990 L.A.Paes *M.Ondruska*	2008 G.Dimitrov *H.Kontinen*
1955 M.P.Hann *J.E.Lundquist*	1973 W.W.Martin *C.S.Dowdeswell*	1991 K.J.T.Enquist *M.Joyce*	2009 A.Kuznetsov *J.Cox*
1956 R.E.Holmberg *R.G.Laver*	1974 W.W.Martin *Ash Amritraj*	1992 D.Skoch *B.Dunn*	2010 M.Fucsovics *B.Mitchell*
1957 J.I.Tattersall *I.Ribeiro*	1975 C.J.Lewis *R.Ycaza*	1993 R.Sabau *J.Szymanski*	2011 L.Saville *L.Broady*
1958 E.H.Buchholz *P.J.Lall*	1976 H.P.Guenthardt *P.Elter*	1994 S.M.Humphries *M.A.Philippoussis*	2012 F.Peliwo *L.Saville*
1959 T.Lejus *R.W.Barnes*	1977 V.A.W.Winitsky *T.E.Teltscher*	1995 O.Mutis *N.Kiefer*	2013 G.Quinzi *H.Chung*
1960 A.R.Mandelstam *J.Mukerjea*	1978 I.Lendl *J.Turpin*	1996 V.Voltchkov *I.Ljubicic*	2014 N.Rubin *S.Kozlov*
1961 C.E.Graebner *E.Blanke*	1979 R.Krishnan *D.Siegler*	1997 W.Whitehouse *D.Elsner*	2015 R.Opelka *M.Ymer*
1962 S.J.Matthews *A.Metreveli*	1980 T.Tulasne *H.D.Beutel*	1998 R.Federer *I.Labadze*	2016 D.Shapovalov *A.de Minaur*
1963 N.Kalogeropoulos *I.El Shafei*	1981 M.W.Anger *P.H.Cash*	1999 J.Melzer *K.Pless*	2017 A.Davidovich Fokina *A.Geller*
1964 I.El Shafei *V.Korotkov*	1982 P.H.Cash *H.Sundstrom*	2000 N.P.A.Mahut *M.Ancic*	2018 C.H.Tseng *J.Draper*

BOYS' DOUBLES CHAMPIONS & RUNNERS-UP

1982 P.H.Cash and J.Frawley *R.D.Leach and J.J.Ross*	1995 J.Lee and J.M.Trotman *A.Hernandez and M.Puerta*	2008 C-P.Hsieh and T-H.Yang *M.Reid and B.Tomic*
1983 M.Kratzmann and S.Youl *M.Nastase and O.Rahnasto*	1996 D.Bracciali and J.Robichaud *D.Roberts and W.Whitehouse*	2009 P-H.Herbert and K.Krawietz *J.Obry and A.Puget*
1984 R.Brown and R.V.Weiss *M.Kratzmann and J.Svensson*	1997 L.Horna and N.Massu *J.Van de Westhuizen and W.Whitehouse*	2010 L.Broady and T.Farquharson *L.Burton and G.Morgan*
1985 A.Moreno and J.Yzaga *P.Korda and C.Suk*	1998 R.Federer and O.L.P.Rochus *M.Llodra and A.Ram*	2011 G.Morgan and M.Pavic *O.Golding and J.Vesely*
1986 T.Carbonell and P.Korda *S.Barr and H.Karrasch*	1999 G.Coria and D.P.Nalbandian *T.Enev and J.Nieminem*	2012 A.Harris and N.Kyrgios *M.Donati and P.Licciardi*
1987 J.Stoltenberg and T.A.Woodbridge *D.Nargiso and E.Rossi*	2000 D.Coene and K.Vliegen *A.Banks and B.Riby*	2013 T.Kokkinakis and N.Kyrgios *E.Couacaud and S.Napolitano*
1988 J.R.Stoltenberg and T.A.Woodbridge *D.Rikl and T.Zdrazila*	2001 F.Dancevic and G.Lapentti *B.Echagaray and S.Gonzales*	2014 O.Luz and M.Zormann *S.Kozlov and A.Rublev*
1989 J.E.Palmer and J.A.Stark *J-L.De Jager and W.R.Ferreira*	2002 F.Mergea and H.V.Tecau *B.Baker and B.Ram*	2015 N.H.Ly and S.Nagal *R.Opelka and A.Santillan*
1990 S.Lareau and S.Leblanc *C.Marsh and M.Ondruska*	2003 F.Mergea and H.V.Tecau *A.Feeney and C.Guccione*	2016 K.Raisma and S.Tsitsipas *F.Auger-Aliassime and D.Shapovalov*
1991 K.Alami and G.Rusedski *J-L.De Jager and A.Medvedev*	2004 B.Evans and S.Oudsema *R.Haase and V.Troicki*	2017 A.Geller and Y.H.Hsu *J.Rodionov and M.Vrbensky*
1992 S.Baldas and S.Draper *M.S.Bhupathi and N.Kirtane*	2005 J.Levine and M.Shabaz *S.Groth and A.Kennaugh*	2018 Y.Erel and O.Virtanen *N.Mejia and O.Styler*
1993 S.Downs and J.Greenhalgh *N.Godwin and G.Williams*	2006 K.Damico and N.Schnugg *M.Klizan and A.Martin*	
1994 B.Ellwood and M.Philippoussis *V.Platenik and R.Schlachter*	2007 D.Lopez and M.Trevisan *R.Jebavy and M.Klizan*	

GIRLS' SINGLES CHAMPIONS & RUNNERS-UP

1947 Miss G.Domken
Miss B.Wallen

1948 Miss O.Miskova
Miss V.Rigollet

1949 Miss C.Mercelis
Miss J.S.V.Partridge

1950 Miss L.Cornell
Miss A.Winter

1951 Miss L.Cornell
Miss S.Lazzarino

1952 Miss F.J.I.ten Bosch
Miss R.Davar

1953 Miss D.Kilian
Miss V.A.Pitt

1954 Miss V.A.Pitt
Miss C.Monnot

1955 Miss S.M.Armstrong
Miss B.de Chambure

1956 Miss A.S.Haydon
Miss I.Buding

1957 Miss M.G.Arnold
Miss E.Reyes

1958 Miss S.M.Moore
Miss A.Dmitrieva

1959 Miss J.Cross
Miss D.Schuster

1960 Miss K.J.Hantze
Miss L.M.Hutchings

1961 Miss G.Baksheeva
Miss K.D.Chabot

1962 Miss G.Baksheeva
Miss E.P.Terry

1963 Miss D.M.Salfati
Miss K.Dening

1964 Miss J.M.Bartkowicz
Miss E.Subirats

1965 Miss O.V.Morozova
Miss R.Giscarfe

1966 Miss B.Lindstrom
Miss J.A.Congdon

1967 Miss J.H.Salome
Miss E.M.Strandberg

1968 Miss K.S.Pigeon
Miss L.E.Hunt

1969 Miss K.Sawamatsu
Miss B.I.Kirk

1970 Miss S.A.Walsh
Miss M.V.Kroshina

1971 Miss M.V.Kroschina
Miss S.H.Minford

1972 Miss I.S.Kloss
Miss G.L.Coles

1973 Miss A.K.Kiyomura
Miss M.Navratilova

1974 Miss M.Jausovec
Miss M.Simionescu

1975 Miss N.Y.Chmyreva
Miss R.Marsikova

1976 Miss N.Y.Chmyreva
Miss M.Kruger

1977 Miss L.Antonoplis
Miss M.Louie

1978 Miss T.A.Austin
Miss H.Mandlikova

1979 Miss M.L.Piatek
Miss A.A.Moulton

1980 Miss D.Freeman
Miss S.J.Leo

1981 Miss Z.L.Garrison
Miss R.R.Uys

1982 Miss C.Tanvier
Miss H.Sukova

1983 Miss P.Paradis
Miss P.Hy

1984 Miss A.N.Croft
Miss E.Reinach

1985 Miss A.Holikova
Miss J.M.Byrne

1986 Miss N.M.Zvereva
Miss L.Meskhi

1987 Miss N.M.Zvereva
Miss J.Halard

1988 Miss B.A.M.Schultz
Miss E.Derly

1989 Miss A.Strnadova
Miss M.J.McGrath

1990 Miss A.Strnadova
Miss K.Sharpe

1991 Miss B.Rittner
Miss E.Makarova

1992 Miss C.R.Rubin
Miss L.Courtois

1993 Miss N.Feber
Miss R.Grande

1994 Miss M.Hingis
Miss M-R.Jeon

1995 Miss A.Olsza
Miss T.Tanasugarn

1996 Miss A.Mauresmo
Miss M.L.Serna

1997 Miss C.C.Black
Miss A.Rippner

1998 Miss K.Srebotnik
Miss K.Clijsters

1999 Miss I.Tulyagnova
Miss L.Krasnoroutskaya

2000 Miss M.E.Salerni
Miss T.Perebiynis

2001 Miss A.Widjaja
Miss D.Safina

2002 Miss V.Douchevina
Miss M.Sharapova

2003 Miss K.Flipkens
Miss A.Tchakvetadze

2004 Miss K.Bondarenko
Miss A.Ivanovic

2005 Miss A.R.Radwanska
Miss T.Paszek

2006 Miss C.Wozniacki
Miss M Rybarikova

2007 Miss U.Radwanska
Miss M.Brengle

2008 Miss L.M.D.Robson
Miss N.Lertcheewakarn

2009 Miss N.Lertcheewakarn
Miss K.Mladenovic

2010 Miss K.Pliskova
Miss S.Ishizu

2011 Miss A.Barty
Miss I.Khromacheva

2012 Miss E.Bouchard
Miss E.Svitolina

2013 Miss B.Bencic
Miss T.Townsend

2014 Miss J.Ostapenko
Miss K.Schmiedlova

2015 Miss S.Zhuk
Miss A.Blinkova

2016 Miss A.S.Potapova
Miss D.O.Yastremska

2017 Miss C.Liu
Miss A.Li

2018 Miss I.Swiatek
Miss L.Kung

GIRLS' DOUBLES CHAMPIONS & RUNNERS-UP

1982 Miss E.A.Herr and Miss P.Barg
Miss B.S.Gerken and Miss G.A.Rush

1983 Miss P.A.Fendick and Miss P.Hy
Miss C.Anderholm and Miss H.Olsson

1984 Miss C.Kuhlman and Miss S.C.Rehe
Miss V.Milvidskaya and Miss L.I.Savchenko

1985 Miss L.Field and Miss J.G.Thompson
Miss E.Reinach and Miss J.A.Richardson

1986 Miss M.Jaggard and Miss L.O'Neill
Miss L.Meskhi and Miss N.M.Zvereva

1987 Miss N.Medvedeva and Miss N.M.Zvereva
Miss I.S.Kim and Miss P.M.Moreno

1988 Miss J.A.Faull and Miss R.McQuillan
Miss A.Dechaume and Miss E.Derly

1989 Miss J.M.Capriati and Miss M.J.McGrath
Miss A.Strnadova and Miss E.Sviglerova

1990 Miss K.Habsudova and Miss A.Strnadova
Miss N.J.Pratt and Miss K.Sharpe

1991 Miss C.Barclay and Miss L.Zaltz
Miss J.Limmer and Miss A.Woolcock

1992 Miss M.Avotins and Miss L.McShea
Miss P.Nelson and Miss J.Steven

1993 Miss L.Courtois and Miss N.Feber
Miss H.Mochizuki and Miss Y.Yoshida

1994 Miss E.De Villiers and Miss E.E.Jelfs
Miss C.M.Morariu and Miss L.Varmuzova

1995 Miss C.C.Black and Miss A.Olsza
Miss T.Musgrove and Miss J.Richardson

1996 Miss O.Barabanschikova and Miss A.Mauresmo
Miss L.Osterloh and Miss S.Reeves

1997 Miss C.C.Black and Miss I.Selyutina
Miss M.Matevzic and Miss K.Srebotnik

1998 Miss E.Dyrberg and Miss J.Kostanic
Miss P.Rampre and Miss I.Tulyaganova

1999 Miss D.Bedanova and Miss M.E.Salerni
Miss T.Perebiynis and Miss I.Tulyaganova

2000 Miss I.Gaspar and Miss T.Perebiynis
Miss D.Bedanova and Miss M.E.Salerni

2001 Miss G.Dulko and Miss A.Harkleroad
Miss C.Horiatopoulos and Miss B.Mattek

2002 Miss E.Clijsters and Miss B.Strycova
Miss A.Baker and Miss A-L.Groenefeld

2003 Miss A.Kleybanova and Miss S.Mirza
Miss K.Bohmova and Miss M.Krajicek

2004 Miss V.A.Azarenka and Miss V.Havartsova
Miss M.Erakovic and Miss M.Niculescu

2005 Miss V.A.Azarenka and Miss A.Szavay
Miss M.Erakovic and Miss M.Niculescu

2006 Miss A.Kleybanova and Miss A.Pavlyuchenkova
Miss K.Antoniychuk and Miss A.Dulgheru

2007 Miss A.Pavlyuchenkova and Miss U.Radwanska
Miss M.Doi and Miss K.Nara

2008 Miss P.Hercog and Miss J.Moore
Miss I.Holland and Miss S.Peers

2009 Miss N.Lertcheewakarn and Miss S.Peers
Miss K.Mladenovic and Miss S.Njiric

2010 Miss T.Babos and Miss S.Stephens
Miss I.Khromacheva and Miss E.Svitolina

2011 Miss E.Bouchard and Miss G.Min
Miss D.Schuurs and Miss H.C.Tang

2012 Miss E.Bouchard and Miss T.Townsend
Miss B.Bencic and Miss A.Konjuh

2013 Miss B.Krejcikova and Miss K.Siniakova
Miss A.Kalinina and Miss I.Shymanovich

2014 Miss T.Grende and Miss Q.Ye
Miss M.Bouzkova and Miss D.Galfi

2015 Miss D.Galfi and Miss F.Stollar
Miss V.Lapko and Miss T.Mihalikova

2016 Miss U.M.Arconada and Miss C.Liu
Miss M.Bolkvadze and Miss C.McNally

2017 Miss O.Danilovic and Miss K.Juvan
Miss C.McNally and Miss W.Osuigwe

2018 Miss X.Wang and Miss X.Wang
Miss C.McNally and Miss W.Osuigwe

GENTLEMEN'S WHEELCHAIR SINGLES CHAMPIONS & RUNNERS-UP

2016 G.Reid
S.Olsson

2017 S.Olsson
G.Fernandez

2018 S.Olsson
G.Fernandez

GENTLEMEN'S WHEELCHAIR DOUBLES CHAMPIONS & RUNNERS-UP

2006 S.Saida and S.Kunieda
M.Jeremiasz and J.Mistry

2007 R.Ammerlaan and R.Vink
S.Kunieda and S.Saida

2008 R.Ammerlaan and R.Vink
S.Houdet and N.Peifer

2009 S.Houdet and M.Jeremiasz
R.Ammerlaan and S.Kunieda

2010 R.Ammerlaan and S.Olsson
S.Houdet and S.Kunieda

2011 M.Scheffers and R.Vink
S.Houdet and M.Jeremiasz

2012 T.Egberink and M.Jeremiasz
R.Ammerlaan and R.Vink

2013 S.Houdet and S.Kunieda
F.Cattaneo and R.Vink

2014 S.Houdet and S.Kunieda
M.Scheffers and R.Vink

2015 G.Fernandez and N.Peifer
M.Jeremiasz and G.Reid

2016 A.T.Hewett and G.Reid
S.Houdet and N.Peifer

2017 A.T.Hewett and G.Reid
S.Houdet and N.Peifer

2018 A.T.Hewett and G.Reid
J.Gerard and S.Olsson

LADIES' WHEELCHAIR SINGLES CHAMPIONS & RUNNERS-UP

2016 Miss J.Griffioen
Miss A.van Koot

2017 Miss D.de Groot
Miss S.Ellerbrock

2018 Miss D.de Groot
Miss A.van Koot

LADIES' WHEELCHAIR DOUBLES CHAMPIONS & RUNNERS-UP

2009 Miss K.Homan and Miss E.M.Vergeer
Miss D.Di Toro and Miss L.Shuker

2010 Miss E.M.Vergeer and Miss S.Walraven
Miss D.Di Toro and Miss L.Shuker

2011 Miss E.M.Vergeer and Miss S.Walraven
Miss J.Griffioen and Miss A.van Koot

2012 Miss J.Griffioen and Miss A.van Koot
Miss L.Shuker and Miss J.J.Whiley

2013 Miss J.Griffioen and Miss A.van Koot
Miss Y.Kamiji and Miss J.J.Whiley

2014 Miss Y.Kamiji and Miss J.J.Whiley
Miss J.Griffioen and Miss A.van Koot

2015 Miss Y.Kamiji and Miss J.J.Whiley
Miss J.Griffioen and Miss A.van Koot

2016 Miss Y.Kamiji and Miss J.J.Whiley
Miss J.Griffioen and Miss A.van Koot

2017 Miss Y.Kamiji and Miss J.J.Whiley
Miss M.Buis and Miss D.de Groot

2018 Miss D.de Groot and Miss Y.Kamiji
Miss S.Ellerbrock and Miss L.Shuker